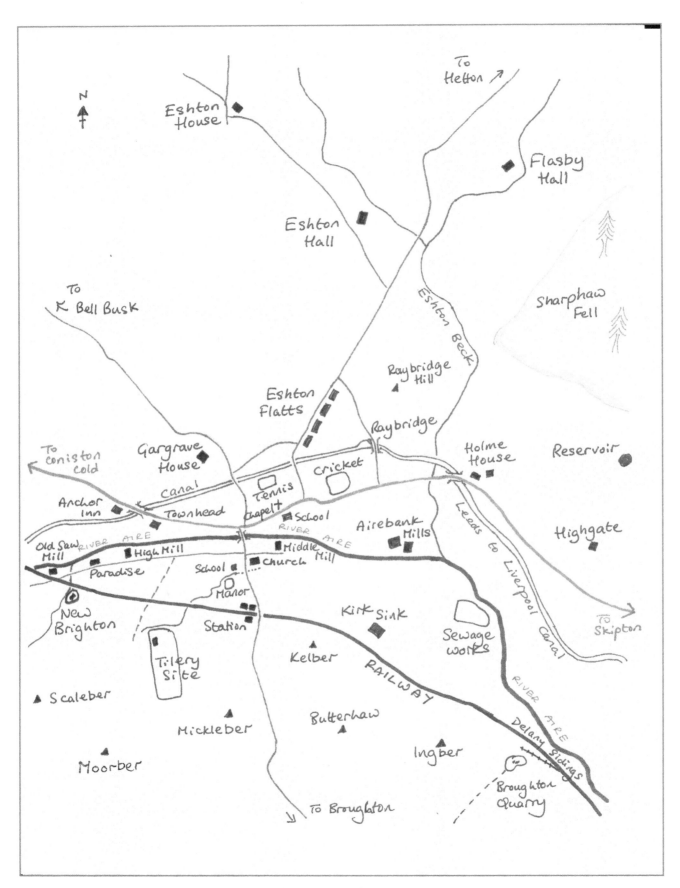

The 'Vill' or 'Parish' of Gargrave
From a sketch map by Sue Lyall

FROM MILLS TO MARCHING AND BACK AGAIN

A History of Gargrave from 1900 to 1925

CO AUTHORS

Sue Lyall

Donavon Slaven

❧

CONTRIBUTORS

George Ingle

Ray Jones

Martin Thompson

❧

COVER DESIGN AND EDITING,

Donavon Slaven

❧

❧

Gargrave Heritage Group
Saint Andrew's Church
Gargrave
North Yorkshire
U.K.

IN MEMORY OF

THE MEN OF GARGRAVE WHO FOUGHT AND
FELL IN THE GREAT WAR OF 1914-1918

This edition published in 2019 by
Gargrave Heritage Group

ISBN 978-1-9161058-0-5

978-1-9161058-0-5

CONTENTS

FOREWORD

This book would not have been possible without access to the Dennis French collection. This comprehensive archive of Gargrave photos, newspaper cuttings, pamphlets, books and films has been collected over many years. Dennis' daughter and son-in-law are now the custodians of this invaluable resource. We are extremely grateful to Cath and Graham for allowing us to use so many of the photos and to Graham for his enthusiasm in helping us to locate information.

We remember with great affection our friend, the late Ray Jones who sadly passed away after a very short illness in January 2017. It was Ray who started us off with the group's research into the fallen soldiers of the Great War. He travelled to the conflict zones of France and Belgium, taking photos of cemeteries, war graves and battlefields. Many of these are included in this book.

Throughout the book, many Gargrave places and buildings are mentioned. Most still exist, some have changed their use and others have disappeared. The maps of the Parish (Frontispiece) and Gargrave village centre (page 384), show their locations.

When we first planned the book it was to be a memorial to those from the village who lost their lives in the First World War. There is already a permanent memorial to them in the village, but we thought that one hundred years after the armistice something more was needed.

Just a list of names was not enough so we planned to give as much detail as possible about who those men were and they were mainly men. We wanted to fit them into village life, what they did, their families and where they lived. It then seemed necessary to give some detail about the village so that people today could understand village life in 1914 and also how the village had changed by 1918. To just concentrate on those four years again seemed inadequate so the time scale was widened to encompass the twenty five years1900 to 1925. The extensive biographies originally penned about the soldiers were edited to fit with the new publication.

So much was happening, nationally and internationally, during those years and we wanted to see how Gargrave adapted and changed over that time. Further thought about our readers and the scope of this book made us realise that we needed to give more information about the village itself.

Why was the village here in the first place. Nothing of great significance had happened in the village over the centuries to provide a well known record in the history books, or did it? So what did the stranger need to know about this place in the Craven area of the Yorkshire Dales.

The fact that Gargrave, like most Dales villages had an industrial past which continues to the present day was important, never mind over a hundred years ago in 1900. We perhaps assume that farming changes slowly but farming in the parish changed fundamentally over the years and attempts to put the clock back during the war were resisted.

The long history of the parish was dominated by extensive land holdings by a few wealthy families over several centuries and was still the same in 1900, but was soon to change. The impact of changes in transport perhaps changed Gargrave more than many other Dales villages. Finally, national developments in areas like religion, education, government, technology and leisure could not be resisted and shaped the village in the years before 1900.

The village has changed again since 1925, but that will be another story.

GARGRAVE'S EARLY HISTORY

ORIGINS OF THE KINGDOM OF CRAVEN

The last Ice Age carved out this area, now known as 'Craven', with easily traversed low, rounded hills. Named drumlins, the hills not only provided timber for dwellings but, when cleared, were found to be very productive. Gargrave occupies a position providing not only land that could be made good for farming and which could be settled readily but also gave easy access to travellers from all directions. People ventured into this northern region

Drumlins near Gargrave
Private Collection - Don Slaven.

of Britain between 11,000 and 10,000 years ago, before the ismuth joining us to Europe disappeared beneath the rising sea.

A series of settlements from the Neolithic times, the Bronze Age, Iron Age, the 1st century Roman invasion, the 6th century Anglo-Saxon, the 9th century Danish, the 10th century Norwegian and the 11th century Norman occupations through to the present day all have left their impressions in and upon the surrounding ground.

Evidence of a Bronze age settlement on Sharp Haw.
Courtesy of Martin Thompson.

Neolithic arrowheads and other implements of that era are regularly recovered from ploughed fields. Evidence of a Bronze Age settlement can still be seen on the slopes of Sharp Haw, a peak just West of present Gargrave.

A strong indication that an Iron Age settlement existed here was discovered during property development on Gargrave High Street during 2003. Preliminary work on the site revealed the remains of three women, two men and a child buried in an unusual ritualistic manner. Radiocarbon dating has confirmed that the burials took place in the late Iron Age or early during the Roman Occupation. This dates the skeletons at between 2,228 and 1,889 years old.

Excavations at Kirk Sink
Courtesy of Craven Museum

The Romans arrived in Britain around 45 A.D. It is about this time that the first settlement on the site known as Kirk Sink was founded. This is the most westerly of the villas in the north of England, most of which were centred on York. The name Kirk Sink, meaning 'buried' or 'sunken' church, was adopted later as it was mistakenly thought that an early church may have been in this location.

Partial archaeological excavations were carried out between 1968 and 1974. This revealed that the earliest houses, which were used well into the villa period, were structures built from wood and turf. These early buildings may have beeen the home of the local pre-Roman ruler of the region. Roman masonry buildings were erected in the second century replacing ealier wooden structures. The villa fell out of use between the end of the third century and the beginning of the fourth. No further development has taken place on the site, but much of the masonry was probably reused elsewhere in the nearby settlements, especially in the constuction of masonry churches, following the Roman christian tradition, in place of the earlier wooden structures of the Celtic church.

After the Romans withdrew in the late 4th and early 5th centuries, various Celtic and Anglian 'kingdoms' emerged, led by warrior kings. One of these realms was the "Kingdom of Craven". A Celtic ruler Arthuis, great-grandson of Coel the Elder, ruled the Kingdom of Dunoting (North Pennines). Dunoting was divided into two areas, Dent and Craven. The title 'Kingdom of Craven' suggests that this region was the more important and held the capital. Dent was designated as the home of the 'Court' of Dunaut. Craven still existed at the time of the Norman Conquest, and it is listed in the Domesday Book as the wapentake of Cravescire, and later as an arch deanery. Several villages in the Dales have evidence of the Anglo-Celtic monastic practice of carving stones, with examples being found in Gargrave.

The incoming tribes from the continent have often been seen as violent, but in the Craven Area they settled and gave names to features and places. They may have taken over the ownership of the land, but it still had to be worked. Outside any land suitable for cultivation, it would have been necessary to control grazing land for cattle, sheep, horses and pigs. Buildings in that era were usually constructed of timber, so very little remains apart from the occasional discovery of a post-hole during site development, and some place names which indicate the language and origin of the settlers.

During the Danish and Norse occupations, two distinct manors were established in the area now occupied by Gargrave. Possibly of Saxon origin, both buildings were wooden structures leaving little behind.

North of the River Aire the manor in the 11th century was held by Thorfin of Ravensworth, a noble of the Kingdom of Orkney. This northern manor, 'Hobury Garth', (roughly translated as 'Fortified Hall in the Mud'), was surrounded by marshland and soon became completely untenable. The manor moved during the 14th century to 'higherland'. This 'new' site, to the right of Higherlands Lock, has been developed and is now populated by residential properties. The original manor site of Horbury Garth lies beneath the houses on North Street and the Village Hall.

The settlement which grew around the northern manor had a different identity to that surrounding the manor south of the river which was held by Gamal Son of Karli, a 'Thegn', who also could claim to have his origins in the Kingdom of Orkney. It is from this manor that the name of Gargrave may have been derived. This manor house was built on land that could provide the means for sustaining a permanent moat. The conditions were similar but not as depressing as the northern site and the house persisted longer. The site is known as the Garris. One explanation for this links the name of a Norman warlord, hailing from Garrison in what is now Northern France with Gargrave. Garri may have been the Lord of the Manor here in Gargrave, however this would have been well after 1066 and unfortunately would have meant that Gargrave did not exist until his name was bestowed on the village. The practise of naming places after a person was not common

Paget Hall ca. 2000
Unknown Author

place until after the 13th century and it would appear that Gargrave held its title well before this date. The site was eventually abandoned in favour of an elevated position a few hundred yards to the east. The outline of the manor house island surrounded by a moat can still be seen. The field where the original site lies has lain undisturbed by agricultural or any building developments.

The 'new' manor house, known as Paget Hall, erected early in the 17th century, still stands intact although it has undergone some modifications during the 19th century and has lost its original limewashed 'slobbered' rendering. 'Slobbering' is the application of an uneven rendering to rubble masonry usually finished with several coats of limewash. Todays conservation practices would have stopped removal of this coating.

It appears that Thorfin held a total of fifty-eight manors in Yorkshire with eight of these located in Craven prior to 1066. The Norman conquest of Britain in that year brought the Scandinavian expansion to an end. By 1068, the two manors, along with the eighty-six manors in Yorkshire held under the name of Gamel, twelve of them in Craven, had been transferred to Roger the Poitou a Norman noble born in the mid-1050s in Normandy. He gained the Poitou addition to his name by marriage to Almodis, heiress of her brother, Boson III, count de La Marche in Poitou, a province on the West Coast of France.

17th Century houses on South Street. The curvature at the right of the building may be the remains of a tower.
Photograph by Don Slaven 2019

The Great Domesday Book shows the land was placed in Roger the Poitou's hands after. The entries on the page for Euruicscire (Yorkshire) relating to the lands in Gargrave held by Roger can be translated as follows:

> In WINTERBURN, Thorfinnr had 3 carucates of land to the geld; "Leuetat" [in Flasby], 3 carucates; Flasby, 4 carucates; GARGRAVE, 2 carucates; Little Newton, 2 carucates; Horton in Ribblesdale, 2 carucates; Selside, 1 carucate.
> In the same place Thorfinnr had 2 carucates of land to the geld.
>
> In GARGRAVE, Gamal had 8 carucates to the geld.

Poitou held these manors until 1102, after which a succession of powerful landlords found themselves in possession.

Prior to 1066, Earl Edwin of Mercia, the Lord of the manor of Bolton in Craven (Bolton Abbey) held land in Gargrave. In 1068, this was transferred to the conquering King William. A building comprising 17, 18 South Street and 25 High Street has been identified by some authorities as a manor house which may occupy the site of an original building built under the aegis of Edwin. The building has been identified by Heritage England as probably from the late 17th century.

The Norman landowners who had been given their landholdings built castles such as Skipton Castle to confirm their power, but for ordinary people it just meant a change of landlord.

A hundred years after the Norman Conquest, the Dales came under monastic control. The monasteries received endowments from the Norman lords and were able to consolidate their holdings through exchange and purchases.

By 1291 the tithes of Stainton, a quarter of the tithes of Gargrave were granted to Sawley Abbey, by Henry de Percy, 1st Baron Percy of Alnwick, son of Henry Percy, 7th Feudal Baron of Topcliffe. In 1313 Henry granted the advowson (right to appoint a vicar) of the church of Gargrave to Sawley Abbey. Henry Percy, 1st Baron Percy died October 1314 aged 41 and on 17 March 1322 the church property including the lands and the great tithes were granted to Sawley Abbey by his widow, Lady Eleanor Fitz Alan Percy and the Archbishop of York, William Melton.

The dissolution of the monasteries between 1536 and 1541 resulted in land holdings changing again with the emergence of the great landowning families. In the 16th century, farmhouses were improved, either by additions or complete rebuilding. Craven was a wealthy area compared with the more northern Dales, and in 1673, the Hearth Tax survey showed that 35% of the houses had more than two fire hearths.

1750 to 1850 was a period of improvement in farming practice, particularly towards the end of the French wars when food became scarce and expensive. Much more thought was given to the selective breeding of sheep and cattle, and experiments were carried out to achieve maximum output from arable and grazing land. In the Craven Dales, this was carried out in conjunction with the enclosure of common land. Enclosure by Act of Parliament was usually promoted by the large landowners.
They benefitted, as they could afford the costs of building walls to enclose their new holdings and the cost of improving the pasture and stock. This improvement and reclamation involved burning the old surface vegetation, draining, and liming to reduce the acidity of the soil.

The Enclosure Commissioners, appointed under each Act, had to assess the various common rights and allocate the land accordingly. The problem for many farm workers was that they no longer had access to the common land and just had to rely on their wages as hired hands. Local society was therefore divided into three classes: landlords, tenant farmers and labourers. For the farm labourers in Gargrave, life was hard with cramped cottages and few alternative opportunities for work. This was to change with improvements in transport and the introduction of new industries.

INTO THE INDUSTRIAL AGE

ROADS AND TURNPIKES

The original roads in Craven would have been animal tracks, used as the best way to move between places, either on foot or on horseback. The Romans built well-engineered roads to link their military, trade and administrative centres. The nearest highway was the road from Ribchester to Ilkley, going via the fort at Elslack. There were minor Roman routes from Grassington for transporting grain and lead down to the main road. One of these routes came through Gargrave, forded the river and went on to Elslack.

From medieval times the need to supply fresh meat to the cities led to the practice of droving – moving livestock on the hoof. The drovers' roads needed to be wide to accommodate herds and flocks and often went over the hills and open land. Overnight staging posts at farms and inns evolved so that men and beasts could rest and eat.

Keighley & Kendal Road marker on the Hellifield Road, Gargrave.
Photograph by Don Slaven 2018

The stone and dirt roads used by pack-horses, were wholly inadequate for wheeled vehicles and too expensive for the local communities to maintain. In 1765 there was an Act of Parliament, which authorised the setting up of turnpike trusts. The Keighley to Kendal Turnpike, founded in 1753, roughly follows the line of the present A65. A toll house was at Holme Bridge just outside the village, this is now a private dwelling.

 One main advantage of the new highway was that with better road surfaces, it needed less than half the number of horses to convey goods by carriage than by those carrying packs. In the first part of the 1800s, the 'Union' stagecoach ran a service every other day but that soon changed to a daily service. Coaching inns were established where the horses were changed, and coach passengers could have refreshments or stay the night. An advertisement for the Swan Inn in Gargrave that appeared in the Leeds Mercury on the 28th of December 1816 illustrates this.

SWAN INN, GARGRAVE.

To be LET by TICKET for a Term of Years,

And Entered to next Spring,

Upon the Premises at Gargrave, in the County of York, on Monday, the 30th Day of December next, subject to such Conditions, as shall be there produced,

ALL that Capital Old and Well-accustomed INN, called the SWAN INN, situate in Gargrave aforesaid, with a good Garden, Yards, and excellent Stabling for Fifteen Horses, and Hay-Lofts over the same, a Granary, and other suitable and convenient Outbuildings. Together with Eight Acres of rich Meadow and Pasture Land, at a convenient Distance from the House.—All which Premises are now in the Occupation of Mr. John Standing, the Owner, who is retiring from Business.

The above Inn has an extensive and well-established Business, being desirably-situated on the Great North Road leading through Craven to Lancaster and Kendal, and is commodious for Gentlemen Travellers and others. The Leeds and Kendal Coaches pass the Door daily, and the Situation is well calculated for establishing a good Posting Connection, and in other Respects worth the Attention of any Person wishing to engage in the Public Line.

Mr. Standing, the Owner, will shew the Premises, from whom further Particulars may be known; or on Application at the Office of Messrs. J. & W. Hartley, Solicitors, Settle.—28th Nov. 1816.

LEEDS AND LIVERPOOL CANAL

The construction of the sections of the Leeds and Liverpool Canal that linked Gargrave with Leeds in 1777 brought about significant changes to agriculture and introduced new industries to the Craven Dales. The changes happened during a period of about twenty years with nearly every town and village being affected. Gargrave played a vital role in these changes. After 1777 when the link to Gargrave finished, the initial funding for the canal was exhausted and work stopped.

Leeds was already linked to Hull via the 'Aire and Calder Navigation', so Gargrave became an inland port for a wide area. The terminus was on the Gargrave side of Ray Bridge where the canal ended in a turning circle, and a bulge in the canal is still evident. In 1791, work resumed continuing westwards towards Lancashire and the stretch as far as Burnley opened in 1796. The canal wasn't fully completed until 1816.

Ray Bridge Wharf - Barge Turning Point
Sue Lyall 2019

To help with the considerable amount of goods now carried by the new canal, five separate wharves were built. Ray Bridge Wharf and Eshton Road Warehouse dealt with Upper Wharfedale; Higherlands Wharf covered local trade while the Anchor and Scarland Wharves dealt with the Settle and Upper Ribblesdale trade. Large warehouses were built at some of these wharves with cobbled yards and a high wall around for security. When textile mills in the Gargrave area were for sale, their proximity to the canal was always mentioned. As the Duke of Devonshire owned much of the land between his lead mines near Grassington and Gargrave he built a road to bring lead from the smelting mills to the warehouse on the canal.

Landowners and merchants from around Bradford needed cheap limestone from the Craven area for their businesses. This was then burnt with coal from the Keighley and Bradford mines to produce lime to improve grazing land, or for building purposes. Later is was used to help smelt iron at the Bradford iron works with the Low Moor Company established there in 1788. The canal was the ideal way to transport heavy cargoes such as stone, coal, lead, agricultural products and textiles. As soon as the canal reached Skipton, the price of coal there fell by 50%.

Hoffman Lime Kiln at Langcliffe, near Settle
Sue Lyall 2019

Most of the limestone quarries were in the Skipton area, and soon there were 40 lime kilns between Skipton and Bradford where the three-mile-long Bradford Canal had joined the Leeds and Liverpool at Shipley.

One horse could now pull a barge containing 40 tons of wheat, instead of just carrying one sack on its back. Suddenly it was possible to bring in cheap flour from the more productive land east of the Pennines rather than struggle to grow wheat in the Dales.

In the other direction as well as transporting coal into Gargrave and then by cart into the Dales the canal assisted with the expansion of the Bradford worsted trade. The problem was the need for hand spinners, as it took five or six spinners to supply enough yarn to keep one hand-loom weaver employed. The worsted manufacturers in the Bradford area had to look elsewhere for hand spinners and the Craven area, including Gargrave, was now accessible via the new canal. The combed 'tops' were sent out regularly to be distributed to shop keepers who were paid a small sum to have them spun locally on the hand-wheel and then returned as spun yarn via the canal. This provided an income for women and children at a time when agricultural wages were low. Soon local people decided that there was money to be made from hand-loom weaving. The availability of cheap transport made it affordable for cloth to be sent for sale in the Halifax Piece Hall. In 1803, Gargrave Parish had sixteen weavers as well as all those who worked part-time at the trade.

Towards the end of the century, water shortages closed the canal for several weeks at a time at a high cost to the canal company. One of the primary sources of water to the canal was Eshton Beck and, to supplement this, a new reservoir at Winterburn was completed in 1891. By 1900, with little money invested for up-keep and improvements, the canal was still in use but in a poor financial state.

Travelling through Eshton Road Locks. Fred Green's Wharf can be seen behind the barge.
Courtesy of the Dennis French Collection

Railways

Gargrave Station late 19th century.
Courtesy of Martin Thompson

The coming of the railway in 1849 impacted on the canal trade. Although not able to compete in the carriage of coal and stone, the railway did take the trade in more general merchandise. Passenger traffic became far higher than initially projected and very profitable.

The first official train to pass through the new Gargrave station was on the 31st of July 1849 during the opening ceremonies. The shareholders had high hopes for this railway, which was planned to offer the shortest route from the West Riding to Glasgow and benefit the inhabitants of the rich grazing districts of Craven. A further advantage would be to bring tourists to Malham and the Three Peaks area. A reporter from a Leeds newspaper riding on the train, described Gargrave village as

'... a very pretty one, with its church in the centre...'

He added that

> "Not withstanding the unfavourable state of the weather, a considerable number of persons had assembled at Gargrave to welcome the traveller; the bridge which crosses the railway a short distance from the station was crowded with spectators."

The line had been incorporated by an Act passed on the 26th of June 1846 with the first sod cut on the 31st of December 1846. The original intention was to construct a line from Skipton to Low Gill on the Lancaster and Carlisle Railway, ten miles north of Kendal, with a branch to Lancaster. However, financial problems meant that this did not happen immediately.

As with the canal the promoters of the new railway came from the ranks of bankers, landowners, mill owners and the gentry in both Lancashire and Yorkshire. Several local mill owners were investors and, as the new railway connected with the Leeds and Bradford Railway at Skipton, the advantages of this line were clear.

George Thornton, an experienced railway contractor who had recently completed work on the London and Brighton Railway, set up his work sites just outside Gargrave and at Niffany near Skipton. He needed places where he could store all the necessary tools and equipment for building the railway but also the materials for its construction. Just outside Gargrave village, on the Marton Road, he found two pieces of land. The larger 16-acre site had a bed of fire clay near the surface and a reliable source of spring water, enabling him to make his own bricks and drainage pipes. This was known as the Gargrave Tilery. Thornton produced thousands of bricks, drainage pipes, roofing tiles, floor tiles, chimney pots and a range of vases and flower pots. The smaller two-acre site was known as New Brighton after the last place where he had lived and worked. Here he built a row of cottages for his senior staff and called them Western Cottages after the railway he was going to construct. The construction workers, or navvies, perhaps had a camp at New Brighton, but no evidence of this has been discovered. It is probable that the workers were housed at Niffany and travelled daily to the place of work. George Thornton himself lived in style at Greenhead (later called The Beeches) in Marton Road.

When Thornton had completed the line from Skipton to Settle, he moved on to his next contract in London. The sites, together with the cottages and all the equipment and materials left from the construction project and his house, were put up for sale. Items for sale included 28 draught horses and a locomotive. The Western Cottages sold quite readily, but the Tilery and the New Brighton depot didn't get sold. Eventually, New Brighton was bought and developed into a Saw Mill, but the Tilery stopped production entirely.

Nearly all evidence of the Tilery has now been lost, although maps from the early twentieth century show a field building marked Brick Kiln Laithe. There are however traces of its existence still in the village.

A Tilery brick in the wall of an outbuilding behind 76 High Street Gargrave
Courtesy of Fred Manby

From the 1st of June 1852 the North-Western Railway was operated by the Midland Railway, although it was not fully absorbed until 1871. The railway was of most importance to the Gargrave farming community with increasing trade in cattle and especially milk supplies to the industrial towns. With the railway built and a regular service provided the single-track railway line was doubled and eventually the Settle to Carlisle line was constructed which meant that Gargrave continued to have a station on an important route.

Passenger traffic increased with the benefit of regular timetables for people travelling for work and special excursions for leisure. The Craven Dales drew townspeople from neighbouring industrial areas to enjoy the fresh air and scenery.

FARMING

The Parish of Gargrave and the surrounding countryside had been formed by farming over the centuries. The good soil, reasonably level ground, easy access to water and a good river crossing provided the basis for the original settlement. The arable fields, ploughed in rotation, were within easy access for the tenant farmers and their labourers. Growing crops, mainly oats, continued until the end of the eighteenth century. The crop returns of 1801 show that 90% of the crops grown were oats and the remaining 10% comprised wheat, barley, potatoes and turnips. Then changes in local transport with the turnpike roads and the canal made arable farming uneconomic, the fields were turned to meadowland, and stock rearing became the norm. The markets for the meat were in the growing industrial towns of East Lancashire and West Yorkshire. Skipton had an annual fair for sheep and cattle from 1779, which Gargrave farmers would have attended.

Skipton in 1830
Scanned from - History Of Skipton by W. Harbutt Dawes -1882

The various enclosure acts redistributed the land amongst fewer tenants and they moved to farmhouses away from the village centre. The Wilson family of Eshton Hall, the Coulthurst family of Gargrave House and the Mason family of Milton House, were the principal landowners in the area. This was still the situation in 1900 when British farming was recovering a little from the 'Long Depression', which had lasted since about 1870.

Meat and grain were now being imported from South America and the USA. Overall prices fell, sometimes by over 50% and farm workers moved away to the towns.

Farming in the area in 1900 was therefore not prosperous. Farmers just about made a living and still employed labourers with the horse as the power behind most of the farming processes. Many farm workers, with their families, had opted for higher wages in the nearby industrial towns. Others had favoured emigration as a way of using their skills for a better reward.

INDUSTRY

MILLS

By the end of the 18th century, the cottage industries of spinning and weaving were being replaced by mills with modern steam-powered machinery. The way was open for anyone with capital, or land with a river or stream with a good fall of water, to build a new mill. Changes to agriculture and transport had made many old corn mills redundant and, as they had dams and goits (water channels), they could be readily converted into textile mills. The map opposite shows the position of the two converted corn High and Low mills and the purpose built Airebank mill.

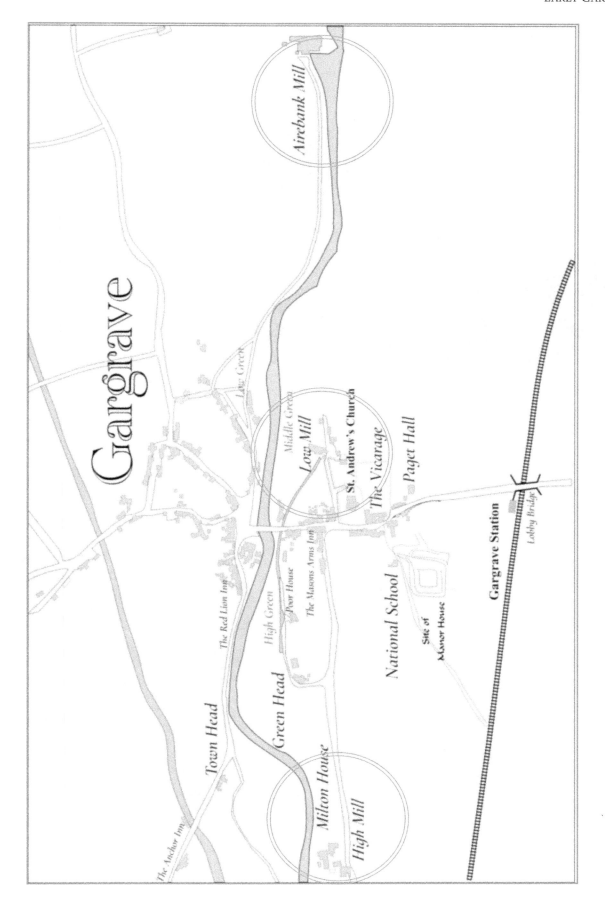

Gargrave

Airebank Mill

Low Green

Middle Green

Low Mill

St. Andrew's Church

The Vicarage

Paget Hall

Town Head

The Red Lion Inn

High Green

Green Head

Poor House

The Masons Arms Inn

National School

Site of Manor House

Gargrave Station

Lobby Bridge

The Anchor Inn

Milton House

High Mill

HIGH MILL

High Mill ca. 1920
Courtesy of the Dennis French Collection

The first of the Gargrave mills to be converted was High Mill, which was bought by Joseph Mason in 1791, but soon handed over to his nephew, another Joseph. This mill was attacked by rioters on the evening of Thursday 27th April 1826. The original rioters came from The Laneshaw Bridge area near Colne and were mainly unemployed hand-loom weavers, intent on destroying the power looms which they felt were taking their jobs.

LOW MILL

In 1798 Betty Hudson the widow of a worsted manufacturer from Keighley took this old corn mill in Gargrave and rebuilt it for spinning cotton. Betty's grandson James Parker and his partner Samuel Gill ran the mill until 1811 when they became bankrupt. The sale notice provides some interesting information about the village at that time. Besides the three storey mill, which we can still see today, were twelve cottages and a spacious garden with fruit trees. It is not clear what happened to this mill during the rest of the century, but by 1900 it was still in industrial use.

Low Mill 1960s
Courtesy of the Dennis French Collection

AIREBANK MILL

Airebank Mill
Airton Studio
Courtesy of the Dennis French Collection

In 1791 Thomas Mason, the cousin of Joseph built Airebank Mill in Gargrave on a new site, just to the east of the village. Thomas senior died in 1810, so the mill passed to his son, also Thomas who continued cotton spinning there for many years. As usual for a cotton spinning mill, most of the employees were women and children who worked long hours from 5.45 in the morning until 7.15 in the evening.

By 1834 part of the mill had been taken by Joseph & Benjamin Smith for worsted spinning and manufacturing, although the latter process was probably still on hand looms. The following year Gargrave was listed as having four mills which explains the division at Airebank. The worsted section stayed in the Smith's hands until 1842 when the complete worsted business was offered for rent. A week following the rental announcement, all the worsted machinery was advertised for sale, including the spinning machinery, bobbins, skeps, weights and scales.

Airebank Mill eventually came into the possession of the Wilson family of Eshton Hall. They let the land and mill to a number of tenants over the years. A major fire in

November 1865 at Airebank Mill resulted in damage to the new building, stock and machinery estimated at £20,000. As everything was insured, the mill was rebuilt and two sixty horsepower steam engines were installed. A fire in an attic room nine years later in 1874 resulted in the destruction of two-thirds of the new building with the loss of 101 carding engines and spinning machinery with 44,000 spindles. About 250 of the 400 workers at the mill lost their jobs until production could start again. Sir Mathew Wilson, from Eshton Hall, the owner, then had it rebuilt, and it was running again by 1875. A gas making plant was built to supply gas to the mill and to the village.

NEW BRIGHTON

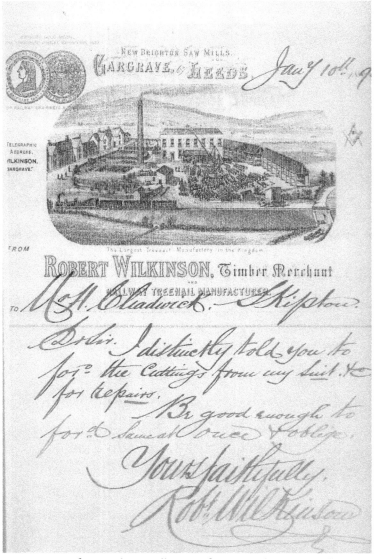

Letter from Robert Wilkinson of New Brighton Sawmill
Courtesy of the Dennis French Collection

By 1900 the now well-established industrial site based on the railway contractors' site outside the village on Marton Road was used as a sawmill and timber yard. From 1881 the site had been occupied by Robert Wilkinson who specialised in making tree nails and advertised his firm as the largest tree nail manufacturer in the kingdom. The early iron bolts quickly rusted in the damp conditions of the sleepers. The constant vibration of rail traffic separated the rust from the bolt which became loose. Compressed wooden tree nails provided a relatively safe substitute, swelling up in the moisture and tightening the grip on the sleeper. They were in use on many railways until the development of better metal bolts.

In January 1893 a severe fire destroyed much of this sawmill, but it was rebuilt, and in 1898 the firm became the New Brighton Saw Mills Co and was taken over by Robert Wilkinson Junior.

The Old Saw Mill
Courtesy of the Dennis French Collection

THE OLD SAW MILL

Just across the road from New Brighton was a long-established sawmill. Little is known about this business, but it was bought in 1876 by James Bell who ran it for many years. In his initial advertisement, he announces himself as a wheelwright and timber merchant and maker of carts. The mill may have previously been used for manufacturing bobbins, as the 1861 census records a high concentration of bobbin turners in the New Brighton and Paradise Cottages.

QUARRYING

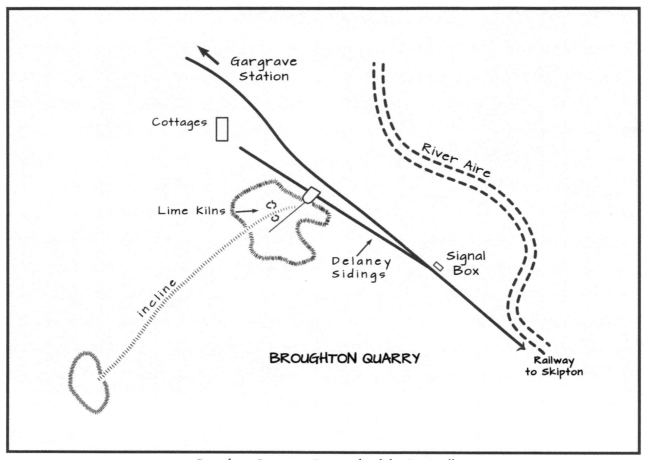

Broughton Quarries - From a sketch by Sue Lyall

Maps from the 1850s show evidence of several small redundant quarry sites, as well as working quarries around Gargrave and Broughton. These latter ones were on land owned by the Tempest family of Broughton Hall and leased to quarry operators. In 1899, John Delaney, who owned quarries at Horton in Ribblesdale and at Threshfield, signed a lease to take over the quarry near Broughton. Four years later, he and his partner John Smith, leased the quarry at Small House pasture, just outside Gargrave. Unfortunately no contemporary photographs have been found.

This one became known locally as Delaney's Quarry, although the official name was Broughton Quarries.

John Delaney had come to Settle in the 1860s to escape from poverty and famine in Ireland. He could see business opportunities and went to study geology at Manchester University before borrowing £40 from a Quaker banker to set up a coal delivery business. He then expanded into quarrying limestone.

OTHER OCCUPATIONS

Trade Directories for the 19th century list a vast range of occupations in the village. For example in 1822 there was a hat maker, a clockmaker, a wheelwright, two blacksmiths, three butchers, four grocers and seven shoemakers. The shoemakers were presumably using leather from local cattle. However, only one farmer and two graziers were mentioned. The village also had all the people to keep it going such as the schoolmaster, the vicar, the surgeon, the postmistress, the insurance agent and several publicans. The self-sufficiency of the times perhaps explains the four tailors. The five public houses for a population of 972 is probably justified by the need for coaching inns where horses could be changed.

One common occupation, particularly for girls who did not want to go into the mill, was domestic service. It was normal for the gentry to have several servants and middle-income families would usually have some help. One advertisement from the Yorkshire Evening Post for the 29th of March 1894 spells out the typical requirements and the yearly wage.

> "Wanted, a strong, active girl as SCULLERY-MAID; age 17- 19; wages £12, all found. Will be required to remain behind three months during the family's absence. Must have been out before and well recommended. – Apply Mrs Coulthurst, Gargrave House, Gargrave."

LONG DEPRESSION 1873 -1898

The "Long Depression" was a contemporary term to describe an economic downturn which took place during the fourth quarter of the nineteenth century. It was a world-wide phenomenon although perhaps "depression" was not the right word, as industry and agriculture did continue, but made little profit. The United Kingdom is often considered to have been the hardest hit, as during this period it lost some of its sizeable industrial lead over the economies of Continental Europe and agricultural production declined.

Gargrave was not immune from what was happening elsewhere. Jobs and incomes were affected by what appeared to be a slowdown in demand for both agricultural and industrial products. The number of farming insolvencies increased nationally, but this was not experienced in Gargrave as most farms were tenanted. Two of the three textile mills were disused by 1896, and the local textile industry was experiencing problems.

One solution at the time in the textile trades was to form combines and try to stop price-cutting and to cut out unprofitable mills. Locally two firms joined the English Sewing Cotton Company Limited in 1897. These were John Dewhurst & Sons from Belle Vue Mills in Skipton and Charles Rickards who had silk spinning mills at Bell Busk and in Skipton. The machinery from Bell Busk was transferred from there to Low Mill in Skipton, and the Bell Busk Mill demolished.

Dewhurst's Sylko thread for machine use.
Courtesy of Donavon Slaven.

LAND OWNERS

In 1900 most of the farms and land in the village was owned by three families, the Wilsons of Eshton Hall, the Coulthursts of Gargrave House and to a lesser extent the the Prestons who at one time lived at Flasby Hall. These families were part of the traditional 'landed gentry' in the country who provided the leaders at both a national and local level. They were magistrates dealing with law and order, they played a leading role in religious and political affairs, they also supported schools and chaired most of the social groups in the village. Their income came from land, but they were prepared to invest in industrial enterprises if it seemed worthwhile. For example, the Wilsons owned Airebank Mills, and Sir Mathew Wilson promoted local railways. The Coulthursts were a landowning family in Craven from at least the 17th century and lived at Gargrave House. The Coniston Cold Estate was bought in 1665, and Henry Coulthurst endowed a free grammar school near Gargrave in 1686. The family was involved with the life of the village until the 1950s and also left a lasting legacy in the form of the Coulthurst Trust which still supports many local organisations.

Eshton Hall ca. 1800
From -"The History and Antiquities of the Deanery of Craven" by Thomas Dunham Whitaker, LL.D. F. S. A. 1885

During the 19th and 20th centuries, members of the family occupied many local positions, with the Craven Agricultural Society, the Education Committee and serving as local magistrates.

Flasby Hall ca. 1900
Courtesy of the Dennis French Collection

Old Gargrave House demolished in 1914
Courtesy of the Dennis French Collection

THE CHURCHES

In Victorian and Edwardian society, church-going was considered an essential part of life. Most people went to the Church of England, but Catholics and non-conformists would co-exist in communities, albeit under a cloud of disapproval from the established church. The rivalry and separation between Church and Chapel continued well into the twentieth century.

ST ANDREW'S PARISH CHURCH

Late 19th century lithograph of St. Andrew's church by Palleyn and Hunt of Leeds.
Private Collection – St. Andrew's Church

The Parish Church at Gargrave had many incarnations since its founding. Some of these are described in Whitaker's History of Craven and in the History of Gargrave Church and Parish by Janet Dinsdale.

The original place of Christian worship, on the site the present church occupies, may have been merely a meeting place in the open but with carved stone markers followed later by a wooden structure in which to pray. A break from the Celtic Christian Church to follow the practice of the church of Rome began in 664 following the Synod of Whitby where King Oswiu of Northumbria, declared that his kingdom would follow the customs of Rome, rather than those practised by the Irish monks of Iona. Wilfrid, Bishop of York between 669 and 677 decreed that the old Celtic places of worship be replaced with church buildings which were more in keeping with the new order.

It is entirely possible that the original stone built church at Gargrave was constructed using masonry from the site of the Roman Villa in the period that Wilfrid was in office. This would not be an exceptional thing as there are many other examples of this happening. Escomb Church, Bishop Auckland, was constructed in 670 with stone from a nearby Roman fort. All Saint's at Brixworth Northamptonshire was built sometime around 670 using Roman bricks from a nearby villa.

The church was rebuilt around 1520. In more recent times, part of the church was rebuilt in 1852. The 1521 tower survived, but as the rest of the old church had fallen into disrepair, the nave and chancel were reconstructed. Along with the additions of some modern facilities, this is the church building that still serves the parish.

Throughout most of the 19th century, there were only two vicars, Anthony Marsden and his son Charles. Anthony died in 1852 and was succeeded by Charles who had been acting as his curate for the previous 14 years. Towards the end of his tenure, Charles and his wife were in failing health, and they retired to Torquay in 1896. The running of the church had been mainly in the hands of his curate, John Rowland Leigh, who often preached the sermon when the vicar was not able to do so. Rev Leigh was a keen cricketer, and a story has been passed down that one Sunday he was in the pulpit sporting two black eyes – the previous day's match having been somewhat eventful.

The Magee family.
Courtesy of Derek Mc Robert

The next vicar was Arthur Victor Magee, a newly ordained clergyman with high church leanings, which didn't always go down well with the parishioners of Gargrave.

OTHER DENOMINATIONS

Much about the religious state of the village can be deduced from what the vicar told the Archdeacon on his periodic visits. In 1764, out of 189 families in Gargrave, three were Popish, one was Quaker, and four were known to be Methodists.

CATHOLICS

The Catholics worshipped at Broughton Hall, where the Tempest family had their own chapel. The next nearest church was St Stephen's in Skipton.

QUAKERS

It is probable that Quakers met in private homes in the village in earlier days, and at some time there were licenced Meeting Houses in Broughton, Gargrave and Airton. An act of Parliament in 1693 granted non-conformists more freedom to worship so they could emerge from their 'secret' churches without fear of persecution. What happened to the Gargrave and Broughton Friends is not known, but the Quakers established their meetings in Airton in the 1650s and in Skipton in the 1660s. These last two are still active. Births, marriages and burials of Gargrave Quakers were recorded at Airton.

WESLEYAN METHODISTS

In 1764, the vicar said that the Methodists gathered in a licenced meeting house and that he had heard that their teacher, Joseph Edmundson was a follower of Mr Ingham. Benjamin Ingham was part of John Wesley's Holy Club at Oxford, but became influenced by the Moravians and developed his own type of non-conformist worship. As his influence declined, most of his followers went back to the Wesley brand of Methodism, which is probably what had happened with the Gargrave group.

Their original meeting place was in two cottages in East Street, and then the Old Chapel in South Street was used from about 1800. This building eventually became the Parochial Hall and is now converted into apartments.

The church flourished and grew, and a new chapel was opened in 1865 on Skipton Road. The land was purchased from Sir Mathew Wilson for £100 and the chapel built at the cost of £2,500. A significant part of the financial support came from the Bracewell family, who lived at Knowles House and ran Airebank Mills.

In the same year, the Wesleyans were responsible for a 'red-hot revival' of religious fervour in the village. The local newspaper reported that many had flocked to the chapel to hear the zealous and eloquent preachers. The vicar (Charles Marsden) was not at all impressed by these outward expressions of feeling and warned his congregation not to be taken in by such fanaticism.

Skipton Road Methodist Chapel in Gargrave
Airton Studio
Courtesy of the Dennis French Collection

The Gargrave chapel was part of the Skipton Wesleyan circuit, and the ministers had a rota for preaching at the various places in the area. As the Wesleyans didn't have a resident minister, the management of the chapel was in the hands of the congregation who elected their church trustees and elders. The circuit superintendent minister would come to functions and to chair meetings, but as the person in this post changed regularly, the consistency was maintained by the church members.

PRIMITIVE METHODISTS

The Primitives split off from the Wesleyans in about 1811 to return to a plainer style of worship and to appeal to the lower working classes – servants and labourers. The Gargrave group moved into premises vacated by the Wesleyans. Firstly they met in the East Street cottages and then in the Old Chapel once the Wesleyans had moved to their new premises in Skipton Road.

Primitive Methodist ladies 'Ranting' outside their cottages in East Street
Airton Studio
Courtesy of the Dennis French Collection

Because of its long association with the Methodists and their vigorous style of preaching, East Street was known locally as 'Ranters' Row'. The Old Chapel closed in 1908 when the building was reorganised and used for the Mechanics' Institute and the Parochial Hall. The Primitive Methodists continued in Skipton, and eventually, in 1932, they put aside their differences and reunited with the Wesleyans to become The Methodist Church.

EDUCATION

Before the Victorian era, education had been only for the rich and privileged. Children would be taught at home by governesses and tutors. The boys would be sent away to public schools and would then progress to university, the armed forces, to the church or would inherit the family estate. Girls remained at home to learn the art of being a lady and preparing for marriage.

The earliest known school in Gargrave was the Free Grammar School, founded in 1686 by members of the Coulthurst family. A charitable trust fund was set up to pay for the building and a schoolmaster. The school was built in a somewhat isolated position on a hill equidistant from Gargrave, Bank Newton and Coniston Cold, so it was accessible for pupils from these settlements. The school could only be reached by walking across fields. The school taught English and Maths and for a fee, Latin, which would be needed for university entrance. Nothing much is known about the fortunes of the school until 1824 when the schoolmaster left, and the building fell into disrepair.

For ordinary children, the only source of education was at the Sunday Schools, run by the churches. The Wesleyan Sunday School started in 1815, and it is thought that the Church of England Sunday School dates from about 1800.

However, a new school, see image on following page, was set up in 1820 by Robert Story, a poet and playwright from Northumberland. Initially, the school was in cottages in South Street and then in a superior residence built for him in North Street by Sir Mathew Wilson and at its peak had 50 pupils. Robert Story lost his enthusiasm for teaching and, as a result of differing views from the local political establishment, found it expedient to leave Gargrave in 1843 for a civil service post in London.

Robert Story - Gargrave's Poet
*Modified Scan of Painting by R. Waller, Engraved by W. O. Geller From
"The Lyrical and Other Minor Poems of Robert Story, with a Sketch of His Life and
Writings" by John James. 1861*

Robert Story's house and school on North Street.
Courtesy of Donavon Slaven 2018

The Victorians promoted the concept of education for all, and in Gargrave, this was delivered by the churches establishing their own schools. Firstly, the Church of England built a school on the site of the redundant tithe barn, opposite the church. The school was supported and funded by Mathew Wilson and John Coulthurst and opened in 1846. This was known as the National School, but this was actually the short version of its full title - "The National Society for Promoting the Education of the Poor in the Principles of the Established Church in England and Wales".

The Catholics had a school in an upstairs room in West Street from about 1850, supported by the Tempest family of Broughton Hall. It was generally referred to as the 'Roman' school and only lasted until 1871. Mr Bracewell (the proprietor of Airebank Mills) sent his part-time workers here until it closed and the children were then transferred to the National School. However, once the Wesleyan School opened, Mr Bracewell sent them there, in keeping with his own religious persuasion.

The Wesleyan Sunday School was first established in 1815 at the Old Chapel. In those days, this would be the only form of education available to most of the children. The youngest children were taught in the basement and the older ones in the floor above. The aim was to teach the children to read, write and know the scriptures. 170 children regularly attended Sunday School. In 1870, the Wesleyan congregation decided to build a school. A piece of land directly opposite the chapel was bought from Sir Mathew Wilson for £80, and fundraising began. When the eventual building costs came in at £1412

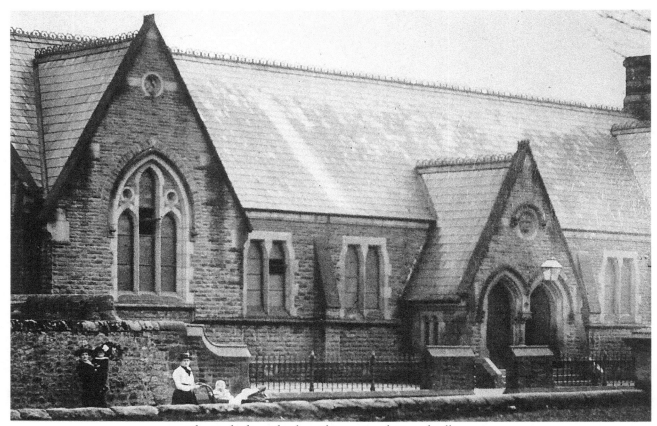

The Methodist School on Skipton Road. Now dwellings.
Courtesy of the Dennis French Collection

(instead of the estimated £1000),
Mr Edmund Bracewell stepped in to make up the difference. The new day (and Sunday) school opened on Good Friday 1873.

The Wesleyan cause was strong in Gargrave and split the village along religious lines. This divide between church and chapel was to persist for many generations. The new chapel had been built in 1865, and with the opening of the school, this completed the removal of all their operations from the 'Old Chapel' in South Street.

Census returns and local directories show that there were some small local 'Dame schools' in the 1800s, as well as the two main schools. One of these, run by the Misses Davis was at Bridgeholme in the High Street in 1881 and had 8 girls boarding there. Miss Elizabeth, Miss Margaret and Miss Jane were the daughters of William Davis, a farmer of Holme House. Their school in Gargrave wasn't long-lived as the 1891 census found them running a similar small girls' boarding school in Knaresborough. The three of them retired back to Gargrave and ended their days at The Hollies in Church Street.

When the National School was set up, probably not many children went to school. Children would be working in the mill from the age of 8 and families would have to pay the 'school pence' which was typically 2d a week for a labourer's child. In 1870, an education act decreed that a child should have at least 5 years of elementary education from the age of 5 years.

The National School. Now converted to dwellings.
Courtesy of Martin Thompson

This didn't make much of an improvement to the school attendance, as parents would send their children to work half time at the mills or just keep them at home to help with household chores.

The removal of school fees in 1891, encouraged more children to attend school, as the state paid 10s a year per child. Some schools charged top-up fees for older pupils.

Much of the following information comes from the headmasters' logs of both schools. These were discovered at Gargrave Primary School and were summarised by Enid French for her dissertation. Mrs French has kindly given us access to her notes.

It wasn't just a simple case of Church people going to the Church School and Methodists to the Wesleyan School. Parents often chose the nearest school to home. The Wesleyan Church was more central, with a larger catchment area than the National School on the edge of the village. The headmasters' logs from both schools show that there was a good deal of swapping between the schools. Back in 1885, there were complaints by the Wesleyan headmaster that the curate was bribing families to transfer and that the vicar had even threatened an employee with dismissal unless he moved his children. Usually, the removals were brought about by the parents. There was considerable gloating when one school gained pupils. However, if parents had the temerity to remove their children, the head was knocking on their doors, demanding to know the reason why.

Often the reasons were to do with discipline. A father would arrive at the National School complaining about his son being caned, and on being told that the lad deserved it, he removed all his children to the other school. One mother so appalled the head of the Wesleyan school with her 'indecent language in front of the other children' that he expelled her son and she transferred him and his siblings to the National School.

THE SCHOOL DAY

The school day started with religious teaching, followed by lessons in reading, writing, arithmetic and singing. The older boys would learn geography, and the girls had sewing lessons. Depending on the interests of the teachers, there might also be nature rambles and trips. The schools only had three classrooms, for the infants, the boys and the girls. One teacher had a large class of mixed ages, but they were usually assisted by pupil teachers. From the age of 13, a capable pupil could start a 5-year apprenticeship as a trainee teacher. After that, on passing an entrance exam, the pupil-teacher could go to a government funded teacher training college. From the headmasters' logbooks, it was apparent that there was a high turnover in the pupil and assistant teachers.

Discipline was harsh, and punishments were given out freely, although it wasn't permitted to hit the infants. A mild punishment would be 500 lines for bad behaviour. Fighting or tearing a book would result in being caned. However, if an offender showed any defiance while being reprimanded, flogging would be administered.

TIME OFF

Attendance at both schools was affected by family finances, parental indifference and by the sickness of the pupils. Even after legislation stopped young children from working and school fees were abolished, some parents still didn't see education as a priority and found excuses to keep their children at home. Several times a year, the schools were closed because of outbreaks of illness. Typical closures would be between one and four weeks for measles, chicken pox and whooping cough and 9 to 12 weeks for diphtheria or scarlet fever.

The school inspectors regularly reported that most of the children failed to reach the required standards by the time they left school. However, the National School inspectors from the Diocese always gave glowing reports on the teaching of the Bible.

The summer holiday was 4 weeks long and timed to coincide with the hay harvest in July / August. There would also be two weeks off at Christmas, and several days for Easter and Whitsun, plus quite a lot of other occasional days. Schools closed for the Gargrave Fair in December, for jubilee celebrations, the otter hunt or visits to the circus. Bostock and Wombwell's travelling circus and menagerie regularly came through Gargrave. Their sights and curiosities were not to be missed by young and old alike.

The schools had their annual summer treats with food and games and, at Christmas time, Lady Wilson provided food and entertainments such as Punch and Judy, a conjurer or a cinematographic show. The pupils would also put on concerts for their families and the patrons of the school. The children at the National School were exposed to the latest technology when Mr Wilkinson brought his gramophone in to entertain them at the end of the autumn term in 1897.

THE MECHANICS' INSTITUTE

Only a few children progressed to secondary education at the Skipton schools. However, there were opportunities for continuing education within the village. In the 1820s industrialists and wealthy benefactors had established Mechanics' Institutes to provide education and constructive leisure activities for their workers. It was intended to steer them away from the evils of drinking and gambling and turn their employees into a better class of worker. In the Craven area, the Skipton Mechanics' Institute began in 1847, and at Grassington, an Institute was founded for the benefit of the lead miners. It inspired other towns and villages to do likewise. The purpose was to provide reading materials, classes and concerts and eventually many institutes became public libraries or colleges of education.

In 1868, a group of young men set up the Gargrave Mechanics' Institute in a cottage in South Street. William Henry Davis, from Holme House Farm, was the driving force behind the enterprise, along with Richard Greenwood, a local solicitor. Another founding member was John Hyde who was only 18 at the time. A reading room was the nucleus of the Institute with books and newspapers from Manchester, Leeds and London, and was open from 9 am until 10 pm.

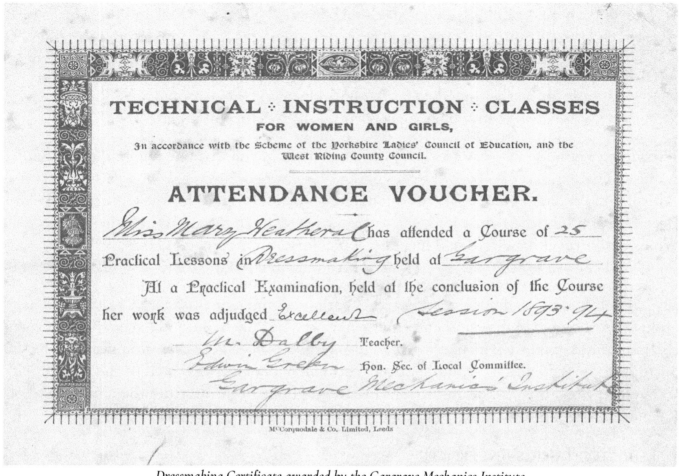

Dressmaking Certificate awarded by the Gargrave Mechanics Institute
Courtesy of Audrey Weatherill

Evening classes were started in Arithmetic, English and Science. Mr Smart, the headmaster of the National School took some of these. Later, there were classes in drawing, geography and dressmaking. A branch of the Yorkshire Penny Bank was available on the premises to encourage saving and organised debates were a regular feature on the events calendar.

In the 1880s the institute was in a crisis, suffering from lack of leadership, poor accommodation and lack of funding. However, it survived and by the end of the century was running a wide range of classes for both men and women. These were usually held in the Wesleyan school rooms, due to lack of space in the South Street cottage.

Eventually, the Mechanics Institute was able to move into larger premises in the Old Chapel, just behind their old cottage.

1900-1914 Life In Gargrave

A new Century A new Beginning?

The new century opened with the whole of Europe at unease.   In addition to the struggle to recover from the Long Depression of between 1873 and 1896, there was a great deal of political instability which would eventually affect the whole world.

In 1888, Wilhelm II, the eldest grandchild of Great Britain's Queen Victoria, became enthroned as Kaiser - "German Emperor" and King of Prussia. He immediately changed the stance of the country to a more aggressive and proactive nature. He refused to renew a policy with Russia and joined with the Austro-Hungarian Empire to achieve a new measure of strength. The Kaiser's actions alarmed the neighbouring countries, which immediately created a series of treaties, pacts and alliances in an attempt to halt the march to war. Britain also felt the threat and formed alliances with European nations promising to aid them in times of conflict. In 1905, the political situation became critical. Earl Roberts, along with other members of the House, made several speeches in the House of Lords about strengthening our armed forces.

Newly retired from the post of Commander-in-Chief of the British Armed Forces, Earl Roberts was in a position to speak with authority. In September 1902, he and the Earl of Midleton, William St John Fremantle Brodrick, had attended German Army manoeuvres as guests of the Kaiser. Much of his insider knowledge was passed to a William Le Queux, a diplomat, journalist, and author who was preparing a fantasy novel "The Invasion of 1910".

The novel was proof read by Earl Roberts and the book released in 1906. It seems that this may well have been a push to get the government to take things seriously.

 The book contained detailed descriptions of the imagined German invasion of Britain in 1910.

Maps and official looking declarations to the "conquered" British citizens as illustrations in the book, may have had some influence on the decisions that were being made with regard to the defence of the realm. Steps were eventually taken to strengthen our armed forces.

PROCLAMATION.

WE, GENERAL COMMANDING THE 3rd GERMAN ARMY,

HAVING SEEN the proclamation of His Imperial Majesty the Emperor William, King of Prussia, Chief of the Army, which authorises the generals commanding the different German Army Corps to establish special measures against all municipalities and persons acting in contradiction to the usages of war, and to take what steps they consider necessary for the well-being of the troops,

HEREBY GIVE PUBLIC NOTICE:

(1) THE MILITARY JURISDICTION is hereby established. It applies to all territory of Great Britain occupied by the German Army, and to every action endangering the security of the troops by rendering assistance to the enemy. The Military Jurisdiction will be announced and placed vigorously in force in every parish by the issue of this present proclamation.

(2) ANY PERSON OR PERSONS NOT BEING BRITISH SOLDIERS, or not showing by their dress that they are soldiers :

(a) SERVING THE ENEMY as spies;

(b) MISLEADING THE GERMAN TROOPS when charged to serve as guides;

(c) SHOOTING, INJURING, OR ROBBING any person belonging to the German Army, or forming part of its personnel;

(d) DESTROYING BRIDGES OR CANALS, damaging telegraphs, telephones, electric light wires, gasometers, or railways, interfering with roads, setting fire to munitions of war, provisions, or quarters established by German troops;

(e) TAKING ARMS against the German troops,

WILL BE PUNISHED BY DEATH.

IN EACH CASE the officer presiding at the Council of War will be charged with the trial, and pronounce judgment. Councils of War may not pronounce ANY OTHER CONDEMNATION SAVE THAT OF DEATH.

THE JUDGMENT WILL BE IMMEDIATELY EXECUTED.

(3) TOWNS OR VILLAGES in the territory in which the contravention takes place will be compelled to pay indemnity equal to one year's revenue.

(4) THE INHABITANTS MUST FURNISH necessaries for the German troops daily as follows :—

1 lb. 10 oz. bread.	1 oz. tea.	1½ pints beer, or 1 wine-
13 oz. meat.	1½ oz. tobacco or 5 cigars.	glassful of brandy or
3 lb. potatoes.	¼ pint wine.	whisky.

The ration for each horse :—

13 lb. oats.	3 lb. 6 oz. hay.	3 lb. 6 oz. straw.

(ALL PERSONS WHO PREFER to pay an indemnity in money may do so at the rate of 2s. per day per man.)

(5) COMMANDERS OF DETACHED corps have the right to requisition all that they consider necessary for the well-being of their men, and will deliver to the inhabitants official receipts for goods so supplied.

WE HOPE IN CONSEQUENCE that the inhabitants of Great Britain will make no difficulty in furnishing all that may be considered necessary.

(6) AS REGARDS the individual transactions between the troops and the inhabitants, we give notice that one German mark shall be considered the equivalent to one English shilling.

**The General Commanding the Ninth German Army Corps,
VON KRONHELM.**

BECCLES, *September the Third*, 1910.

One of the Proclamations displayed in the book.

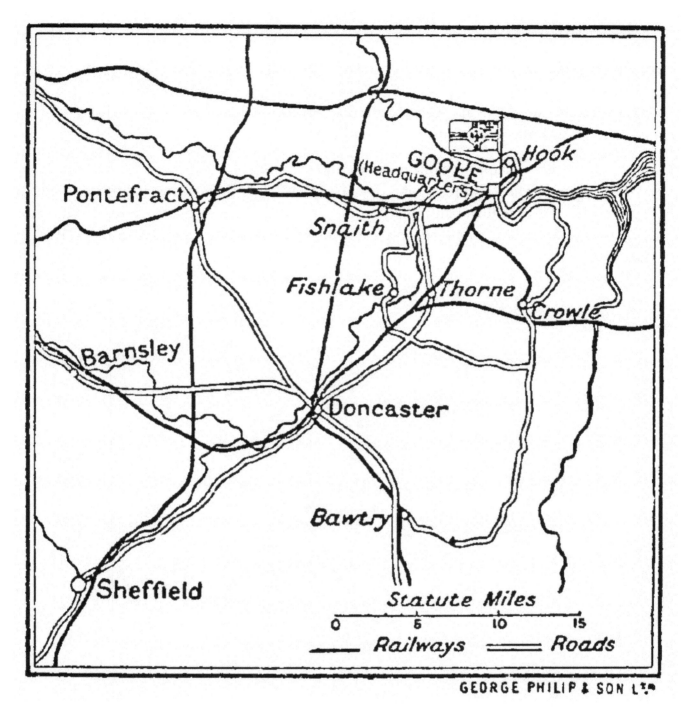

Map from "The Invasion of 1910" Showing the Imperial German Flag flying over Goole.

Gargrave could not escape from witnessing its own military 'invasion', which took place in 1912, and was also to face a number of local catastrophes in the years to follow.

LIFE IN GARGRAVE

Tom Airton, a signalman for the Midland Railway, had a passion for photography which left Gargrave with a wealth of pictorial records. In his spare time he went out on location recording village life capturing street scenes, people and recording village events. He turned part of his home into a studio for family portraits.

His most iconic photograph was one of an elephant, and a dromedary pulling a wagon through Gargrave. They had just come past The Swan, heading towards Skipton. Pulling the wagon with a dromedary helping is a young female Indian elephant called Dixie. The three boys on the left of the photograph are Walter Hudson, Maurice Hudson, and Rufus Bradley.

Bostock and Wombwell's travelling circus and menagerie. High Street Gargrave ca. 1910.
Courtesy of the Dennis French Collection

Unfortunately, Tom's time as Gargrave's official photographer was to come to a tragic end. He helped at the Liberal Club as a caretaker, and on 27 September 1914 he was attempting to light the acetylene gas lamps.

Acetylene lights are bright, but dangerous if not used correctly. No-one was sure what happened, but Tom had struck a match, causing an explosion and the carbide container hit him in the face, fracturing his nose and skull. On hearing the explosion, William Lofthouse rushed in from next door to find Tom lying unconscious and bleeding on the floor. Dr Cameron came at once from his house across the road, but he could do nothing to help Tom. He died at his home a short while later.

On the day of his funeral, many villagers attended. The coffin was carried by four uniformed signalmen and house blinds, and shutters were closed as a mark of respect. The inscription on his grave says:

"In the midst of life, we are in death."

We are indebted to Tom for the many photographs used in this book. A selection of Tom's work is shown on the next pages.

Barges at Fred Green's Wharf
Airton Studios
Courtesy of the Dennis French Collection

South Street ca. 1900
Airton Studios
Courtesy of the Dennis French Collection

The Early Co-Op on South Street,
Airton Studios
Courtesy of the Dennis French Collection

Assing About - South Street ca. 1905
Airton Studios
Courtesy of the Dennis French Collection

Higherlands Lock ca 1902
Airton Studios
Courtesy of the Dennis French Collection

Eshton Hall ca 1902
Airton Studios
Courtesy of the Dennis French Collection

Church Lane ca. 1905
Airton Studio
Courtesy of the Dennis French Collection

Troops marching over Gargrave River Bridge 1912
Airton Studios
Courtesy of the Dennis French Collection

River Bridge, Gargrave.
Airton Studios
Courtesy of the Dennis French Collection

POPULATION

At the start of the 20th Century, Gargrave was a village of 1261 inhabitants. This figure had remained unchanged since the 1891 census, but by 1911, the population had decreased to 1165. More information about the changes in population over the years can be found in Appendix A.

Lack of employment caused this decline as families moved to Lancashire or abroad to find work. The prosperity of the village rose and fell depending on the success of its employers, chiefly the large cotton spinners at Airebank Mills.

INDUSTRIES

The mills provided work for a high proportion of the village. Outdoor employment was provided by the estates, quarries and farming. The Gargrave Sanitary Laundry in West Street, employed about 20, mostly female workers. The New Brighton Saw Mill was the only other industry of any size.

In 1901, 35% of the workers were employed at Airebank Mills, 21% in agriculture and other outdoor work, 19% in retail, trade and services and 10% in domestic service.

Opposite Page
Ladies from the mill in their work clothes.
Top - from left to right
Back row: Rebecca Langstroth; May Langstroth; Margaret Wiseman; Polly Saunders; Jane Harrison
Middle row: Hannah Metcalfe; Mary Ellen McQueenie; Ms Knight; Mary Bradley; Lizzie Summergill; Sarah
Elizabeth Langstroth Front row: Mrs Hargreaves; Hilda Saunders

The image belowshhows the ladies from the mill in their Sunday best at the old cricket pavillion. Not all of the ladies in the lower photograph are known.
Both images Courtesy of the Dennis French Collection

AIREBANK MILLS

The main employer was still the Airebank cotton spinning mill. Sons and daughters followed their parents to work in the mill. The school leaving age had been raised to 13 in 1899, but some 12-year-olds in Gargrave were half time at school and half time at work. By the age of 13, provided they had the required number of attendances at school and were healthy enough, they worked full time at the mill. A young lad would earn 5 shillings 4 pence for a 56 hour week. In 1911, 39% of the village was working there as doffers, rovers, winders, spinners, beamers, frame tenters, piecers, drawers, overlookers, mechanics and stationery engine drivers. Descriptions of some of the cotton industry jobs and processes can be found in Appendix B.

The business had been run by the Bracewell family since 1847, but by the turn of the century, it was in decline and eventually ran out of capital in 1904. It was taken over by William Cecil Slingsby and John Arthur Slingsby of Carleton, and gradually the former workers were re-employed. The Slingsbys had spinning and weaving mills at Carleton, but at that time, they were carrying out significant alterations and may have needed an alternative site to produce their thread. However, there were difficulties ahead, as 1909 was recorded as a poor year with the workers on short time.

> "Working during the year in the principal industry – cotton spinning - has been somewhat of a mixed character, and just now 35 hours per week is the standard time."
>
> Craven Herald review of 1909.

Thomas Whittle and John Brindle took over as tenants of the mill towards the end of 1911 in a wave of optimism. Thomas Whittle had previously been a manager at Carleton Mill and John Brindle had managed a mill in Lancashire.

> "The dying year will leave Gargrave with rosier prospects commercially than it found it. The chief source of employment is, of course, the extensive cotton spinning and doubling works at Airebank Mills, and here the long-drawn-out uncertainty of regular employment had now given place to full time since the advent of Messrs Whittle and Brindle and Co Ltd to the business. Full time is now being worked, and the cottages, which were emptied by migrating families, are gradually being let again."
>
> Craven Herald Review of 1911

However, the good times proved to be short-lived, as the mill was all but destroyed in the disastrous fire of 14 November 1912, plunging the village into despair and unemployment. The mill had been working full time, and there was a large stock of cotton bales on the premises.

The fire broke out at about 4.30 p.m. in the spinning room rope race on the first floor. It ignited suddenly, with no warning smoke and spread rapidly to the looms, the ceiling and then to the rest of the building, due to a lack of fire-proof doors and construction materials. Once the alarm was sounded, all of the workers managed to escape unharmed, although some of the female staff fainted from shock after they reached safety. The mill's fire brigade sprang into action, but it quickly became evident that this blaze was far too big for them to tackle and help was summoned from the nearby fire stations.

The Keighley fire brigade arrived at 5.30 with their modern motor pump, having made the journey in 30 minutes. No crew from Skipton attended, as no request for help had been received although the men were available.

The Craven Herald described the scene:-

> "The fire cast a lurid glare over the heavens for miles around, which could be plainly discerned at Skipton, and motors and cycles were requisitioned to convey persons to the scene of the conflagration."

> In fact, a huge crowd of spectators gathered – from those concerned for their livelihoods to the merely curious.

> "The scene was one of awesome grandeur, and not without a trace of weirdness, accentuated by the hoarse cry of the buzzer which was not stopped from the time it was set going to give the alarm until the steam in the boilers was exhausted and the flames subsided to a dull red glow."

In an attempt to reduce losses, cotton bales were thrown out into the field, the wooden gangway from the main building was hacked away to save the adjacent grinding shed (the older part of the mill).

The gas making plant was turned off to prevent explosions. As the mill also supplied Gargrave with gas, the village was plunged into darkness, so the residents had to revert back to candles and oil lamps for lighting.

The shell of the burnt out mill. Note the cigarette smoker

Courtesy of the Dennis French Collection

By midnight, the fire had burnt itself out, leaving a tangled mess of machinery and only the walls standing, although a large part of one of the gable ends had partially collapsed, narrowly missing a group of firefighters.

The mill was the property of Sir Mathew Amcotts Wilson and it was insured, but the loss of some 300 jobs was a devastating blow to Gargrave.

A disaster relief committee was promptly set up to raise funds and assist the unemployed.

The ruins of the mill proved to be quite a tourist attraction. Photographs of the scene were taken and quickly made into souvenir postcards for sale. A local resident, sent a card of the ruins to her friend in Lothersdale to wish her a Happy Christmas!

Courtesy of Martin Thompson

Throughout the early months of 1913, the Mill Fire Distress Committee reported on their work, which involved fundraising, providing interim financial support and help in finding alternative employment.

Ten men were found work in the local area, one on the Eshton Hall Estate, three on the Gledstone Estate, three at Hellifield Peel, two at Knowles House and one at Milton House. The railway fares for the workmen travelling to Hellifield were paid out of the relief fund.

At a meeting of the village's unemployed men at the end of January 1913, the chairman said that it was almost impossible for the relief fund to last long, as little work would be available for eighteen months to two years. Several firms in Lancashire had written to offer employment, so it was thought it best to call the unemployed together to consider the situation. Some of these firms were only providing jobs for girls and had no work available for the men. The relief fund gave help with removal expenses, and by this time, fifteen families had already left for the nearby Lancashire towns. The Cuba Mill Co Ltd had provided work and prepared cottages for three families, and in March the families moved to Ramsbottom.

At the end of February, some good news was imparted to the committee by John Brindle and reported in the Craven Herald.

> "Mr Brindle announced that he had taken over the mill which would be rebuilt, and, he expected to be working again in about eight or nine months. The announcement was received with applause.
>
> His partnership with Thomas Whittle had ended, and John Brindle was now the sole tenant of the mill.
>
> Mr Brindle also stated that he considered everybody concerned was greatly indebted to Sir Mathew Wilson, Bart, who, he said, "has come to our aid, and has met us manfully."
>
> We understand that Mr Brindle is forming a limited liability company, who will rebuild the mill upon modern lines – partly two storeys and partly one. The area of land covered will exceed that upon which the old mill stood. The number of spindles will be about the same, viz, 30,000, but two thirds will be ring spindles and one third mule spindles. The work of reconstruction will be put in hand forthwith, and, given ordinary conditions, the machinery will be running in about eight months."

There was some hope that a weaving shed would be built, but this was not to be the case and the eight months' estimate to starting up again was somewhat optimistic. It wasn't until November 1914 that the mill engines started again for the opening ceremony.

Once the engines were started up, Mr Brindle named them Albert and Janey, after his son and daughter. The assembled company of directors, management and representatives from the village drank a toast to the success and prosperity of the business.

The whole of the building was now fireproof. Girders and concrete floors had been substituted for the wooden ones, and the rope pulleys, where the last fire was said to have originated, were in a fire-proof chamber apart from the engine house. The roof of the main building was of concrete, and it was suggested that it could make a good skating rink in winter.

Arthur Reeder at Airebank Mills
Courtesy of the Dennis French Collection

John Hyde was one of the invited guests at the celebration dinner and said that probably his position in that room was unique, as he had seen the mill built up four times and burnt down three times, which no-one present had done.

Arthur Reeder started up the engines. He and his family had left Gargrave to work in Barnoldswick but returned so Arthur could resume his job running the engines, which he did for many more years. With orders on the books and cotton supplies bought, the mill started partial production in early 1915. By then, many of the young men had enlisted and gone away to war, but the remaining workforce had the skills and experience to make Airebank Mills work again.

HIGH MILL

Joseph Mason's cotton spinning business was long gone by 1900. After this, the mill was often let to more than one company at a time, on a 'room and power' basis and there was a regular turnover of tenants.

There was a fellmongering business in the mill at the beginning of the century, run by the Platt family. Fellmongers processed animal skins, particularly sheepskins together with animal parts which could be used in the manufacture of products such as bone meal fertiliser, tallow for soap and lanolin to name but a few. The Platts were an itinerant family and don't seem to have been in Gargrave for long, apart from Harry, who married local girl Rebecca Langstroth and stayed.

This picture shows the tannery workers at High Mill. Three of the Platt family are in the photo
Harry (second from the left), James (second from the right) and Samuel (seated on the right).
Courtesy of Robin Platt

John Gaunt's Cycloplane

William Gaunt and his son John operated the Ventilated Collar Band Company from 1901 to about 1911. John became obsessed with flying. He developed the Cycloplane – a wing assisted bicycle. Not satisfied with the bicycle, John and two assistants kept busy building an aeroplane in the company premises at High Mill. In 1910 his father died, the Collar Band Company ceased to exist, and John and his aviation ambitions removed to Southport. After a few setbacks and the move to Southport, the small team eventually finished the production of a small bi-plane which he flew along the foreshore in 1911.

In another part of the mill, Charles Henry Spencer was making tramway braking systems and appliances from about 1908. Why he chose Gargrave is not known, but his interest in tram brakes can be traced back to his birthplace of Halifax.

His father, Frederick Spencer had been the manager of the Halifax Corporation Electric Tramway since its start in 1898 and Charles had worked for them as the stock car electrician.

John Gaunt depicted flying his 'Baby Biplane' at Southport 23rd August 1917

Halifax was a hilly and dangerous place for a tram system, so accidents and derailments were regular occurrences as the braking systems were inadequate. Charles Spencer was working to improve this and had filed a patent in 1904 for better tramcar braking. Whether his improvements ever got implemented is doubtful. After two severe accidents in 1906 and 1907, involving multiple fatalities, both father and son left Halifax and came to Gargrave. The company at High Mill was only in existence until about 1916. However, Charles Spencer's time in Gargrave was not wasted, as he met and married Jane Ellen Hartley (daughter of Samuel Hartley the painter and plumber) and they went off to live in Shipley.

The next tenant was J H Cleave, manufacturers of athletic goods and billiard tables, who had previously been operating in Bradford and brought several new families into the village in 1913. Unfortunately, they went into receivership in 1914, but Robert Wilkinson from New Brighton Saw Mills saw this as an opportunity to diversify, bought the company, and continued to run it from High Mill for a few more years.

LOW MILL

Low Mill (later referred to as Middle Mill – as it was situated on Middle Green) had been a cotton mill in the past, but at the beginning of the century it was unoccupied and appearing to struggle to find tenants. In 1908, parts of it were let to the Meridian Lighting Company (manufacturers of acetylene gas lighting apparatus) and to Wright's aerated mineral water company. Arthur Wright also ran the grocery and drapers shop in the High Street. Both of these companies had moved out or ceased trading by the start of the war.

NEW BRIGHTON SAW MILLS

This was a consistently successful company run by Robert Wilkinson that made tree nails for the railways. As well as their main business, Wilkinson also manufactured charcoal and naphtha (a flammable hydrocarbon product used as a solvent or basic gasoline fuel). As the demand for tree nails diminished, the company diversified by buying J H Cleave and after the war, were making billiard tables and tennis rackets.

THE OLD SAW MILL

The old sawmill, situated on the banks of the river just across Marton Road from the New Brighton works, was an older and separate business. It was run by James Bell for many years, but nothing much is known about this company, during this period in time, so it was probably merely preparing timber for joinery and building.

QUARRYING

Broughton Quarry
Courtesy of the Dennis French Collection

The limestone quarry near Gargrave was run by John Delaney and his business partner John Smith. John Delaney also had quarries at Horton-in-Ribblesdale and Threshfield and a fleet of railway wagons to transport his products.

The Gargrave quarry was situated between Small House Farm and the railway line, about a mile from the station, going towards Skipton. An extension to the quarry (Smellows) and some sort of track was built to connect the two parts. The correct trading name was the Broughton Quarry Company, but locally it was called Delaney's Quarry.

The quarry had its own sidings and signal box, cottages and a track connecting the upper and lower parts of the quarry. The blue limestone extracted in this area was hard-wearing and was used as road stone.

According to the census of 1901, one cottage was occupied by Thomas Wood (the manager), his wife and 13 children. The other one housed Robert Thompson, the quarry engine driver and his family. Both families also had quarry workers boarding with them.

John Delaney became a devout Quaker and was known as a strict but fair employer. When he died in 1921, he left each of his workers £5 in his will.

FARMING

James Dawes Taylor watching George Lowther ploughing at Friars Head, Winterburn about 1910.
Courtesy of Dennis French collection

In response to economic pressures in the 19th century, corn and crop farming had mainly given way to raising animals. Some crops were still grown, as oats could survive the Yorkshire climate. Gargrave was (and still is) surrounded by farms. Some of the farmers had houses and barns in the village itself. The barns are all now converted into housing, but the arches of the large barn doorways are still in evidence.

Good employment was to be found in farming as it was still labour intensive. Sheep and cows were raised around Gargrave, so the jobs were for stockmen, farm labourers and dairy workers.

OTHER OUTDOOR WORK

The 'Lords of the Manor' had always provided local employment. The big houses at Eshton Hall, Flasby Hall and Gargrave House needed gardeners, drivers, gamekeepers, forestry workers and carpenters. They even employed teams of carpet beaters. Vacuum cleaners were not as ubiquitous as they are today. Many men in Gargrave worked on the railways, as plate layers, signalmen or porters, as Gargrave had a busy station for transporting goods and livestock. The Leeds and Liverpool Canal Company employed lock keepers and canal carpenters. There was also a watcher for the River Aire.

The Craven Hunt employed John Tobin as their huntsman in charge of the hounds. The kennels were situated just near Holme Bridge and are now in ruins.

Craven Hunt Kennels near Holme Bridge
Courtesy of Sue Lyall 2019

The images on the following pages show how the estates and houses relied on a large workforce.

Logging on the Eshton or Flasby Estate
Courtesy of the Dennis French Collection

Group of Estate Workers at Eshton Hall.
Left to Right - Fred Hayton, Mudd, unknown, unknown, David Walker, Ted Rodgers
Courtesy of the Dennis French Collection

Group of unknown Carpet Beaters at Eshton Hall.
Courtesy of the Dennis French Collection

Sheep dipping at Flasby about 1910.
Courtesy of Edith Parker

Domestic Servants

The big estates were run with indoor staff, both male and female. Quite young girls were working as housemaids, kitchen maids and nursemaids. Most of the live-in staff came from other parts of the country, and some could have been placed there by workhouses or orphanages. Advertisements for domestic staff were placed in the regional newspapers such as the Yorkshire Evening Post.

In 1909, Mrs Bramwell from Greenhead required a cook and a young house/sewing maid. Mrs Lund at Knowles House was looking for an experienced kitchen maid. They were to apply, supplying references and stating age and wages required.

Even smaller households might be able to afford a live-in servant. Professional people – doctors, clergy or businessmen – would undoubtedly have servants, maybe some living in and some local daily help. Rev Magee had a nursemaid for his children who had been brought up in a children's home in Hertfordshire. Even the curate had a nanny for his children. For young Lily Greening, coming to Gargrave changed her life as she met and married Arthur Reeder and stayed here for the rest of her life.

Nannies and other household staff were in demand Sorry, names are not available!
Courtesy of the Dennis French Collection

THE SANITARY LAUNDRY

Laundry wagon in North Street.
Courtesy of the Dennis French collection

This was built in 1894 by Sir Mathew Wilson and Mr Coulthurst. The laundry employed about 20 women and girls. Presumably, this was mainly to service the big houses and the professional families in the village. The laundry also had three baths for public use and an adjacent barber's shop.

In 1910 the laundry was modernised and relaunched as Gargrave Laundries Ltd, but the baths closed in 1914.

EMIGRATION

When times were hard at home, some families decided to seek a better life abroad, Canada being a popular destination. During the pre-war period, there was a lot of encouragement to find work abroad. An article in 1910 advised that Canada needed farm workers and female servants, New South Wales required farmers and stockmen, New Zealand had jobs for male and female tailors, and South Africa had opportunities for builders. Advertisements and advice appeared in the Craven Herald and agents were on hand to help would-be emigrants.

The two houses built on North Street in 1904
Courtesy of the Dennis French Collection

The new buildings in Coronation Square.
Courtesy of the Dennis French Collection

HOUSING

The majority of the village workers lived in terraced houses. Some dated back to around 1700, and others dated from a building boom around the 1860s when River Place, Airebank Terrace and more homes in East Street were constructed. However, very little new building took place in the pre-war years, as industries were stagnating and people were starting to move away.

Larger houses in the High Street, Church Street, Marton Road and Knowles House were occupied by managers, clergy, doctors and other professionals.

During this period, the village was still largely owned by the Wilson and Coulthurst families. Sir Mathew Wilson employed Mr John Broughton as his estate manager and rent collector, working from the Estate Office in West Street. He dealt with complaints from tenants, including a disgruntled John Gaunt, who had problems with "Sunnyside" on the High Street.

John Gaunt sent a cheque for rent and gas but gave notice to quit in another six months because

> "...we cannot see our way to facing another winter in such a damp house,
> which apart from being so unhealthy, is ruining furniture and pictures. I
> have previously drawn your attention to this and also that the greenhouse
> still remains unpainted."

Some of the bigger houses were rented by mill owners and managers from further afield. Often, these were the sons of business owners, who, once married would look for a home of their own out in the countryside away from the West Yorkshire industrial centres. Commuting to work from Gargrave could easily be done by car or by train. Examples were Norman England at Townhead (family worsted mill in Bingley), Reginald Lund at Knowles House (Montserrat Mills, Bradford) and Godfrey Ermen at Milton House (manager of Dewhurst's mill in Skipton).

Other people renting in the village were widows, daughters and sisters of wealthy families and also local businessmen. Old Hall Cottage was the home to the three single Cookson sisters in 1901 – they were also related to the Wilsons of Eshton Hall. Two of them made advantageous marriages, and the sisters moved away. Ethel Cookson married Ernest Illingworth Holden, later Baron Holden. After his wife's untimely death in 1912, Baron Holden paid for the carved oak chancel screen in St Andrew's church to be erected in memory of his wife. The next tenant of Old Hall Cottage was Alfred Rickards, son of the proprietor of the former Bell Busk silk mill, and a silk dealer in his own right.

Luckily for John Gaunt, he found a residence more to his liking, and the 1911 census found him living at Endsleigh House. His next-door neighbour at Bridgeholme was Charles Thomas, a retired indigo planter from India.

Very little building took place in this era, apart from replacing a few of the older cottages. The old house at Church Gates was demolished in 1903. James Hunt, the shoemaker, had run his business from here. Three new homes were built in its place.

The Coulthurst Estate built a pair of houses in North Street. Pre 1900 maps show that there was a building on this site, which may have been a barn. Three new homes were built on The Square in 1909 by the Wilson Estate. Other building work was confined to extensions and improvements. For example, the Wesleyan School was modernised in 1911 as one of the conditions that the West Riding County Council would take over the management of the building and the educational services it provided.

Above, 1903 newly built houses at Church Gates replacing the old building shown left.
Airton Studio Images - Courtesy of the Dennis French Collection

Infrastructure

The water supply for Gargrave usually came from springs on Sharp Haw Fell. A collecting tank (later enlarged to become a small reservoir) stored the water which was then piped to the village. At times, this water supply would run low, and it was supplemented with water from a well near Airebank Mills. The villagers didn't like the harder water from this source, but it was better than having none at all.

Nothing is known about when the sewage system and treatment plant was constructed, but it was certainly in operation before 1900. It was extended to reach Paradise Cottages, and when Gargrave House was rebuilt at the beginning of the war, a new sewer pipe was laid under the canal to join up with the main village network.

Gas was supplied and sold to the village by the gas works at Airebank Mills. As the mill building was owned by Sir Mathew Wilson, the gas plant was under the control of the Eshton Estate. Gas street lights were in operation from about 1870. Later improvements to the gas mantle produced a better quality of lighting. Homes that could afford to do so installed gas lights, but it was seen to be too expensive for any other use, so coal was still generally used for heating and cooking.

At times, the gas pressure would fall, and this caused concern. In the spring of 1903, the Parish Council conducted pressure tests before and after lighting-up time. The Parish Council sent their findings to John Broughton, Sir Mathew's agent. They had measured the pressure at the mill, Mr Walker's house in South Street, the church, the kitchen at the Mason's Arms and Mr Fred Robert's house in Church Street. They concluded that the 3-inch pipe was inadequate and should be enlarged. This was done at a later date.

Electricity didn't come to Gargrave until the 1930s. Before the war, there had been discussions about generating hydroelectric power from the river. The Parish Council investigated a similar scheme installed at Kettlewell in 1913. However, the war intervened, and this scheme was shelved. Eshton Hall, however, established its own electricity system in 1910 when the new 3rd Baronet (Sir Mathew Amcotts Wilson) implemented some home improvements.

Residents had to pay rates – the equivalent of today's council tax – to cover the cost of local amenities. The Parish Council employed rate collectors to bring in the contributions toward lighting, sanitation and care of the poor.

COMMUNICATIONS

The postal system was very good with two collections and deliveries a day. The Post Office, which was also the Telegraph Office has been in its present position since the middle of the 19th century. Telegraph messages were relayed by a network of overhead wires to a machine in the post office. The news was then handwritten onto a telegram form and promptly delivered by a lad on a bike.

Miss Dorothy Varley was the postmistress from 1900 to 1920, having taken over from her mother Isabella (in charge from 1871). The post box was emptied at 11.25 am and 7.40 pm. The postmen made their delivery rounds at 8 am and 3 pm and also on Sunday mornings.

From Left to Right - Miss Lily Varley, relative, Miss Dorothy Varley
Courtesy of the Dennis French Collection

One winter evening in 1913 a telegraph boy had a fright while taking a telegram from Gargrave to Coniston Cold. A group of men, apparently tramps, jumped out in front of his bicycle, but seeing that he was only a youngster, said: "Let him go, he's nobbut a lad."

Telephones were coming into use at the turn of the century but were only affordable by larger businesses, and the landed gentry. The telephone exchange was in Skipton, so all the Gargrave subscribers had Skipton phone numbers. The early phones in Gargrave were:

11   Airebank Mills
13   CA Rickards
17   Leeds & Liverpool Canal Company
18   Dr Knowles
18Y John Broughton - Estate Office
19X The Mason's Arms
19Y A E Wright - Draper & Grocer
23   Dr Wales
29   Fred Green & Sons
46   New Brighton Saw Mills
49   J W Bairstow - Endsleigh
55   Reginald Lund - Knowles House
097 The Swan
0102 The Grouse
162 The Vicarage

The telephone at the Estate Office was installed in 1904 at a yearly rental of £6. The apparatus was supplied by the National Telephone Company, and the contract was for one wall telephone in connection with a party line circuit to the company's Skipton Exchange.

TRANSPORT

Horses and bicycles were the general forms of transportation. It was possible to get a ride on a delivery cart to Skipton; otherwise make the four-mile journey on foot.

Delivery cart at Higherlands Bridge.
Courtesy of Barbara Preston.

The railway network provided useful links to more distant destinations. Excursions and day trips could be made on the canal or by char-à-banc (an early bus or motor coach). Other road users complained that the 'charas' drove too fast and often in the middle of the road. There were very few private cars or motorbikes.

Char-à-banc 'Tourists' visiting Gargrave about 1910.
The vehicle is parked in front of Endsleigh House, High Street. Tourists unknown.
Airton Studio Image - Courtesy of the Dennis French Collection

Gargrave Station in 1905
Courtesy of the Dennis French Collection

The earliest known car in the village was photographed at the Eshton Estate office in West Street in 1900.

A 1900 Clement Panhard Vis-a-Vis in front of the Wilson Estate Office
Courtesy of the Dennis French Collection

From 1903, motor vehicles had to be registered and display number plates. Drivers also had to pay 5s for a licence, but there was no driving test.

Another early car was owned by Miss Alice Emily Garnett-Orme from 1906 until 1910. She lived at Airton and didn't drive herself, but employed a chauffeur. As a member of the tennis club in Gargrave, she and her car would have often been seen in the village. The vehicle was registered in Bradford. It was a 1904 De Dion Bouton with an 8 HP single cylinder engine. The bodywork was painted green with white lines, and the upholstery was red.

Miss Garnett-Orme's car and chauffeur at Scosthrop Manor, Airton
Reproduced by kind permission of the Ellwood family, Mrs V Rowley and North Yorkshire County Council, Skipton Library

The speed limit was 20 mph, having been raised from 14mph by the 1903 Motor Vehicle Act. This limit was frequently flouted, and the police would set speed traps to catch offenders. On a half a mile stretch of road between Skipton and Kildwick, the police timed William Spencer driving at 30 mph. Mr Spencer, the chauffeur to Reginald Lund of Knowles House, was fined 20s. In his defence, he said he didn't think there was any danger in travelling fast on a straight road.

The railway station, as well as being used for passengers, transported goods and livestock. There were cattle pens at Gargrave station. The staff must have taken pride in the station, as it was awarded a prize in 1901 for the flower displays.

The canal was still used for the transport of heavy and bulky goods, such as coal and grain, but dry weather could cause the canal to be closed causing disruption to traffic.

Bank Newton Locks
Airton Studio
Courtesy of the Dennis French Collection

SHOPS AND TRADES

In common with other small communities, Gargrave was a mainly self-sufficient village, with retail shops and trades to cater for everyday needs. In the 18th and 19th centuries, the Swan Inn was a major stop on the coaching route, so the necessary services were to be found in the High Street – blacksmiths, saddlers, ironmonger, shoemakers, tailors and a telegraph office. When horse-drawn coaches were replaced by the railways, these trades dwindled to one or two providers rather than the previous three or four. In 1900, there was probably only one motor car and a couple of motorbikes in the village, so horsepower was still essential for farmers, carters and private transport. At this time, James Wade was the only saddler (following in the footsteps of his father Thomas), and Jonathan Dodgson was the blacksmith.

Jonathan Dodgson's High Street forge in about 1900
Airton Studio - Courtesy of the Dennis French Collection

There were two butchers, Luke Gill at Bridge House and Richard Driver in West Street. Small grocery shops were at 4 River Place (Isabella Procter), High Street (Alice Gregson) and Mrs Holmes on West Street – the earlier ones were usually converted from old cottages.

Luke Gill, the butcher and his daughter Olive - about 1910
Courtesy of the Dennis French Collection

East Street grocery about 1905
Courtesy of the Dennis French Collection

Barbara Preston
14 Coplow View
Clitheroe
Lancashire
BB7 4SG

Dear Vivienne

.   Here is my address which
I tried to send to you before!
When I returned from posting
the first card I found the
sticker on the floor! so I will
try again. Love Barbara xx

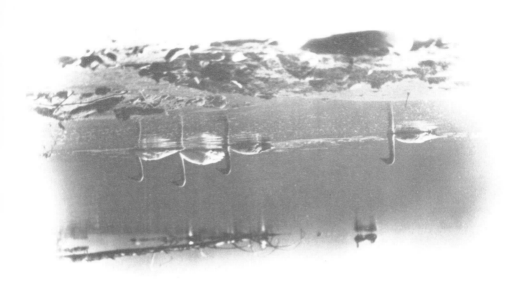

"TRUMPETER SWANS" ©1985 • SANDI ALLIN • CAMPBELL RIVER, B.C.

During the village expansion of the 1860s, Sir Mathew Wilson constructed two purpose built, double fronted shops at 9 East Street and in South Street. Both display date stones for 1863. Mrs Wiseman had the East Street grocery shop initially, and Tom Pighills took over at the turn of the century.

Unfortunately, his tenure only lasted for 5 or 6 years, he became bankrupt, the shop closed and it was changed to a private residence.

The Middlebrook family ran the South Street grocers along with their shoemaking business next door. Both enterprises had passed through several generations, but when Sarah Middlebrook died in 1902, her son Herbert concentrated on shoes. Bert Middlebrook was well-known in Gargrave for taking care of the cricket pitch and the tennis courts for many years. Bert's wife Stella provided catering services.

Bert Middlebrook tending the cricket pitch in front of the old pavillion. Ca. 1905
Courtesy of the Dennis French Collection

Sometime after the death of Sarah Middlebrook, Stephen Reeder and his family took over the grocery shop.

The Gargrave Industrial Co-operative Society occupied three adjacent cottages in South Street, including their grocery and drapers departments. The Gargrave branch had been founded in 1872. The shop was a local enterprise, being run by a management committee with half-yearly open meetings and published accounts. In 1908 they acquired the next cottage along, which had previously been occupied by the Mechanics' Institute, to make a row of four shops. The Co-op was to stay here until 1935 when the present High Street premises were built.

25. South Street in about 1912. Miss Hilton's tea room on the left, then the Co-op
Courtesy of the Dennis French Collectionh

THE GARGRAVE INDUSRTRIAL CO-OPERATIVE SOCIETY LIMITED.

ESTABLISHED AND REGISTERED JUNE 22ND, 1872.

FIFTY-EIGHTH HALF-YEARLY
REPORT AND BALANCE SHEET

From November 24th, 1900, to June 1st, 1901.

PRESENT OFFICERS OF THE SOCIETY.

President :
MR. GEORGE BALDWIN.

Secretary :
MR. ANTHONY CLARKE.

Treasurer :
MR. BENJAMIN C. WALLS.

Auditor :
MR. WILLIAM SWALLOW, LEEDS.

Bankers :
YORKSHIRE BANKING COMPANY.

COMMITTEE'S REPORT.

TO THE MEMBERS,

We have pleasure in presenting you with the following Statement of Accounts, which we hope will meet with your approval and adoption.

The Receipts are : Grocery, £2912 15 1 ; Drapery, £491—total, £3403 15 1 ; an Increase on corresponding period of last year of £252 9 7½, in Grocery, and £25 in Drapery. Total increase of £277 9 7½. The average weekly takings are £126 1 3½. The nett profit on Trade, after adding balance from last half-year £12 9 6, and allowing Interest on Share and Loan Capital, and all other charges, is £565 4 9, which we recommend to be apportioned as follows : 4/- in the £ on Members' Checks, and 2/- on Non-Members'.

The total number of Members is 220.

Yours truly,
THE COMMITTEE.

ATTENDANCE OF COMMITTEE.—POSSIBLE NO. 27.

MR. GEORGE BALDWIN 27
*MR. GEORGE NICHOLSON ...25
*MR. JOSEPH WALLS 25

MR. ANTHONY CLARKE...27
MR. HENRY HASTINGS ...24
MR. WILLIAM CLARKE ...23
MR. BENJAMIN HILTON...21

MR. JOHN GREY 25
MR. EDWIN GREEN............25
MR. BENJAMIN WALLS 23

Those marked with an asterisk retire, but are eligible for re-election.

NOTICES.

The General Meeting will be held in the Primitive Methodist Chapel, on Wednesday, June 19th, 1901, at 7-30 p.m.

PROGRAMME OF BUSINESS.

1.—Minutes of last Half-Yearly Meeting.   2.—Report and Balance Sheet.   3.—Election of Officers and Two Committee-men.   4.—Other business.

Dividend and Interest will be paid at Stores on Saturday, June 22nd, 1901, from 6 to 7 p.m. No Dividend or Interest will be paid after Saturday, June 29th, 1901. Members are expected to clear their accounts every week.

Co-Op balance sheet for 1900-1901
Courtesy of Marie Wolfenden

The double-fronted shop, shown below, in the High Street (next door to the present pharmacy) was also a grocers and drapers. At the turn of the century, the shopkeeper was J Howarth, but it changed hands in 1905 and was run by Arthur Edward Wright for 15 years. During their time in Gargrave, Arthur Wright and his brother also manufactured aerated mineral water at Low Mill.

High Street with Hyde's ironmongers seen on Park Place facing High Street.
Courtesy of the Dennis French Collection

This view of the High Street is from around 1910 and shows Wright's grocers on the left and the Liberal Club (with flagpole) in the centre. The Swan is hidden behind the tree, and the building facing up the street is the ironmongers on Park Place.

The West Street butchers also changed hands in about 1909 when Frank Hardisty (a blacksmith's son from Skipton) took over and remained for many years. The premises are now the back part of the Dalesman Café.

The newsagents at the corner of High St and West St. The name above the door has changed from Hyde to McKell. 1913
Courtesy of Martin Thompson

Staff of West Street butchers with next weeks Sunday roast?
Courtesy of the Dennis French Collection

The Reeder family were involved with the grocery trade. When Isabella Procter retired from running the corner shop at 4 River Place, Stephen Reeder took it over. Miss Procter continued living next door, earning a living as a dressmaker until her death in 1906. Then Stephen moved his family up from number 36 to live at number 3. Soon, they acquired another shop across the road at 21 South Street and transferred the grocery business there, but keeping number 4 River Place. Eventually, the South Street shop was run by son George, and number 4 became a fish and chip shop.

The shop at 4 River Place run by Stephen Reader.
Courtesy of the Dennis French Collection

Fresh fruit and vegetables were grown in the heart of the village on the plot of land where the Co-op now stands.

John Horsman's granddaughter, Enid White, recalled a family tale that all the family would help with harvesting. At pea picking time he insisted that everyone whistled while they worked because if they were whistling, he knew they weren't eating the peas.

This market garden had been run for many years by John Horsman until he died in 1909 and the business was taken over by Anthony Clarke.

The Market Garden taken from High Street
Courtesy of the Dennis French Collection

Anthony Clarke & Sons. Fish & Fruit Salesmen. High Street.
Courtesy of Martin Thompson

Shoemakers and repairers were in god supply. As clogs were the essential daily footwear, Stephen Metcalfe had a clogger's shop at Trees Terrace. Photos taken from Coronation Square show the shop on the end of the row, with a clog sign above the door.

Trees Terrace clogger's shop
Courtesy of the Dennis French Collection

Other shoe and boot makers in the village were Sarah Middlebrook and her son Herbert in South Street and the Maudsley family near the Swan Inn. There was also James Hunt (who came to Gargrave in 1860 as an apprentice to Abraham Bateson) ran his business from Church Gates, but the site was redeveloped in 1903 and James moved to one of the cottages at Mill Hill (near Low Mill). His business carried on, in a wooden workshop near Luke Gill's house at Bridge End.

Although there was a good choice of clothes to be found in Skipton, there was no need to leave Gargrave. John McKell was the village tailor, as was his father Robert before him. He lived and worked from premises just near the post office.

There were probably several dressmakers, although the trade directories listed two ladies, Sarah Lofthouse, next to the Liberal Club in the High Street and Miss Every Wolfenden (and her assistant) in West Street.

For household needs, the grocery shops had soaps, polishes, brushes and toiletries. Coal could be bought from Fred Green and Son at the Eshton Road Canal Warehouse (as it is to this day). Actually, Fred Green only ever put in the initial finances for the business and it was his son Basil who ran it; Fred being involved with his own decorating business in Colne.

Eshton Road canal bridge and Fred Green's Warehouse
Courtesy of Martin Thompson

Domestic accommodation adjoining Fred Green's Warehouse about 1905
Courtesy of the Dennis French Collection

The 1901 census shows Basil Green aged 19, coal and corn merchant living in the house next door to the warehouse along with a manservant/carter. A few years later, Basil, his wife and two children were living at Airebank House, and a manager was living at the warehouse, so the business must have been thriving.

In those days, smoking was common. Tobacco products were stocked by John Hyde who ran the newsagents and stationers at the corner of West Street and High Street (where the Dalesman Café is now situated).

Absalom Hilton and his wife had a similar shop next to the Co-op in South Street. After Absalom's retirement, his daughter Ann ran the shop and also a tea room on the premises, as Gargrave attracted good numbers of visitors at Whitsun and in the summer months.

The Misses Hartley had a confectionery business in the High Street, in what is now the left-hand part of the Bollywood Cottage restaurant. Previously, it had been a grocery shop run by Alice Gregson and before her by Thomas Middlebrook. Samuel Hartley (the painter and decorator) who lived next door, had several unmarried daughters. Maggie Hartley was in Harrogate in 1901, working as a confectioner. Having learnt her trade, she returned to Gargrave and set up shop in the former grocers, next door to the family home. One or more of her sisters helped her in the business.

Pots and pans were available from the ironmongers at Park Place (the part of the High Street to the right of the Swan). This business had been run by the Parkinson family for many years, and at the turn of the century, the proprietor was Robert Parkinson. Having no sons, his apprentice and assistant was his nephew John Hyde and later on his great-nephew Thomas Hyde. John Hyde changed career after his marriage to Sarah and went

High Street with Hyde's ironmongers facing toward the camera. Various metal containers are on display.
Courtesy of the Dennis French Collection

on to run a newsagents, tobacconists and a stationery shop on the corner of High Street and West Street.

Later, the running of the newsagents passed to his daughter May and her husband, William Henry "Harry" McKell. Harry was working as a tailor with his father John McKell but changed career when the opportunity to take over the shop arose. John Hyde and his wife Sarah moved back to the ironmongers business in Park Place.

John Hyde was the maker of the "tin cup" a local football trophy, a founder member of the Mechanics' Institute and the Gargrave correspondent for the Craven Herald and Pioneer.

The first Tin Cup competition was held in 1900, contested by local teams representing Airebank Mills, the Conservative Club, the Mechanics' Institute, Broughton Quarry and New Brighton Saw Mills. Victory went to the Liberal Club team, and William Lofthouse and Robert Kirkbright filled the cup with some unspecified beverage for a celebration.

Samuel Hartley

The principal man for painting, decorating and plumbing was Samuel Hartley. He was born in 1849 into a farming family and came to Gargrave in the 1870s.

He ran a family business spanning several generations, with a house in the High Street and later on a shop and showroom. His son Harry joined the firm and later on, so did his grandson.

Samuel Hartley's portrait still hangs in his former shop, and this is reproduced here by kind permission of the Dickinson family, who occupied the premises in later years.

Fred Roberts in Church Street was a joiner and builder. The Franzees (father and son) were cabinet makers and upholsterers. The Franzee family lived on North Street in Story's House, part of which was their workshop. Rudolph Franzee was German by birth and had been in Gargrave for many years after marrying a Cracoe lass in 1846. His son Clemence was born here and carried on the business after his father died in 1902 before retiring in 1920 at the ripe old age of 70. Clemence and his father were very much involved with the Wesleyan Church.

There was no chemist until the war years. Back in the 1870s, William Tranter was a surgeon's assistant and chemist, but after his death, no-one performed this function. Medicines were bought directly from the doctors, if people could afford them and if all homegrown remedies had failed to work.

For more specialist shopping, a trip to Skipton would be needed to buy jewellery, spectacles, music supplies, books and furniture, to visit the dentist or to get a bicycle repaired.

The locations of the Gargrave businesses can be found on the map in Appendix D together with a timeline of the proprietors. In some cases, the dates when the shops changed hands are difficult to determine, but it gives an idea of who was running which business and when. This covers the whole time-span of the book 1900 – 1925.

TOURISM

Gargrave has always attracted tourists. At Whitsuntide, most people had the Monday and Tuesday off work, so the long weekend gave the residents of Gargrave a chance to get away to Morecambe or Blackpool. People from the nearby industrial towns of Lancashire and West Yorkshire would come to Gargrave for a breath of fresh country air. The railway company would run special excursion trains over this period. As private motoring was only available to the rich, the ordinary working folk came on char-à-banc trips or on their bikes, as cycling had become a popular pastime. The photograh reproduced below shows the first char-à-banc excursion from Gargrave. The trip which took place in 1912 was paid for by Mr Norman Hartley.

During the summer months, all the towns had their own holiday weeks, so the visitors were spread out over a more extended period. Accommodation could be found at the inns, but also in private houses. The Bownass family advertised holiday accommodation at Winterburn during the summer of 1908.

One Saturday afternoon in 1913, the Barnoldswick Brass Band organised a trip via the Leeds and Liverpool Canal to Gargrave.

*"It proved a great success as nearly four hundred passengers paid their
"nimble sixpence", a most reasonable charge for the double journey. The
weather was favourable, a brisk wind adding zest to the few hours "life on
the ocean wave". Arriving at Gargrave, many visited the ruins of the burnt
out Airebank Mills, and the band played on the Low Green for dancing,
which was well patronised and altogether a remarkably pleasant afternoon
was spent, while Gargrave caterers and shopkeepers benefited by the influx
of the trippers."*

char-à-banc at Broughton Hall
Private Collection

SOCIAL LIFE

By the turn of the century, there were four pubs in the village. Three are still in operation – The Swan, The Mason's Arms and The Anchor. The 'lost' pub was The Grouse at the corner of High Street and West Street. This was converted to housing in the 1970s. Between them, these venues provided accommodation for travellers, meeting rooms for organisations, as well as places to drink. The big upper window on the West Street side of the Grouse shows the room where court sessions were once held and where other functions carried on in later years.

The Grouse Hotel, High Street
Courtesy of the Dennis French Collection

The Summer Seat (on The Square) has always been a place to sit and gossip. The original version was double-sided, with another seat looking towards the river. At some point, access to the river-facing side was blocked off. This was to discourage "goings on". The original was replaced with a single sided version in the late 1920s.

A still later version of the Summer Seat is now standing in the same place, providing shelter and a meeting place.

The original Summer Seat.
Courtesy of Martin Thompson

Entertainment was mostly 'home-grown', except for the occasional cinematographic shows, lantern slide shows and visiting theatre groups. One performance, the play "East Lynne", had a seven-night run in the summer of 1913 at the Victoria Hall. This was a popular and sensational tale of infidelity and double identity.

The people of Gargrave loved to dance, act and make music. The village was fortunate to have several good venues for these activities –

- Victoria Hall in the High Street (above what are now the florists and antique shops)

- The Parochial Hall, just off South Street (now converted to the St Andrew's Court flats)

- The Wesleyan School Rooms in Skipton Road (later the Methodist Chapel and now a small development of houses)

The events at these venues were split between the religious, secular and political. Most of the villagers would go either to church or chapel. Both churches held regular meetings and events. There were seasonal events at New Year, Easter, Harvest and Christmas. These would take the form of supper with a concert.

The Wesleyan Methodists staged their concerts and plays at the school room, opposite the chapel. St Andrew's held their events in the Victoria Hall until the Parochial Hall opened in 1908.

Other village societies would use the Victoria Hall for their activities. Whist drives were very popular, usually followed by dancing to a local band of musicians. The Conservative Club and various sports clubs would use this hall, and the Liberals had their own meeting rooms, further down the High Street.

People took pride in their gardens and allotments and competed at the annual flower show. The show became known as the Gargrave Horticultural Show from 1903 to reflect the fact that more fruit and vegetables were being grown. It was held on the first Saturday in August on the cricket ground. After the war, livestock categories were introduced, and this was the birth of our Agricultural Show.

There were other organised groups, not attached to the churches, for example, the Gargrave Male Voice Choir, the Gargrave Musical Society and the Drama Group. A full account of the Musical Society's summer 1912 production of 'The Merry Men of Sherwood' was reported in the Craven Herald. This was an open-air production held in the grounds of Gargrave House with an impressive cast list of actors, singers and musicians. It seemed that a large part of the village was taking part, watched by an audience of 300.

"Merry men of Sherwood" 1912
Courtesy of the Dennis French Collection

"Shortly before three o'clock, the wide expanse of lawn in front of the house was dotted with groups of ladies and gentlemen, the vari-coloured dresses of the former standing out in bold relief against a backdrop of shrubbery, heavy with foliage. In the distance, ensconced in the corner of the lawn, was the "theatre", surrounded on two sides by tall trees, and on the third by a rich meadowland. This was a playhouse where everything associated with the adventurous life of Robin Hood and his Merry Men was to be seen in the brushwood in the rear of the stage, the waving grass in the adjacent meadow, and the gnarled trunks and frowning branches which commanded the entire scene.

Dr Wales was a chivalrous Will Scarlett, whose courage was not even damped when he walked with measured step to pay the last penalty for a crime of which he was falsely accused. As Robin Hood, Mr T B Wane gave a fine exposition of the outlaw's most famous characteristics. His rescue of Scarlett from the scaffold provided one of the most thrilling moments in the production. The other principal parts were sustained by Miss Winn as Maid Marion, Mr G D Hunt as Friar Tuck, Mr T E Butler as Much, the Millar's son; Mr P Dodgson as Little John; and Mr G Wane as the Holy Palmer.

During the performance, some clever Morris and Maypole dances were introduced. At the close, refreshments were served, after which dancing was indulged in."

POLITICS

Nationally, the government had alternated between Conservatives and Liberals for the previous 40 years. At the turn of the century, the country was in the hands of an alliance between the Conservatives and the Liberal Unionists (who had broken away from the Liberal Party in 1886). This alliance won both the 1895 and 1900 elections and Labour was represented for the first time in 1900, with two members of parliament. Voting in these days didn't take place on just one day; it was spread over several weeks.

In common with the rest of the country, Gargrave was a two-party village. The Conservative Association met in Victoria Hall, and the Liberals had their club rooms further down the High Street. As well as promoting their political ideals, both organisations held social events – dances, concerts, whist drives, lantern lectures and outings. Both the Conservatives and the Liberals had billiards and football teams, so these organisations were essential to the social life of their members.

A popular night out with the Conservatives was a Smoking Concert, or "Smoker". Smoking Concerts were for the purpose of introducing new forms of music to the audience. The men present would be smoking and discussing the politics of the day. The musical taste of the Gargrave group ran to comic songs such as 'The Quack Doctor' and 'Step on the tails of me coat'. The discussions were usually critical of the rival Liberal party and their performance in government.

The Craven Herald reported extensively on politics both local and national. Although regional and national newspapers were available in the Mechanics' Institute reading room, the residents were perhaps more likely to read their local paper.

In the early 1900s, the public became disenchanted with the government in power for many reasons. The Boer War had dragged on for longer than expected, and proposals for trade tariffs provoked fears that food prices would increase. There was real poverty, particularly in the cities, and it was shocking to find that one in three potential army recruits were rejected on medical grounds. The general election of 1906 returned the Liberal Party to power with a convincing majority, and the Labour Party was starting to increase its following with 29 MPs.

The Skipton constituency had been staunchly Liberal since its creation in 1885 with Sir Mathew Wilson as the first MP. In 1900, Frederick Whitely-Thompson was elected and William Clough in 1906, both Liberals. William Clough held on to the seat in 1910, but Conservative opposition was growing.

This pre-war period was one of intense political activity in the Craven area with rallies and meetings, even in the villages, with great interest shown in trade tariff reforms. In contrast, the 'Votes for Women' campaign didn't appear to have made much of an impact in the Craven area. In 1908, Adela Pankhurst and Nellie Kenney addressed local meetings. In Skipton, Miss Pankhurst had a hard time as a large part of the crowd were opposed to her views and she was pelted with flour and 'pellets of objectional substance'. Miss Kenney spoke in Ilkley and said that she realised that it was a beautiful place and the residents might not understand the plight of women and children in the city slums and how important it was to give women a voice. There was heckling from the crowd, but she gave back as good as she got, saying "If politics did not meddle with women, women would not want to meddle with politics."

In Gargrave, hardly any references have been found to the suffragettes. A visiting preacher at the Parish Church condemned them saying

> "The Holy Spirit did not make fighting, screaming, window-smashing suffragettes, of that I am certain."

A lady who attended the consecration of Archdeacon Kilner as Bishop of Richmond in 1913, remarked that when she arrived at York Minster,

> "The official at the entrance, seeing the satchel that I was wearing, asked me kindly to leave it behind. That made me realise that suffragettes were to be guarded against, even in such sacred precincts."

ROYAL OCCASIONS AND CELEBRATIONS

North Street decorated for the 'Relief of Mafeking' celebrations.
Courtesy of the Dennis French Collection

The beginning of the 20th century was a busy time for royal events – two funerals and two coronations in the space of eleven years. Celebrations and processions were held throughout the country whenever a major national event occurred. The people of Gargrave joined in heartily and patriotically, and the children had time off school.

The Anglo-Boer War was still in progress, and although it wasn't the end of the war, the Relief of the Siege of Mafeking in May 1900 was big news and led to huge celebrations and a national holiday on 23 May. The village was decked with flags and pictures of Colonel Baden-Powell. There was a fancy dress parade, sports, fireworks and dancing. An effigy of the South African leader was burnt on a bonfire.

Joe Langstroth, who was 12 at the time, recalled in a radio interview when he was 92, how he was carried through the village on a stretcher, dressed as a wounded soldier. The ladies from the Sanitary Laundry dressed up as nurses. Spectators told him afterwards

Joe Langstroth on the stretcher – 1900 Mafeking Day
Courtesy of the Dennis French Collection

Joe's Watch
Photograph by Martin Thompson 2010

that he made a realistic Tommy Atkins (soldier) and looked to be in real pain. Joe replied that he was in pain, as he really needed to go to the toilet and couldn't get off the stretcher!

Joe worked as a half-timer at Airebank Mills from the age of 11. During the Boer War, he used to call in at the Post Office to find out the war news and relay it to the other mill workers. To show their gratitude, the mill over-lookers clubbed together to buy Joe a watch and this was presented to him at the time of the relief of the Siege of Mafeking in 1900. He treasured this watch all his life and it's still in the possession of his family.

The closing years of the previous century had seen the joyful celebrations of Queen Victoria's Diamond Jubilee, held in 1897, but in a few short years, the nation was in deep mourning when she died in January 1901. The churches held solemn memorial services.

The following year, everyone was celebrating the coronation of King Edward VII. Gargrave decided to erect a lasting memorial to this event and a lamp post and drinking trough was installed and the Square itself was renamed Coronation Square. The drinking trough proved to be a problem, as the local children were always messing about in it and a few years later, a hole was bored in it to enable it to be drained and cleaned. The village coined a nickname for this monument – "The Gawmless".

The Gawmless
In the background can be seen Weatherill's disused "Ice Cream and Hot Pea Saloon". Demolished ca. 1909.
Courtesy of the Dennis French Collection

In May 1910 when Edward VII died, there was a procession from Coronation Square to the Parish Church for a memorial service. Unusually, the denominations were united, as it was led by both the Vicar and the Wesleyan church secretary. People dressed in mourning, flags were at half mast, the chancel rails were draped in black, and Beethoven's Funeral March was played.

*The Giant
Coronation Bonfire.
Height 25 ft Girth 57 ft
Weight 25 ton,*

Courtesy of the Dennis French Collection

With another royal coronation to mark, Gargrave once again organised celebrations for the new King George V in 1911. The usual parades and sports took place, and a huge bonfire was built.

Gargrave Bletherhead Band
From left to right:
Back row. *Jack Grey, Jim Warne, Bill Adams, Harry Lord, Dick Black, Harry Birtwhistle, Wallace Bradley.*
Front row. *Charlie Kirkbright, George Horner, Tom Bradley*
Courtesy of the Dennis French Collection

The Coronation procession was headed by the Gargrave Bletherhead Band. These were comic bands, particular to Yorkshire and the name bletherhead meant a person who talked nonsense.

The members dressed up (and sometimes blacked up) and played such things as the concertina, a Tommy Talker (kazoo) and a variety of home-made instruments.

Other events that brought the village to a standstill were the funerals of Sir Mathew Wharton Wilson in 1909 and Sir Mathew Amcotts Wilson in 1914. There was genuine sadness at the passing of two 'lords of the manor' who had contributed so much to Gargrave and the wider Craven area. The mills and the schools closed and the community went into mourning.

The event that caused the biggest effect that the village had experienced was the Military Exercise, simulating a battle between two opposing forces.

The exercise commenced on Sunday the 28th of July 1912, a spectacle the like of which which had not been seen since the Scottish raids. A horde of armed men, 9734 officers and men, 295 horses, 129 vehicles and 44 guns of crossed the Lancashire Yorkshire border into Craven. The troops travelled by specially chartered trains at Gisburn, Skipton, Elslack and Gargrave, a fantastic piece of organisation by the Midland Railway and the Lancashire and Yorkshire Railway, something virtual impossible today. Nearly fifty special trains were involved. Soldiers of the Manchester Regiment, from Patricoft, Leigh, Wigan, Blackburn, Burnley, Nelson and Colne plus Royal Signals and Field Ambulance from Manchester, Bolton and Burnley, and many others arrived, at Skipton, East Marton and Gargrave in pouring rain and thunderstorms for last of their annual summer training camps that would be held for some time.

Manchester Regiment marching past the Methodist Chapel on Skipton Road 1912
Courtesy of the Dennis French Collection

The exercise was the last training exercise the Territorial Force were to take part in before the onset of war in 1914. The camp at Gargrave was situated on the hillside overlooking Coniston road bridge but no doubt many of the fields between there and the Anchor Inn were used.

Contemporary post card depicting the mood of the 'Happy Campers'!
Courtesy of the Dennis French Collection

The wet start is vividly apparent from the many photographs that have come to light. One subtitled *"Fishing for Fine Weather at Gargrave "* sets the scene.

A comment on the back of one card says

"We are camped amongst the mountains"

The troops were engaged in a simulated battle where an enemy army had landed on the east coast of Yorkshire and was advancing on the industrial towns of Yorkshire and Lancashire. This bears striking similarity to the events which unfolded in the book by William Le Queux, "The Invasion of 1910" mentioned earlier.

Courtesy of the Dennis French Collection

On Monday, the 29th of July a tremendous thunderstorm washed out the 'battlefields' and the camps, leaving wet tents and bedding. Many of the soldiers became ill. A group at the East Marton camp, sheltering from a thunderstorm, when a bolt of lightning hit the bayonet attached to the rifle that Private Hutton from Darwen was holding. The bolt ran down the rifle and burst the butt. Twenty-three year old Pte. Hutton died instantly. Weapons held by the witnessing troops were hastily thrown to the ground to avoid the same fate. A total of other twelve men were injured, three seriously.

Private Hutton was taken to the mortuary at Skipton and later his remains were carried on a gun carriage from the mortuary to Skipton station prior to a military funeral in Darwen.

The people of Gargrave and Major Tottie from Coniston Hall rallied round to open up barns, village halls and private houses to give shelter to sick soldiers. Others provided hot food to supplement the camp rations and give comfort to the men. This 'invasion' was a big event in the life of Gargrave, with troops seen marching to and from their camp and exercise ground.

SPORT

There have been sporting activities in Gargrave for many years. Certainly, many of these were well established by the end of the nineteenth century.

For most of the 1800s, the average working man or woman had no time for leisure or sport. Such pastimes were only for the likes of the gentry who had money to spend and time to spend it. In Gargrave, there was hunting, golf and tennis for the elite and the more accessible activities of football and cricket didn't really feature until nearer the end of the century.

THE CRAVEN HUNT

Craven Hunt members meeting in front of Eshton Hall
Courtesy of the Dennis French Collection

Hunting had for centuries been a favourite pastime of royalty and the nobility, and in Craven, the local landowners carried on this tradition. The Craven Hunt had its origins with a pack of hounds bought by Mathew Wilson of Eshton Hall in the 1830s. New kennels were built at Holme Bridge in 1851, which are still standing, but in a ruinous state. The big event of the year was the 'Gargrave Great Hunt' held on 12th December, the second Gargrave Fair day. For this event, anyone who could find something to ride would take part. Originally, the hunt would meet on Kelber Hill and chase hares, but this venue was abandoned after 1881 as the increased number of trains made it too dangerous to cross the railway line. The December Fair had ceased to function by 1914, and the annual hunt was eventually changed to Boxing Day.

The first huntsman was Jack Holmes, succeeded in 1874 by John Tobin from Ireland and later by his son John. In 1887 Mathew Amcotts Wilson took over as Master from Captain Henderson.

CRAVEN GOLF CLUB

The Craven Golf Club was a short-lived enterprise, founded on the 22nd April 1893 on Stony Butts field, between the river and canal, just off the Hellifield Road. The club membership was open to the gentry, clergy and other prominent gentlemen. However, it only had a lifetime of three years before moving to Skipton.

CRAVEN LAWN TENNIS CLUB

Founded in 1879, the Tennis Club, although situated in Gargrave, drew its membership from a wider area. The membership was very exclusive, as an early list reveals. The ladies and gentlemen from wealthy and prominent families joined the club – Wilson, Bracewell, Preston, Dewhurst (from Skipton), Roundell (from East Marton), Robinson (from Thorlby) and also the vicar of Gargrave.

Initially, the club was situated on the cricket field but soon moved to its present location on Smithy Croft. The highlight of each year was the annual summer tournament, which lasted from Tuesday until Friday. The prizes were of excellent quality, but there was a rule that a player could not win more than one prize. If a victorious player reached a second final, he or she would withdraw and give the chance of winning to another member.

CRICKET

The history of cricket can be traced back to 1852 when the workers at Mr Bracewell's Airebank Mills played on a field next to the mill. After a temporary home at Heber Bottom, the Rev Leigh (curate and keen cricketer) negotiated to rent a field from Sir Mathew Wilson, and so the club was established in 1888 at the place where it still plays to this day. The club was then named as The Gargrave Cricket Club.

In 1892, Sir Mathew paid for a pavilion to be built. This had changing rooms on the lower level and rooms for socials and meetings above. The Wilson family were always involved in the life of the club, and the cricket ground became the venue for many sporting and social activities.

Up until the war, matches were arranged as friendlies between local teams, but during the conflict, cricket and many other sporting activities were suspended.

Gargrave Cricket Team about 1900
Courtesy of the Dennis French Collection

The cricket team in the photo are – standing from left to right: H Birtwhistle (umpire); A Townson; Phillip Preston; T B Wane; W Lofthouse; A Slater; Bill Parkinson and G Baldwin (in the suit). Seated: Bill Clark; Jim Capstick; Tom Wane; John Edward Fishwick and Bill Langstroth.

ASSOCIATION AND RUGBY UNION FOOTBALL

There had been a Rugby Union Football Club in the village, formed in 1890, but this had ceased to exist by the turn of the century. The photo of the rugby team dates from about 1895. Dr Snell, the president, is in the middle of the picture wearing the top hat. Vice presidents of the club were the sporting curate, Rev John Leigh and Mr Arthur Bracewell, one of the proprietors of Airebank Mills.

Rugby was overtaken in popularity by Association Football, and several local teams were in existence by 1900 when the first 'Tin Cup' competition took place. The teams taking part were from Airebank Mills, Delaney's Quarry, the Mechanics Institute, the Conservative Club, New Brighton Saw Mills with the winner being from the Liberal Club.

Gargrave Rugby Union Team c 1895
Courtesy of the Dennis French Collection

The old tin cup 1900

The tin cup trophy was made by ironmonger John Hyde, who unfortunately broke his leg during the final.

Over the years several different football fields have been used. Starting off in a field below the churchyard, a field near the Anchor Inn, Chapel Meadows and eventually the football field came to its present location on Skipton Road.

Matches were not without controversy. In 1907, Gargrave were playing against Barnoldswick, an important game as they were in joint top position in the Skipton & District League. The referee's decisions were not popular with the Gargrave side. The complaints were that he wore a top coat throughout the match and kept too great a distance from the play to be able to judge it correctly. The home side lost 5 – 4 and the home crowd booed, hooted and behaved in such a menacing way, that the referee had to be escorted off by officials and the police. The mob followed them up Church Lane to the changing rooms at The Mason's Arms, booing and shouting all the way.

Gargrave Football Team about 1907
Courtesy of Martin Thompson

HOCKEY

The hockey club started up in 1901 at the instigation of the curate, Rev Hugh Tupholme, who was also the club captain. There was no subscription, but the players had to provide their own equipment. Their home field was near the Anchor Inn, and the side went on to compete with considerable success against some of the best teams in Yorkshire and Lancashire. Away games were played against the likes of Wakefield, Bradford, Morley, Shipley, Whalley and Burnley. A great deal of effort was taken to get to these fixtures, the team would have their kit ready on Friday night, so they could leave quickly after their Saturday morning shift at work and catch the 12.15 train from Gargrave.

Left to right. Back row: Albert Gray, Joe Ayrton, Rev Hugh Tupholme, John Gaunt, Ernest Townson, John Hyde. Middle: Matt Lucas. Front: Thomas Wane, Harry Carpenter, Arthur Jones, George Reeder, Tom Knight.

Unemployment caused by the Airebank Mill fire of 1912, followed by the outbreak of the war led to the demise of the Gargrave Hockey Club.

Gargrave Hockey Team 1905
Courtesy of the Dennis French Collection

BOWLS

The bowling green has always been at its present location behind The Mason's Arms since its founding in 1899. It was the brainchild of Mr Alfred Horner, who was the landlord at that time. An inaugural match was played between two teams from the Craven Green in Skipton. At the time, Mr Horner was praised for his admirable and tastefully laid out grounds. However, there was a warning that the green had a 'fiendish crown' which would be challenging for all players. Lady members would not be admitted for another 60 years.

Mason's Arms Bowling Green about 1910
Courtesy of the Dennis French Collection

ANGLING

Trout fishing was popular along the stretch of the River Aire, downstream from Gargrave Bridge. The Aire Fishing Club was founded in 1838 and was indeed in existence until at least the mid-1960s. Nowadays, this stretch of the river is fished by the Bradford City Angling Association. The canal was also used for angling competitions.

PIGEON RACING

There was a pigeon racing club, and its members had considerable success in the North West Yorkshire Federation's race in April 1910, which started in Rugeley, 84 miles from the Gargrave lofts. The overall winner was a bird belonging to Mr G Parkin of the Gargrave Club with an average speed of 1104.5 yards/minute (38 mph). Other speedy birds belonged to E McQueenie, J Kirkbright, J Nuttall and the Walker brothers.

THE CHURCHES

St Andrew's Parish Church

When the young and enthusiastic Arthur Victor Magee took over this, his first parish in 1896, he reinstated the daily services, formed a Communicants Guild and generally busied himself getting the church back on track. There were some concerns that he might not approve of the annual Parochial Tea and Entertainment, held each New Year, but he was won over by the excellence of the ham sandwiches and the tradition continued.

Whoever wrote the account in the Parish Magazine about the vicar's first experience of this event, made a pointed comment that Northerners could show Southerners how good they were at eating, drinking and being merry.

Arthur Victor Magee
Courtesy of Derek Mc Robert

"It was not only a Northern Tea, it was a Great Northern Tea, conducted on the main lines of hospitality and good fellowship."

The entertainment included a piano duet by Lady Wilson and her daughter Beatrice, many songs from the church members and – shockingly for present-day readers – songs from the 'Gargrave Nigger Troupe'.

St Andrew's had always been involved in overseas missionary work, and this was revitalised by Rev Magee. St Andrew's Day (30th November) was designated as the start of Missionary Week, with a fundraising rummage sale, special services and meetings and the Children's Entertainment organised by Miss Jackson, the infant school teacher. Many of the children already had collecting boxes for missionary work at home, but the vicar extended this work by asking the children in the Sunday School to join a children's Foreign Mission Society, entitled "The King's Messengers". The obligations were to put contributions in their collecting box and to make two pieces of work a year to be sold in Missionary Week. The church also supported two children in an orphanage in India.

Other church activities included the men's Bible classes, the clothing and coal club (to help those in need in the village), the bell ringers, the Church Lads Brigade and the Band of Hope (for both adults and children). The school treat was held at the beginning of August, involving a procession around the village, a church service, tea and then games and sports on the field at Paget Hall.

A great deal of effort was put into the Temperance Movement to enter the new century. Such was the concern by the churches about the evils of drunkenness that the Anglicans and Wesleyans got together to hold joint meetings and rallies. The Parish magazine for July 1902 contained a lengthy report about the first annual United Temperance Demonstration. There was a procession from the Church school through the village to Low Green for a meeting where Captain Preston of Flasby Hall, in his capacity as chairman, started the proceedings by recalling his time in the army when drunkenness was normal amongst the soldiers. Other speakers then recounted their experiences of working with parts of society which were degraded by drink and misery. Mrs Tomkinson from the British Women's Temperance Association lamented the increase in drunkenness among women and concern for the fate of their neglected children. Afterwards, tea was provided in the Wesleyan school, followed by another meeting and more speeches. On the following day, the Sunday sermons carried on with the theme and came up with some helpful guidelines – keep children away from the public house and from intoxicating liquor, stop drinking at funerals, join a Temperance movement and to try and reform any weak brother or sister who is falling victim to the craving for drink.

Many 'signed the pledge', this example was issued by the Yorkshire Band of Hope Union.
Courtesy of the Dennis French Collection

118

As time went on, there were more activities specifically for the ladies and girls of the church, such as the Mothers' Meeting and the Girls' Friendly Society. A girls' choir was formed to sing at the Wednesday evening service (but not on Sundays.)

IMPROVEMENTS TO THE CHURCH BUILDING .... AND TO THE CLERGY

St Andrew's had always been fortunate to have wealthy patrons. Charles Marsden, the previous vicar and his wife, had both died in their retirement home in Devon. Their daughter, Miss Lucy Marsden made several gifts to the church in their memory. She paid for a new reredos behind the altar and also for two new stained glass windows in the South Porch. These windows were designed by Baron Arild Rosenkrantz, who was related to the Marsden's by marriage. Rosenkrantz was Danish, but often worked in London and was famous for his paintings as well as his stained glass work. The carved oak chancel screen and clergy stalls were donated to the church by Sir Ernest Holden in 1912, in memory of his wife.

Archdeacon Kilner
From the Collection of St. Andrew's Church

Rev Magee had been criticised for holding very elaborate services, described by some of the congregation as being too 'popish'. He'd made a big impact in the district by marrying one of Sir Mathew's daughters but in 1906 had moved to a parish in London. This was a High Anglican Church, better suited to his religious inclinations, and the London social life would have been preferable for his family. His successor was Rev Francis Charles Kilner, who also had the role of Archdeacon of South Craven. Archdeacon Kilner was well respected and liked in the parish. He proved to be tolerant of the Wesleyan Church

and did much to build bridges between the two congregations.

Archdeacon Kilner was promoted in 1913 to become Suffragan Bishop of Richmond, and he was succeeded by Arthur Crosbie Blunt who would serve St Andrew's for 35 years.

Rev Arthur Crosbie Blunt
From the Collection of St. Andrew's Church

CHURCH MUSIC AND THE BELL RINGERS

The job of the church organist was most important in the life of St Andrew's. There were several services a week, weddings, funerals and special occasions, so the organist was a busy man. When Edward Burlend succeeded Samuel Thornton in 1901, the stipend was £15 a year. The organist was assisted by the organ blower who hand pumped the bellows in the days before electricity.

Edward Burlend was also the headmaster of the Church School. He was only in charge of the school for a few years but remained the church organist until 1926. His term of office is commemorated on one of the brass plaques next to the organ.

The church bells were rung on Sundays and on special occasions, sometimes for several hours at a time. Up until 1880, there were six bells. The two oldest (and largest) of the original bells dated back to 1703 and 1747, and they have been tuned and refurbished over the years. Two more bells were added in 1880, making the set of eight bells that are still being rung to this day. The church bell ringers were paid £15 a year for their services.

Joe Langstroth's Yorkshire Change Ringers Membership
From the collection of of Saint Andrew's Church

One name forever associated with the bells is that of the Langstroth family. Christopher 'Kit' Langstroth was a bell ringer for seventy years, and his son Joe followed in his footsteps. Joe, born in Gargrave on the 18th of June 1887, started bell ringing at an early age. He was quite small and before he perfected the ringing technique, had a few mishaps when he was carried up on the bell rope and hit his head on the ceiling. Once Joe had completed 720 changes, he was eligible to become a member of the Yorkshire Association of Change Ringers. His membership certificate, dated 1905 (when he was just 18) still hangs in the church. Other notable bell ringers were John McKell, Arthur Jones, Henry Lofthouse, Henry Birtwhistle and his son William.

The church has a set of hand bells that were in use in the early 1900s. Not much is known about when they were rung, apart from the recollections of Joe Langstroth. When he was a young man, a group of 6 or 8 would carry the hand bells and a table and play at the big houses on Christmas Day afternoon. They walked along lanes and across fields to Newfield Hall, Eshton Hall and Flasby Hall to entertain the families and their guests and hope to get some treats for their efforts.

The Choir

The size and membership of the church choir have yet to be determined, as so far, no records have come to light. It is known that Thomas Bentley Wane was a choir member for 65 years and that postmistress Dorothy Varley and her sister were also singers. The boys in the choir had their rewards in the form of trips and outings. These were noted in the school log books, as the headmaster and the organist/choirmaster were often one and the same. Days out were spent at York, Bridlington or Morecambe and there was even a trip to Leeds to go to cricket and then to watch Barnum and Bailey's circus.

Wesleyan Methodists

Coming into the first part of the 20th century, the Wesleyans had a flourishing church and social scene. Entertainment was home-grown and was often centred around music, which had always been a vital part of the Methodist tradition.

One of the Wesleyan Sunday School classes
Courtesy of the Dennis French Collection

One of the main social gatherings was the annual 'At Home' event, which took place early in the year and comprised of food, entertainment and a Sale of Work. Similar celebrations were held for Harvest Festival and Christmas. Throughout the year, the Wesleyan Guild held social functions with visiting speakers, plays and concerts.

The Day School was in competition with the Church School. More about this rivalry can be found later on in this chapter in the section on education.

Every July, the Wesleyan Sunday school had their annual parade round the village, stopping to sing at various locations. Afterwards, there were refreshments in the school room and sports and games in a nearby field. Local photographer Tom Airton captured the 1912 games with his camera.

In 1915, Benjamin Walls compiled an anniversary booklet, looking back on the previous 100 years of the Chapel. He mentioned many of the people involved in the life of the church. Jonathan Dodgson (one of the village blacksmiths) was a leading light, being the church secretary for many years. James Hunt (shoemaker) was one of the church stewards. Other family names associated with the chapel were Bateson, Wellock, Middlebrook, Tranter, Lofthouse, Wiseman, Walls, Cuthbert, Bargh, Walker, Laycock and Gill. Miss Jane Bracewell was particularly remembered for her work in the Sunday School and in running classes for the ladies. Miss Louisa Tranter was the church organist and music teacher. Benjamin C Walls was a talented musician and bugle band leader.

Higherlands Canal Bridge
Courtesy of the Dennis French Collection

Marching down the High Street
Courtesy of the Dennis French Collection

Park Place
Courtesy of the Dennis French Collection

Church Street
Courtesy of the Dennis French Collection

Coronation Square
Courtesy of the Dennis French Collection

The Sports Field. Probably behind Paget Hall
Courtesy of the Dennis French Collection

The Sports Spectators.
Courtesy of the Dennis French Collection

ELEMENTARY EDUCATION

At the turn of the century, all other schools were gone and only the Anglicans and the Wesleyan Methodists were left to educate the young of Gargrave.

Differences in attitudes towards religious education and the demon drink caused friction. A family removed their children from the Church School because they taught too much religion and had recently appointed a publican to the school management committee.

Disagreements over discipline still caused problems. Dick Black had to be corrected for fighting with Horace Aldersley, and Mrs Black stormed up to school to complain. Dick Black's mother would intervene to help him in another nine years when he was 18.

Thomas Wood (son of the Broughton Quarry manager) was caught hitting another boy and causing his nose to bleed. He was caned across the shoulders, much to the fury of his parents who threatened the school with a summons. They removed Thomas and his many siblings to the Wesleyan School, where the headmaster Job Cockcroft was pleased to have them.

Wesleyan School class 3 May 1901
Courtesy of Barbara Preston

Children generally started school at the age of 4, although a few may have started earlier, as there is a mention of the Wesleyan School buying cots for the 'babies' – possibly for 3-year-olds for their nap after lunch. The infants department was for 4 – 7-year-olds and the upper classes from 8 to 13. Various Education Acts had raised the school leaving age, and from 1899, it was set at 13, but with conditions. 11 and 12 years olds were allowed to work part-time at the mill, although not all children did so if their families could manage without the extra income. At 13, provided the child had an attendance record of at least 350 days over the previous 5 years and had passed a medical, he or she could work full time at the mill. Otherwise, they would have to stay on until 14. The more capable pupils could take the scholarship exams to continue their education at the Skipton Grammar schools.

In 1902, there was an initiative from the Local Education Committee to introduce organised Physical Training into schools. The teachers went on a training course every evening for a week. This resulted in the children being out in the playground doing drill exercises, marching and Indian club swinging.

Attendance and Achievements

The numbers on the school rolls in 1904 were 96 at the National School and 128 at the Wesleyan School. By 1913, the numbers were 83 and 101 respectively, this being the year after the mill fire when families had moved away to find work. Even though school was more accessible, attendance was mediocre at the beginning of the century.

The School Attendance Officer was supposed to monitor this, but both the headmasters complained that this system was ineffective. However, by 1913, things had improved, absentees were being chased up, and the average attendance was around 90%.

The last resort to get children to attend was to take the parents to court. In December 1912, the parents of seven-year-old Evelyn had to explain why she had only been to school three times since she'd started eighteen months ago. Although they stated that Evelyn was too sick and frail to go to school, they had failed to get a doctor's certificate. Their other excuses were that they had fifteen children and only one was working, and another four had been put out of work by the Mill fire. The bench showed leniency and gave the family another chance.

Neither school was rated as good by the inspectors because achievements were hampered by high staff turnover, and closures for sickness. Edward Burlend who took over as headmaster of the National School in 1900 was helped out by his children. His son

Edward Ernest was an assistant teacher for a while and his daughter Ethel, although only 17, was acting informally as a teacher.

Exceptionally, there was one teacher who stayed at the National School for many years. This was Sarah Jackson, who taught the infants. She retired in 1914 after 41 years at the school and was presented with a sterling silver tea set.

Miss Jackson with Nellie Jones, her youngest pupil, and Thomas Burrow, aged 45, her oldest former pupil.
Courtesy of the Dennis French Collection

This retirement photo of Miss Jackson was taken by Tom Airton. The child is Nellie Jones, her youngest pupil, who was only three. The man is Thomas Burrow, aged 45, the oldest of her former pupils.

Sarah Jackson lived out the rest of her life in her home in Church Street. She died in 1933 at the age of 84 and is buried in St Andrew's graveyard.

Both schools had their own management committees, but this was an era when the state started to become more involved with the faith schools. Local education sub-committees were set up to receive regular performance reports and oversee the running of the schools. In 1907, the National School was renamed Gargrave Church of England School. The Wesleyan School was taken over by West Riding County Council in 1909 and was then called the Council School.

Mechanics' Institute and Evening Classes

The Mechanics' Institute had been in a small cottage in South Street for 40 years which was restricting their activities, but this all changed in 1908. The Primitive Methodists had vacated the Old Chapel, just behind them and a part of it was being used by the Co-op. With the agreement of Sir Mathew Wilson, who owned the

John Herbert Weatherill County Minor Scholarship 1907
Courtesy of Audrey Weatherill

buildings, an exchange was organised. The Co-op moved into the small cottage, which being next to their existing stores, gave them a bigger frontage onto South Street. The Mechanics' Institute relocated into the ground floor of the Old Chapel. Here they had a reading room, billiards room, smoking room, kitchen and offices. The upper floor, which was reached by an external staircase was converted for use by St Andrew's Church as their Parochial Hall.

Thomas Wood and the Parkinson brothers probably hadn't achieved much at school, but to their credit, had come to evening classes to improve themselves. John Herbert Weatherill had done well at school and was now taking extra subjects to further his career. The following extract from an evening class register of 1908 - 9 shows their achievements.

West Riding County Council.

Session 1908—1909.

Register No.	Date of Entry	NAME (Surname first)	ADDRESS	OCCUPATION	Date of Birth	Preparatory Work done prior to Enrolment	Group, Course, Subjects and Stages approved for	ATTENDANCES Possible / Actual	Examination Claimed upon for Success; Body, Stage and Class	Fee paid Exhibition Letter and No.
71	Sep.t 21/08	Wood ___	The Quarries ___	Quarries ___	21.4.93	from Eng	I			
72	Sept 21/08	Parkinson Smith	Water St Gargrave	mill hand	4.5.95	from Reg School	Arith 26 24 22 / Draw 26 23 / Eng. 26 25 13 / Geog. 26 22		7/6
73	Sept 21/08	Parkinson Alfred	___	mill hand	26.3.94	from Reg School	Arith 26 22 / Draw 26 22 / Eng. 26 13 / Geog. 23 13	I	
74	Sept 30/08	Metcalfe John	Eastonbrook James Gargrave	Clerk	3.4.95	from Reg School	Arith 26 25 / ___	I	7/6

Evening classes, offering a range of courses were well attended. Some of the students and courses are shown in this register for 1908–9.

Courtesy of the Dennis French Collection

HEALTH, WELFARE AND CARE OF THE POOR

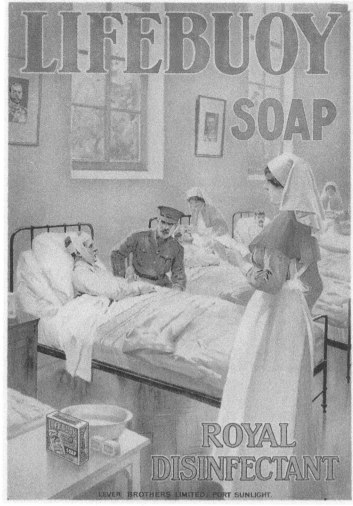

WW1 advert ©IWM

Doctors were self-employed and charged for medicines and for their services, which was not something that could be afforded by the ordinary working families. Natural and herbal remedies that had been used for centuries were still the first choice for curing many ailments. Grocers shops sold patent medicines, pills and cod liver oil.

Lifebuoy was an antiseptic carbolic soap introduced into Britain in 1895 and was a useful tool for combating germs. Other 'remedies' were Beecham's pills for digestion, Kaputine for headaches and Clarke's Blood Mixture to expel impurities from the blood and fix a variety of skin conditions. Ladies were advised to correct 'irregularities' with a course of Horton's Pills.

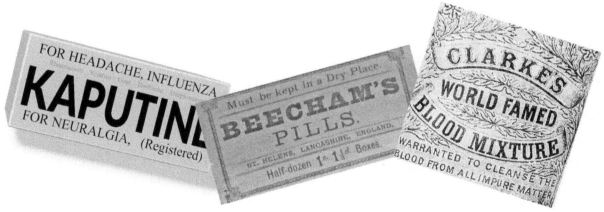

Cure all medications of the period.
Facsimilies of original packaging by Don Slaven

GARGRAVE'S DOCTORS

Mevell Hall. Dr Snell and his wife can be seen looking out of the window above the left bay.
Courtesy of Martin Thompson

Dr Snell in his garden
Courtesy of the Dennis French Collection

Mevell Hall in the High Street was the home of one of the village doctors for many years.

Up until the 1850s, the building was The Red Lion Inn, and then changed its use, as immortalised in this little ditty.

> *Near Gargrave's top, the Red Lion stood*
> *And many went to drink its blood*
> *Where lads and lasses went for pop*
> *Has now become a doctor's shop.*

The incumbents of Mevell Hall in the nineteenth century were Doctors William Harrison, Joseph Hilles and John Snell. They were assisted by an apothecary or by a young doctor. Dr John Snell arrived in 1890 and soon became involved in the villages sporting activities. He was vice president of the cricket club and was remembered as the man with the starting gun at the athletic events.

Dr Snell was replaced in 1905 by 30-year-old Herbert Wales, whose fine singing voice made him much in demand at concerts and social events.

Another medical practice opened in 1893 at The Crofts (now Kirk Syke) in the High Street. This was run by Dr Thomas Knowles until 1914 when he retired, and Dr Alexander Cameron took over.

The village doctors carried out vaccinations and minor surgical procedures as well as treating diseases and ailments. More complicated cases could be referred to Skipton and District Hospital in Granville Street or to Leeds General Infirmary. All this came at a price and was unaffordable for many. Doctors could take on public positions, for example, Dr Knowles was the medical officer for the Skipton Workhouse.

NURSING

In the nineteenth century, nursing was considered an activity not requiring skill or training and was done by servants or family members. It was considered an immodest job and not suitable for more genteel ladies. This gradually changed as the Victorian era progressed, as hospitals were set up and nurses began to be trained appropriately. However, there was an increasing concern for the poor who could not afford hospital care. Charities and philanthropists provided limited funds to care for the sick and poor in their communities, but this was by no means universal.

In Gargrave, there were discussions after Queen Victoria's Diamond Jubilee in 1897 about starting a District Nursing Scheme, using money raised during the celebrations. Skipton was just about to start such a scheme, but it wasn't until 1904 that the Gargrave and Coniston Cold District Nursing Association was launched.

The ladies of the committee were: Mrs Coulthurst (Gargrave House); Mrs Magee (vicar's wife); Mrs Preston (Flasby Hall); Mrs Tottie (Coniston Hall); Mrs Tupholme (curate's wife) and Lady Wilson (Eshton Hall). The first nurse to be engaged was Miss J W Mc Ritchie who was found lodgings with Mr and Mrs Lund in West Street. The nurse's services were free to those who subscribed to the scheme. The charges were quite reasonable, being typically 1s a year for an individual and 2s 6d for a family. This wouldn't be enough to cover the full costs, and the expectation was that the wealthier residents would support the scheme financially. In the first six months of operation, Nurse Mc Ritchie made 355 visits to 35 cases. The scheme carried on through the war years and beyond, but often struggled for money. Fundraising activities helped to keep it going, as did Mrs Coulthurst, who often stepped in to cover any deficits.

FRIENDLY SOCIETIES

There was no state provision for healthcare, so people had either no provision or had to make their own arrangements, by subscribing to one of the many Friendly Societies. Some of these mutual associations had been in existence since the 18th century. Members paid subscriptions which gave them access to medical care, pensions, savings schemes, sickness benefits and funeral costs. Meetings were held (in the local pub or church hall) and were a mix of social activities and informative sessions about insurance and money matters. Societies would also engage the services of a local doctor and pay him to treat members and provide sick notes.   Some Friendly Societies are still in existence, either to provide savings and investments or as social and support organisations (for example, the Three Links Club in Skipton).

Gargrave's longest-established Friendly Society was the Airedale Lodge of the Independent Order of Peaceful Doves, who met at The Mason's Arms. It was suspected, in some quarters, that these meetings were just an excuse to drink lots of beer, so temperance Friendly Societies provided a different option. There had been a society linked to the Primitive Methodists – the Independent Order of Good Templars. The Gargrave branch went by the rather off-putting name of the Hard Struggle Lodge. They obviously lost their struggle and were wound up in 1894.   In 1889, a local branch or "tent" of the Independent Order of Rechabites Salford Unity was set up in the village. They were a temperance based society and therefore in tune with the principles of the Wesleyan Methodists and held their meeting in the Wesleyan School Rooms. Their local groups were called "tents" after the biblical references where God had commanded the sons of Rechab to live in tents. The Gargrave branch was called the "Sir Wilfrid Lawson" Tent, and its medical officers were Doctors Snell and Knowles.

The Peaceful Doves finished in 1912, and their place was taken that year by the Loyal Pride of Gargrave Independent Order of Oddfellows Manchester Unity who had their lodge room at The Swan. Both the Rechabites and the Oddfellows had their rituals, conventions, officials and regalia similar to the Freemasons.

The Liberal government ran the country until the First World War caused a National Coalition to be formed. Their notable achievement was that they instigated the beginnings of the Welfare State, setting up systems for old age pensions and benefits for sickness and unemployment

OLD AGE PENSIONS

The first step towards a Welfare system was the provision of pensions for the aged poor, starting at the beginning of 1909. Anyone over 70 with an income of less than 10s a week could apply, but they had to be of good character. Those receiving poor relief, criminals and lunatics were excluded. Application forms were filled in at the Post Office and passed to a locally appointed pensions committee who approved the claims. Pensioners were issued with a book of coupons that were redeemed at the Post Office. The weekly payment was 10s each or 15s for a married couple. When the pension scheme first launched, there were 18 worthy and eligible claimants in Gargrave.

1911 INSURANCE ACT

Before this, insurance was in the hands of private companies such as the Prudential or Sun Life. Inspired by the German system, David Lloyd George, the Liberal Chancellor of the Exchequer, drew up a bill to raise money by taxing the rich to help the poor. This was not popular in some quarters, and the House of Lords initially blocked it. This triggered a general election, and an act of parliament to stop the Lords interfering in budget matters, so the Insurance Act didn't come to fruition without a struggle.

There were two types of benefit – health and unemployment. All workers earning less than £160 a year could be insured against sickness. The weekly premiums were:

> Employee 4d
>
> Employer....................3d
>
> State............................2d

The beneficiary would receive free medical treatment and 10s a week for 3 months, then 5s a week for a further 3 months. The Liberal Party slogan to promote this benefit was "Ninepence for fourpence."

These benefits were all managed at a local level by Friendly Societies (the Oddfellows were approved for this), trades unions, and county health committees. It is interesting to note that the Manchester Unity Oddfellows only started accepting women members in 1911, as one of the conditions to become an approved organisation to administer the National Insurance benefits. Local doctors were approved (and paid) by the Friendly Societies for their services. Another society came into being in Gargrave at this time. This was the National Deposit Friendly Society and may have had links with St Andrew's Church, as the vicar was on the committee.

CARE OF THE POOR

Traditionally, each parish was responsible for looking after its own poor and destitute. In 1834, the Poor Law Reform Act changed this arrangement, and the Skipton Poor Union was created to cover 41 parishes in the Craven Area. Gargrave had its own Poor House located by the Damside path on High Green. Gargrave's Poor House was made redundant after the Skipton Union Workhouse opened in 1840. Robert Story, the Gargrave poet, wrote this about the new facility:

> They've built a House on yonder slope
> Huge, grim and prison-like, and dull!
> With grated walls that shut out Hope,
> And cells of wretched paupers full.
>
> And they, if we for help should call,
> Will thither take and lodge us thus;
> But Ellen, no! Their prison wall,
> I swear it, was not built for us.
>
> We've lived together fourteen years
> Three boys and four sweet girls are ours;
> Location of the Gargrave Poor House
> Shall they put on their prison dress?
>
> My dear, my dear – THEY SHALL NOT GO.

For destitute people, the only way to get a roof over their heads would be to go into the workhouse. This was a desperate situation for families in particular, as men, women and children were separated into different sections. The responsibility for running it rested with the Board of Guardians, which had representatives from the parishes in the Union. The social stigma attached to going into the workhouse was a terrifying prospect for people. Certainly, by Edwardian times, the address of children born in the Skipton Workhouse was given as '16 Gargrave Road', to protect them from being disadvantaged later in life.

Another function of the Board of Guardians was to appoint local overseers of the poor. Their job was to set and collect the poor rate from the residents and to distribute contributions to the poor. Gargrave was fortunate to have another source of relief which helped to keep the very poor in their own homes. Over the space of a couple of hundred years, wealthy landowners and businessmen had made donations to support the poor of the parish. Interest from the rental incomes on farmland in Gargrave and Hellifield, and of the Black Horse at Hellifield was used for this purpose. Eventually, many of these properties passed to the vicar and churchwardens of Gargrave and were consolidated to become the Gargrave Poor's Lands Charity. The interest was distributed each New Year, and in 1910, 88 sums of money were given out, ranging from 10s to 30s

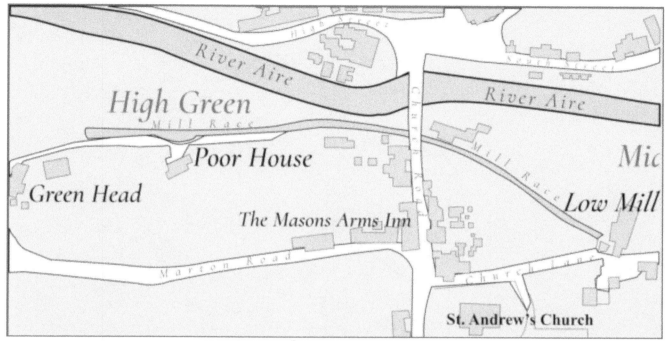

Location of Gargrave Poor House 1834
From an original sketch by Sue Lyall

The Gargrave Poor's Lands Charity is still in existence and provides financial assistance to permanent residents of Gargrave, Eshton, Flasby, Winterburn, Coniston Cold and Bank Newton.

In 1930, control of Skipton workhouse passed to the West Riding County Council, and it became known as a Public Assistance Institution. It later became Raikeswood Hospital and was subsequently converted into housing in the 1990s.

A map of the centre of the village showing the locations of the shops and businesses is shown overleaf. A list of owners and businesses between 1900 and 1929 can be found in Appendix D together with a copy of the map.

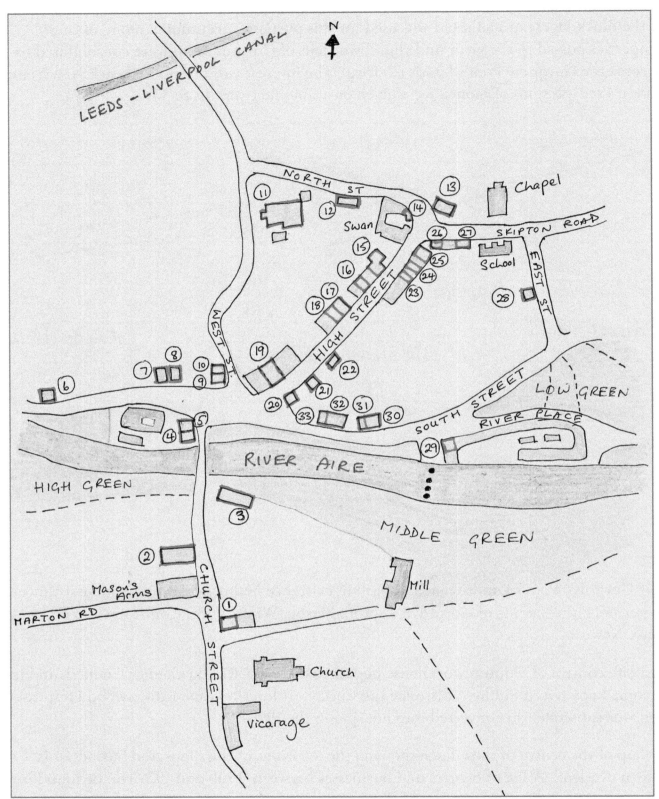

Sketch map showing positions of businesses - Not to Scale
(The key to this map can be found in appendix D.)
From an original drawing by Sue Lyall.

THE WAR YEARS

WHAT EVENT LAUNCHED THE WAR

The trigger incident which started the conflict was the assassination of Franz Ferdinand of Austria, the heir to the Austrian Empire on the 28th June 1914.

The killing was carried out by a Gavrilo Princip, a member of Young Bosnians, a group armed and trained by the Black Hand. The Black Hand was a Secret Serbian Military society, not recognised by the government of the Kingdom of Serbia, but formed by a group of senior officers of the Serbian Armed forces.

Austria, with support from Germany, declared war on Serbia for non-compliance with unacceptable demands by Austria. Austria then asked Russia for help with the Serbian war. Russia refused, as it was in support of the Serbian cause. (Russia was the first to mobilise for war according to some academics.) Germany, giving support to the Austrians, declared war on Russia and later France for having an alliance with Russia. Britain joined in by providing support to both Belgium and France and declared war on Germany. France had a treaty with Russia that brought that country into the conflict. Turkey, being allied with Germany, was also declared at war with Britain. Nearly the whole of Europe was quickly engaged in what we now know as the Great War.

On the 7th of August 1914, the British Government drew on an alliance that Britain held with Japan from 1902, to ask for assistance in controlling the Imperial German Fleet activities in the Pacific. Given the option of taking Germany's Pacific territories, Japan agreed.

On the 23rd of August, Japan declared war on Germany. Austria's refusal to remove one of their cruisers, the SMS Kaiserin Elisabeth from Qingdao, one of Germany's Pacific ports on the Chinese coast, caused Japan to declare war on the Austro-Hungarian Empire on the 25th August 1914.

World War One had now indeed begun.

LIFE IN THE VILLAGE DURING THE WAR

Bantam Recruitment Poster ©IWM

VOLUNTARY RECRUITMENT

When war was declared on 4th August 1914, there was an initial rush of volunteers in the Armed Forces. The expectation was that the young, fit and single men would enlist. Probably many of them saw this as an adventure, and anyway, the politicians said the war would be over by Christmas. The requirements were that men were between the ages of 18 and 30, at least 5 feet and 3 inches tall, with a minimum chest measurement of 34 inches and be fit enough to serve. The youngest recruits were not supposed to be sent abroad until they reached 19. A few weeks later, the age limit was raised to 35. As the war progressed, men between 5 feet and 5 feet 3 inches (but not too skinny) could join the specially formed Bantam Battalions.

A popular anonymous verse about the Bantams was:

"Each one a pocket Hercules

five feet and a bit,

a kind of Bovril essence

of six feet British grit."

In the initial recruitment wave, 20 young men from Gargrave enlisted. Most of them joined the local Company, of the 6th Battalion, Duke of Wellington's West Riding Regiment which, was based in Skipton. Those with particular skills could become drivers, engineers, cavalry men or signallers, and those with previous military experience were in demand as officers and to train the new recruits.

It was possible to join other regiments. The choice of the recruit could be based on past family connections or because the regiment had a better uniform or a good reputation. After conscription in 1916, there wasn't a choice, and recruits were allocated to the regiments that needed the numbers.

Some older men had been in the Regular Army and seen action in South Africa or India. Others were part of the Territorial Army, part-time volunteers who could be mobilised if needed. This required them to attend training days and a 15 day annual summer camp to practise extended military exercises. Their original agreement with the Army was that it would not force them into overseas service but they could volunteer to go and at the outbreak of war, some of them did. Their part-time training meant that they needed a shorter period to make them battle ready. The first line 1/6th Battalion was deployed to France in April 1915. The raw recruits formed the second line 2/6th Battalion and needed more training, so they didn't go abroad until 1917.

One of the regular soldiers living in Gargrave at the outbreak of war was Herbert Gladstone Rhodes. Born in Leeds in 1881, he'd enlisted at Richmond in 1903 into the Princess of Wales' Own Yorkshire Regiment (the Green Howards) and had seen action in India and Africa. He was placed on the reserve list in 1910 and then worked as a French polisher for J H Cleave, makers of sports equipment. Herbert came to Gargrave in 1914 when his employer relocated from Bradford to High Mill. He quickly became renowned in the area as an athlete, having won many trophies for running. On the day after war was declared, he was recalled to his regiment and in October he was fighting in the first battle of Ypres. His war record survives (many were lost during WW2) and it tells how he was buried in a trench, injured in the right forearm, and his right eye was damaged as a result of concussion. After a period in hospital, he was sent back for home service, being deemed capable of garrison or orderly duties. Herbert Rhodes was discharged from the army in January 1916, having come to the end of his period of engagement, at the age of 35 and with the rank of Lance Corporal. Once back in Gargrave, he became a founding member of the Gargrave Volunteer Platoon and continued his interests in athletics.

Two men with some military experience from the end of the Anglo-Boer War were Norman England and Godfrey Ermen. They were both sons of wealthy industrialists, had been privately educated, and could be fast-tracked to officer class. They played an important part in training the new recruits to the 2/6th Duke of Wellington's. Sadly, Captain Ermen died from pneumonia in 1915, but Captain England later served abroad with his men and was awarded the DSO and the Croix de Guerre.

No _____

ARMY FORM B. 104—82

_____ Record Office.

_____

_____ 191

_____

     It is my painful duty to inform you that a report has been recieved from the War Office notifying the death of :—

(No.) _____ (Rank) _____

(Name) _____

(Regiment) _____

which occurred _____

on the _____

The report is to the effect that he _____

_____

     By His Majesty's command I am to forward the enclosed message of sympathy from Their Gracious Majesties the King and Queen I am at the same time to express the regret of the Army Council at the soldiers death in his Country's Service.

     I am to add that any information that may be receive as the the soldiers burial will be communicated to you in due course. A separate leaflet dealing more fully with this subject is enclosed.

        I am,

        _____

        Your obedient Servant,

        Officer in charge of Records.

        PTO

Facsimile of Army Form B. 104-82,
Notification of Soldiers Death

For the first couple of years, Gargrave was relatively untouched by the war, as many of the men were still training on home soil. Six men were lost in 1915 and 8 in 1916, but once more men were deployed abroad, the numbers rose to 19 in 1917 and 15 in 1918. For the families at home, it was an anxious time, waiting to hear if their son or husband had been injured or killed.

The official means of notification for a deceased soldier was a standard army form, shown on the previos page. The families of officers would also be informed by telegram. Other ranks' families might only receive the form, but some might also get a letter from a friend, the chaplain or even a commanding officer.

If a soldier was wounded and not able to write, a friend or the chaplain would send word to the family on their condition and progress.

Some Gargrave lads became prisoners of war, including Jack Parkinson and Charles Hutton.

GARGRAVE FAMILIES AT WAR

Many people in the village had more than one family member in the forces. The Craven Herald of 9 July 1915 writes of "A Patriotic Gargrave Family", praising the four sons of Mr and Mrs David Walker of Airebank Terrace who had joined up. James and William enlisted in the Army Service Corps, responsible for supplying food, equipment and ammunition to the troops. Ralph joined the 10th Duke of Wellington's and David went into the Navy. Later in the war, Ralph was discharged due to injuries which resulted in the amputation of his right leg just above the knee and later in the war, their younger brother Robert joined the Navy. All survived.

William Chester, a joiner from Mill Hill (in Church Lane) had five sons away fighting. Richard joined the 3rd Battalion of the Duke of Wellington's Regiment, Edward was in the Navy on patrol ships guarding the convoys, Charles enlisted in the horse transport section of the Army Service Corps, Harold in the Royal Field Artillery and Thomas Wilfred in the 8th Duke of Wellington's. Thomas (usually known as Wilfred) was killed early in 1917 after only 7 months service, but the other brothers came home.

John and Clara Weatherill had their three eldest boys away in the war. Jack joined the Duke of Wellington's Regiment (and later on was in the RAF), Henry, known as Harry, was a ship's radio officer and Stanley joined the Royal Artillery. Their youngest, Ted was too young for this war, but went on to serve in the Second World War. Both Jack and Stanley were wounded, but all the brothers came through the war.

The extended Wane family provided five of their boys to the war effort. George Anthony Wane enlisted in the Army Service Corps and went to the front early on in the war. A letter he wrote home telling of his initial experiences is reproduced later on in this chapter. His brother Thomas was in the Yorkshire Regiment (Green Howards) and their cousins Richard and Christopher went into the Navy. Christopher was one of the casualties of war and his story can be found in the next chapter. A more distant cousin, John was in the Royal Engineers.

Men from Gargrave who had left these shores to escape from unemployment and build a better life, also heeded the call the join up. News came that John and Walter Horner, who had emigrated to Canada in 1907, had enlisted. Doctor Snell's son, John Simeon Snell went to Alberta in 1909 to start a life as a farmer and signed up with the Canadian Overseas Forces in the last year of the war. John Naylor and his wife Gladys left for Canada in 1908 to find farm work. He also came over to fight with the Canadian Forces early on in the war and afterwards returned to his family in Ontario. John's brothers Sam and George were two of the Gargrave soldiers who lost their lives in the conflict.

A local man who had gone to New Zealand was James Herbert Preston, the son of Robert and Annie Preston of Park House. James was 52 when war broke out and served as a sergeant in the New Zealand Home Service section at the Trentham Military Camp in Ashburton. Sadly, he died after injuries sustained by a fall and was later buried at Ashburton Cemetery.

After the initial rush to join up, numbers dwindled. The recruiters held an open-air recruitment meeting in Coronation Square in June 1915, trying to boost numbers. 250 territorial soldiers from Skipton, headed by the band of the 6th Duke of Wellington's West Riding Regiment, paraded through the village playing inspiring patriotic music. Mr Fred H. Garnett of Knowles House urged every young fellow to come forward and do his best in this great crisis. Mr Garnett himself offered to work for six hours a day in Bradford doing clerical work for the Army Services Corps.

Soldiers with the recruiting team refuted questions about bullying in the army. No-one signed up on the day.

SEPARATION ALLOWANCE

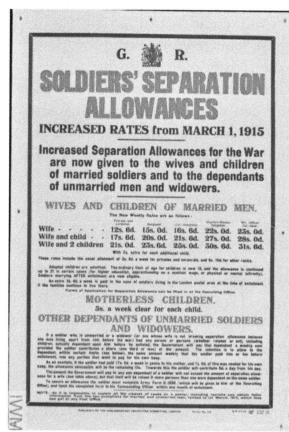

Separation Allowance Information Poster @IWM

The wives of serving soldiers were paid an allowance to make up for their loss of income. Part of this allowance came from the soldier's pay. The rest was made up by the government. The wife was expected to behave dutifully, otherwise her allowance could be stopped if any infidelity or misbehaviour took place.

A widow who relied on her sons for support could also claim the separation allowance, so those left behind would not become destitute.

A scandalous story appeared in the Craven Herald and was a cautionary tale for all wives. Two women in Earby were supplementing their incomes by prostitution and had their allowances stopped. The women were operating a bawdy house, for the benefit of servicemen on leave. After a tip-off from the neighbours, the local police observed the comings and goings for 90 days, before arresting the enterprising duo. They were both imprisoned for 3 months and the one with children had them removed.

CONSCRIPTION

Conscription was introduced in 1916 as voluntary enlistment wasn't providing enough fighting men. The upper age limit was increased to 41 and was extended to include married men, but there were exemptions for those in essential jobs, known as reserved occupations. There had been considerable preparation beforehand, as the potential need had been identified early in 1915. In August of that year, a type of census was taken, called the National Register. In Gargrave, the enumerators were Harry McKell for the south of the river and Bank Newton, and John McKell for the north of the river. On August 15th all people between the ages of 15 and 65 were required to fill in a registration form and received a registration card.

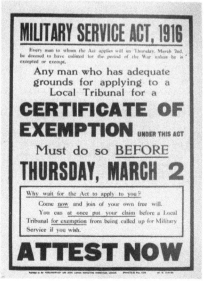

Military Service Exemption poster.
@IWM Art.IWM PST 5042

145

Kitchener Recruitment Poster
Public Domain - Eybl, Plakatmuseum Wien

The data collected was filed by type of occupation, in order to identify the pool of skilled labour that could be utilised for war work, and those required for essential work at home, and also to root out the 'shirkers and slackers'. All men between the ages of 18 and 41 then had their details entered onto a pink card. Those working in essential jobs, who might be exempt from military service, were starred. The pink cards were passed on to the military authorities and the information was later used as a basis for shaming men into volunteering and eventually for conscription.

Men and employers could appeal against conscription, and to deal with this, local Military Tribunal courts were set up. The Craven Herald ran weekly reports of the Skipton Tribunal hearings, but no-one was actually named. They also listened to complaints and allegations of men being exempt for no good reason. A Gargrave woman complained about a young man, a grocer's assistant, "swanking" about the village who had been exempted on the need to support his family. She was furious that her son was serving, and she had no-one to look after her. Whatever the rights and wrongs of the case, it was obvious that bitterness and resentment were setting in.

It was possible to defer conscription. A Gargrave steam wagon driver, age 31 and married, was granted temporary exemption. No further details were given about his circumstances. A representative of an estate at Winterburn was concerned that their only woodman might be conscripted. It transpired that the man had twice been rejected and been classified as C3 (only suitable for sedentary work at home camps), but even so, he would still need to apply for an exemption certificate. He was granted conditional exemption, but would have to join up if needed.

UNDERAGE SOLDIERS

At the beginning of the war, many lads lied about their age in order to enlist. If they met the height, build and health requirements, and looked old enough, they were accepted. The enlisting officials didn't need to see proof of age and anyway, they were paid 2s 6d for each recruit, so had no incentive to turn young lads away. The result was that boys were on the war front below the age of 19, which was the minimum age for going overseas. In the middle of 1916, the War Office decided that if parents could supply a birth certificate and prove their son's age, he could be brought back from the front for home duties.

One such parent was Mary Black of South Street. In May 1915, her son Dick had gone to the recruiting office in Keighley and enlisted in the Duke of Cornwall's Light Infantry. He stated that he was 19 years and 1 month old, two years older than his actual age. At a height of 5 feet 7 inches and with a chest measurement of 34 inches, he would easily pass the physical requirements. It was quite common for underage boys to join a regiment far from home, where their true age was less likely to be discovered.

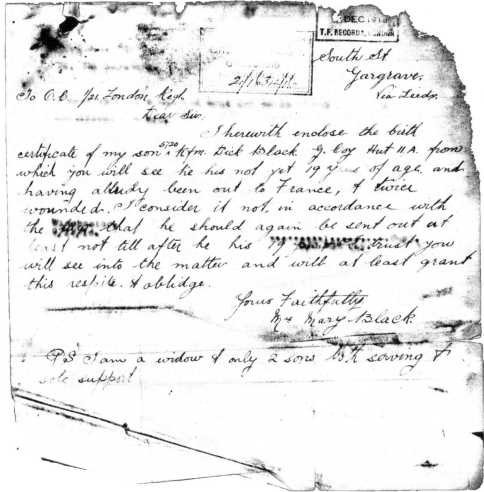

Mrs Black's letter to the War Office. The text is transcribed on the next page.

The letter shown reads;

> *"Dear Sir,*
>
> *I herewith enclose the birth certificate of my son 5720 Rifleman Dick Black. G. Coy hut II. A., From which you will see he is not yet 19 years of age and having already been out to France and twice wounded. I consider it not in accordance with the fact that he should again be sent out at least not until after he is 19 years old. I trust you will see into the matter and will at least grant this respect and oblige.*
>
> *Yours faithfully,*
>
> *Mrs Mary Black.*
>
> *PS I am a widow and only 2 sons, both serving, for sole support."*

After a period of training in Bodmin, Dick was deployed on the Isle of Wight at Freshwater Bay. In June 1916, he was transferred to the 21st Battalion of the London Regiment (1st Surrey Rifles) and sent to France. By the time Mary Black's request was received, he was already at the front and had sustained a gunshot wound in the leg.

The correspondence between Mrs Black, the War Office and Dick's adjutant went on for several months. Once his regiment was satisfied that he was too young to be on overseas service, he was transferred back for home duties in October with a reassurance that he would stay there until he reached 19. As soon as he was old enough, he went to Egypt in July 1917. Although Dick survived the war, Mary's older son from her first marriage, Thomas Wilfred Davis, lost his life. Mary Black was well known for defending her children – she and Dick are also mentioned on oage 130.

LETTERS AND CARDS HOME

The wartime postal system for the men at the front was a remarkable undertaking, dealing with up to 12 million letters a week. A huge wooden sorting office was established in London's Regents Park and mail went by lorry to Southampton or Folkestone. It was then shipped to French ports, where the Royal Engineers Postal Section had the task of getting the mail to the soldiers. The letters only took 2 or 3 days to reach their land destinations. Mail was sent to ships as well, but this was a longer process and some mail was lost at sea when ships were sunk. Letters from France and Belgium had no charge, but would take longer to get back to the UK due to censorship and delays if a major battle was ongoing.

It was vital that the men at the front didn't divulge their whereabouts, so letters were opened to check that no operational details leaked out. If a soldier didn't have time to write properly, they could send a standard field postcard to say how they were doing.

Jack Weatherill's proforma card home.
Courtesy of Audrey Weatherill

This one is from Jack Weatherill letting his family know that he was wounded but 'going on well'. He came home to recuperate, and once fit enough, was back in action.

"WW1 Silks" were embroidered cards that were very popular with the soldiers. They were stitched by French and Belgian ladies in their homes and then sent to factories to be made into cards. The pictures were patriotic and sentimental, and a beautiful keepsake for the families back home. Jack sent one to his mother and one to his sweetheart. These are shown on the next page.

Early in the war, the local paper printed letters from soldiers to give the readers a taste of the tribulations of war. As time went on, fewer of these appeared, as the Craven Herald columns became filled with the official government war reports, details of the dead and wounded, and the proceedings of the Military Tribunals.

These embroidered cards were sent by Jack Weatherill to his mother Clara and to his sweetheart Connie.
Courtesy of Audrey Weatherill

Herbert Rhodes wrote to his wife from the No 8 General Hospital, having been wounded in the First Battle of Ypres in October 1914.

"It is a very nice place where I am now, not many miles from sister Annie, so you will have an idea of where I am. I am going on all right, my wound is not serious, no bones being broken. I think I shall be here a week or two and suppose I shall be then sent to a convalescent camp for a few weeks. The battle I was in is the worst that the British had ever been in in English history. Our losses are terrible. By Jove, we have copped it. I shall tell you all about it when I come home, as we have to be careful about writing."

In the spring of 1915, Corporal George Wane (in the Army Service Corps) wrote to his friends in Gargrave from "Somewhere in Flanders".

"Since I left old England, I have had some very unique experiences. Our up-country journey from Le Havre was something like 250 miles, and this, of course, was done by rail – and what railways they are, to be sure! No system or skill like the Midland, no automatic signals, green grass growing thick between the four foots, and the hedges and ditches in wild confusion. Still all this goes to make nature pretty I suppose. For the past five months we have had a nerve trying time and, I am pleased to say, no casualties in our Company. We have a great leader in Captain Briggs, and a man whom the Company feels proud of. He is as fearless as a tiger and night after night leads our wagons to the trenches. We had a horse shot in the neck last night, bombs and shells flying around wholesale. I wish some of my Gargrave friends could see all, or part of this. The beautiful white walls of churches, farmsteads and cottages, now masses of ruins; dead cattle and horses about the fields and big holes in the ground like duck ponds. The trees in some parts are pierced by shells, while in other parts they are lovely and green and a sight never to be forgotten. We are at present in the ruins of a lovely old church, only the four walls standing. Another church that we used to occupy is down to the ground now, as are hundreds more. We saw this fine place go down and had to clear out helter-skelter for our lives, as our billet was struck no less than eight times, whilst we were in it, and getting out of it. How we escaped alive, God only knows. We are living in good hopes of a quick and sudden ending to this awful affair."

Sergeant Arthur Nicholson, 5th Yorkshire Regiment, formerly chauffeur to the Rev Arthur Blunt, Vicar of Gargrave, wrote home to a friend at Gargrave, on May 12th 1915, saying:-

"Well, I will try to tell you all I can about what has happened since leaving England. We left Newcastle on April 17th and spent the remainder of the night and the next day in a camp on the top of a hill where we could just see the white cliffs of England. The following night we marched to a railway station and entrained, about 45 men in a truck. It was beastly cold, and we were lying on top of each other. I think it was about the worst ride I have ever had. At the end we had a big march. I managed to stick it, but only just, it turned out so very hot. The next three days we were staying at various farms, which were all right.

On Friday, the 23rd, we were ordered to pack and were rushed right up country in motors, going into the reserve trenches at night. We lost a few men here from shell fire. At noon next day we had to 'move up'. Bullets and shells were flying all around, but no one hung back, and we were out in the open all the rest of the day and night, rain pouring all night. Just before dawn on Sunday, the 25th, we had to move again and by the time we had got to our position we had lost a good many. I think this Sunday was the roughest anyone had experienced. We worked hard and made a decent trench which sheltered us fairly well. We hung on here a day and a night, and then had another move further up to relieve some other troops, who had been fighting for days. I don't think we ever knew the value of water until now.

The men would leave the trench and go and fill bottles at a ruined farm a quarter of a mile away, taking no notice of the shells. All this time we lived on hard biscuits and tinned meat. By Jove, I could just enjoy a real good square Gargrave dinner. It is hard to describe what a battlefield is like, everything is in ruins. Before the war, this seems to have been a thickly populated district of farms and small holdings. They are some three or four hundred yards apart, and now in ruins; dead horses lying about, and towards night, men as well. The men are gathered up and buried during the night. At the end of five days and nights we were relieved, and I was jolly thankful, but even when we got to the camp we were shelled every night. I don't think that I shall ever forget this country and the state it is in. The bullets are not so bad, but the shells! They make a whistling noise, which gradually gets louder, and then they burst with an awful crash.

I should like to tell you where I am, but, of course, we are forbidden to do this. I am quite well and fairly comfortable and we were able to get cigs and plenty of milk. Just had some Standard bread, which people here seem to live on. Jove, I could enjoy a good square meal, then I should be happy. Bully beef is all right sometimes, but one gets tired of too much of a good thing. The country here is very much like England, but very flat and uninteresting, although some of the district we came through was simply lovely. I like England better than this country, and Gargrave best yet. I received a Skipton paper the other day, and I see that Gargrave is starting the cricket season again. I wish I could play again before the season ends."

From the war diary of the Green Howards, the battle he referred to was at St Julien (north east of Ypres) and the camp was at Brielen (just to the north west). During their last few days at St Julien, the troops had to rely on emergency rations because their supplies and transport couldn't get through to them. Arthur was wounded, the following year, in September 1916 at the Battle of Flers-Courclette. This was part of the third phase of the Battle of the Somme, also credited as being the first battle where tanks were deployed. He received the Military Medal for his bravery and ended the war as an instructor at the Bisley School of Musketry.

STRANDED SOLDIERS AT SKIPTON

When soldiers came home on leave, if they got to Skipton station late at night, they often missed the last train to their village. Rather than have them spending the night at the station, the Craven Herald launched a scheme to get them home. A subscription fund was launched and people with transport were mobilised to carry the soldiers from Skipton to their homes, paid for by the fund.

VOLUNTEER TRAINING CORPS

At the beginning of the war, worried about the possibility of a German invasion, many towns and cities formed their own unofficial volunteer defence associations. This enabled older men or those with business or family commitments to give some sort of service, without actually enlisting. Units had to be financially self-supporting and members had to provide their own uniforms and weapons. Sometimes they could get dummy rifles for drill purposes from their local Territorial Regiment. Locally, Keighley formed a Volunteer Training Corps (VTC) at the end of 1914 and raised money to buy uniforms, rifles, ammunition and even a field ambulance.

Poking fun at the Volunteer Platoons
Private Collection

In 1916, the War Office gave formal recognition to the VTC, and they were renamed to be associated with the local regiment, in this case, the Duke of Wellington's. The members were now allowed to wear khaki uniforms (if they could afford them) and had armbands with GR on them, standing for Georgius Rex. The force was sometimes ridiculed by the public; there were jokes that the "GR" on their armbands stood for "Grandpa's Regiment", "Gorgeous Wrecks", "Government Rejects" or other variations. Once conscription was introduced, the Military Tribunals had the power to make those rejected from service join the local volunteers instead.

The Gargrave Volunteer Platoon was formed in May 1916. It was part of the Keighley Volunteer Battalion of the 6th Duke of Wellington's Regiment. The purpose of the volunteer battalions in general was to dig anti-invasion defence lines, handle munitions, transport wounded soldiers, carry out fire-fighting, assist the police with any civil disorder and help with harvests. It is unlikely that the Gargrave unit was needed for these activities, but they did do a lot of training with rifles, both in Gargrave and in Keighley.

At the inaugural meeting, 38 out of the 48 members turned up at the Council School where police Sergeant Marshall led the first drill session in the school yard. As the numbers grew, drill sessions were held on three evenings a week at the tennis courts. A few months later, thanks to the money raised by local subscribers, they were able to buy four rifles. The numbers had risen to 61, Charles Thomas was elected Platoon Commander and Edward Burlend became the secretary. They advertised their presence in Gargrave by doing such things as marching for 7 miles around Eshton and Flasby, led

Gargrave Volunteers
Courtesy of the Dennis French Collection

by the Boy Scouts drum and bugle band. Benjamin Walls, the scout leader was also in the Volunteer Platoon and some parents expressed concern that being in the scouts was a preliminary training for a military life. It did seem that the volunteers, and the scouts were often on parade together.

The volunteers were trained to become proficient in drill, signalling, and handling rifles, bayonets and bombs. They also went away for camps at holiday times, and spent Whitsun of 1917 at Ripon, where it was reported that they had a splendid time and were looking forward to the next camp. That summer, the platoons from Gargrave, Skipton, Silsden and Crosshills went again to Ripon to train with the Gordon Highlanders. Notable members of the platoon included Herbert Rhodes (ex-army), who was a very good runner, and represented the platoon at sports events, also Job Cockcroft, the headmaster of the Council School.

BELGIAN REFUGEES

3,000,000 BELGIANS ARE DESTITUTE in BELGIUM

They must not starve.
SUPPORT THE LOCAL FUND.

Belgian Refugee poster
Courtesy of the Library of Congress, LC-USZC4-12694

When the Germans over-ran Belgium in August 1914, many of its citizens were forced to flee from their homes. Britain took in an estimated 250,000 of them. All across the country, fund-raising committees were set up to help.

Skipton had a Belgian Refugees Relief Committee, and it was recorded that by November 1915, 22 adults and 12 children were being housed in Skipton. Gargrave had its own sub-committee and in December 1914, welcomed their own Belgian family. The Lanslot family were housed in Airebank Terrace in a cottage provided rent free by the Wilson estate. They were described as a 'respectable family of 6' and by mid-1915 as 'largely self-supporting'.

On arrival, they were offered free use of the facilities at the Mechanics Institute and library. To help with their integration, the Rev Bethell of the Skipton committee offered Miss Philomena Lanslot a place on the English classes for Belgians at St Monica's Convent. To make this possible for her, she would be provided with free lessons, dinners and a railway pass.

The Lanslots moved away in October, as Mr Lanslot's brother had found work for him in London.

A public meeting had been held to discuss whether the village could accommodate another 1 or 2 families. There was enough money in the fund and the Wilson estate had offered another cottage. Gargrave had been asked to help a family of 'superior tradesmen' or 'destitute gentlefolk'. However, the feeling of the meeting was that they would prefer to offer hospitality to a working class family, so the matter was put in abeyance.

Nothing was resolved by the end of 1915. The feeling was that interest and support for the refugees was waning. No further Belgian families came to Gargrave, although quite a few were living in Skipton.

After the war, the majority of the Belgian refugees were speedily repatriated. The British government wanted to ensure that jobs were available for returning soldiers and the Belgians wanted their citizens to return and re-build the country.

VILLAGE LIFE

Many aspects of life went on as normal, in spite of the war. Gargrave was fortunate that its rural situation distanced its inhabitants from the worst effects of the conflict. Events in other parts of England, however, did impinge on life in Yorkshire. From early in 1915 until 1917, the Germans launched bombing raids on southern and eastern coastal towns, and also on London and Edinburgh, using Zeppelin airships. These operated at night, so the government ordered that all buildings should be blacked out and streetlights dimmed, to make targets harder to find. No Zeppelins ever came near Gargrave, but the lighting restrictions still applied.

The Parish Council had many debates on how to comply with the regulations on street lighting. To prevent the lights being seen by a passing airship, the top 10 inches of each light was to be blackened and the lower part tinted in green. The Council decided that this would render our lights totally useless and opted to turn them off earlier in the evening instead. Householders were expected to black out their windows and enforcers patrolled the village at night. The Craven Herald issued warnings that some houses were still showing lights and urged the inhabitants to stand outside at night to check for chinks of light.

Some other vital matters discussed by the Parish Council that made it into the pages of the local news were:

> Frequent bad smells in Water Street
>
> The appointment of a collector for lighting and sanitary rates
>
> The boring of a hole and the installation of a plug in the Coronation trough to make it to easier to clean.

EVACUEES

There was an evacuation from Scarborough, when the Westland Girls' School relocated to Eshton Hall for the duration of the war. Sir Mathew Wilson was by now spending more time away from here and the Hall was vacant. There is little information about how much the school interacted with the village, but the girls did put on a performance of "The Rivals", a comedy of manners by R B Sheridan, in February 1917 at the Council School.

Scarborough would seem an unlikely place to need evacuating, but there was a good reason. In December 1914, three German battleships patrolling along the coast opened fire on Scarborough, leaving 18 dead, many injuries and extensive damage. The ships then went on to attack Whitby and Hartlepool. There was great outrage at these attacks on civilians and understandably the inhabitants wanted to ensure the safety of their children.

HOLIDAYS AND TOURISM

In the early years of the war, some aspects of life went on as before and people still took holiday breaks and made trips. Bank holiday traffic congestion was seen as a problem for Gargrave, even back then. Over one long Whitsunday weekend *"on the road was an endless stream of cars, wheelmen, char-à -bancs and conveyances to and from the West Riding towns and Morecambe and the Lakes."*

The Whitsun holiday had always been a time when rail excursions to the Lancashire coast were popular and char-a-banc trips came to Gargrave and the surrounding areas. This continued during the war until 1918 when petrol shortages and reduced rail services changed the holiday makers' habits. People were still determined to take a break and instead of going to the coast, stayed nearer to home. Visitors were coming by bike and horse-drawn waggonettes from Keighley, Leeds and Bradford and bringing great benefits to the local hotels and cafés. Cycling groups had been common for many years, but the sight of hikers with back-packs, carrying their own rations, was hailed as a new phenomenon.

EDUCATION COMMITTEE

This met regularly to discuss teacher appointments, school attendance and management. One matter that surfaced in 1915 was a national economy measure requiring that small schools of less than 30 pupils should be amalgamated. As the National school roll was 81 and the Council School 85, it was unlikely that the Gargrave schools would be required to join together. This was a relief all round, as there would certainly be conflicts about the number of hours (and the nature) of the religious teaching needed each week.

RECREATION AND SPORT

Spirits were kept up as the village activities carried on. Music, dancing and sport were regular features on the social calendar as well as lectures and discussions for the enlightenment of the residents. The proceeds from many of these events were donated to patriotic causes.

The Wesleyan Guild concerts and musical evenings were regularly reported. For example, on Good Friday, the Band of Hope organised the children to present a long programme of 80 hymns, melodies, recitations, piano and violin solos, dialogues and part songs. There was more of the same at Harvest and Christmas.

The Wesleyans didn't seem to do much dancing, but others in the village made up for it. An evening combining a whist drive with some dancing was a popular form of entertainment. J R Preston and T Rhodes were the leaders of the dance bands who provided the music. Each November, the Conservatives and Liberals got together to hold a patriotic whist drive and dance, to raise money to send Christmas hampers to the Gargrave lads on the front or in hospital.

The folks of Gargrave could attend lantern lecture evenings at the Parochial Hall or the Wesleyan School Room and be enlightened on such subjects as the work of the British and Foreign Bible Society in Times of War or Belgium in Peace and War. The Society for the Propagation of the Gospel in Foreign Parts told the audience all about the manners and customs of the Indians and Chinese and the efforts made to convert and educate them! Another lecture was on "The Genius of Tennyson".

Some sporting activities were suspended because football and cricket players were in short supply as the war continued. Billiards competitions still went on in the Mechanics' Institute and the Conservative and Liberal clubs.

WORK

Airebank Mill, now being run by John Brindle, had been rebuilt after the disastrous fire of 1912 and started partial production at the beginning of 1915. It must have been a great relief for the village, as jobs were gradually reinstated, particularly for the female workers who could get back to work and help to support their families. Production seemingly increased, as throughout the war years, advertisements appeared asking for grinders, drawers, rovers, ring spinners and mule piecers. Removal expenses were offered for families wanting to relocate to Gargrave.

No information has been found about who the customers were for the yarns produced at the mill. John Brindle had previously worked in the Manchester area and several of his directors had business interests over there. It is possible that through his contacts, he sold the yarn to Lancashire weaving firms, but this is just speculation.

From a Magazine advert of the period.
Private Collection

J H Cleave moved to Gargrave from Bradford just before the war, bringing their sports goods business to High Mill. They made cricket bats, tennis rackets and billiard tables. However, less than a year after their arrival, they went into liquidation.

The New Brighton Saw Mills saw an opportunity to diversify and took over the business, still running it from High Mill, as well as continuing making other wooden items at New Brighton. Towards the end of the war, all the production was moved down to the New Brighton site.

The Sanitary Laundry carried on as usual with its mainly female workforce. The only change was that the slipper baths were closed in November 1914.

There was still a need for some domestic staff. The better-off families could afford to hire help. Mrs Wales (the doctor's wife) and Mrs Garnett (at Knowles House) advertised for housemaids, cooks and nurses and governesses for their young children. There would have been fewer jobs available at the Eshton Estate and at Gargrave House. The Wilsons were no longer living at Eshton Hall and the Coulthursts were rebuilding Gargrave House.

TRANSPORT

Motor cars were becoming more widely used before the war, but this progress stalled as factories concentrated on war production. There were no scheduled bus services, so most people walked or cycled everywhere, or took the train for longer journeys. Gill and Gott had a business in Gargrave selling and maintaining bicycles. After the war, their garage was carried on by Walter Gill and expanded to sell and service motor cars.

The canal was still being used to transport goods, but as canal workers went away to fight, the Leeds and Liverpool Canal Company found it difficult to keep enough boats running. They had to turn to home service soldiers or volunteers to keep essential supplies moving and train them to become boatmen.

The railways provided a vital service throughout the war years, moving supplies and soldiers.

FACILITIES

The village shops managed to keep going during the war years. There was a new addition on the High Street, when James William Hardman opened a chemist's shop in 1916. The premises still have the same use, as the present Gargrave Pharmacy. The other change was that A E Wright's grocery shop came under the management of Stockdale and Helm, who already had a shop in Sheep Street, Skipton.

House building stopped altogether, although it hadn't been much of a brisk trade even in the pre-war years. The only construction activity was the demolition and replacement of Gargrave House and improvements to the Wesleyan School.

DOING THEIR BIT

Responding to patriotic causes was the order of the day. In April 1915, the Craven Herald promoted the Tobacco Fund in response to desperate pleas from the front for cigarettes and tobacco. Out in France and Belgium, men of the 6th Battalion Duke of Wellington's West Yorkshire Regiment complained that *"Cigarettes here are as scarce as gold and no one has an English smoke."*

Appeals went out to provide "soothing weed" for the soldiers. The lady employees from Airebank Mills rallied round by organising a "Soldiers' Solace" social and dance. An evening of *'sustained hilarity and music'* carried on from 8 pm till 2 am, raising £2-7s-2d for the fund.

Sailors and Soldiers Tobacco Fund poster Not politically correct nowadays!
Private Collection

Some thought it inappropriate to hold the 1915 Horticultural Show in times of war, but the event went ahead anyway, with excellent displays of sweet peas and the profits were donated to patriotic funds. As the war progressed, more importance was placed on food production.

The Parish Church held an egg service in 1915. The target was 360 eggs, but the hens must have been busy as 1330 eggs were collected to send out to Malta. The egg collections were a regular event and in June 1917 it was reported that 600 eggs were going to wounded servicemen. By this time, there were many more soldiers and sailors in hospitals in England, and the eggs were bound for local hospitals.

Eggs for the Injured poster
© IWM (Art.IWM PST 10825)

It would be reasonable to presume that there were plenty of hens in and around Gargrave.

The ladies of the village got busy with their knitting needles and made socks, scarves and sweaters that were much in demand in the trenches. Later in the war, probably when yarn supplies were running short, Frederick Garnett from Knowles House, provided the wool. Mr Garnett was a mill owner with a worsted spinning and weaving business in Bradford and did much to support the war effort.

KEEPING SPIRITS UP

Each January, Frederick and Kathleen Garnett treated the families of the servicemen to a meal and entertainment. As well as a slap-up roast dinner, presents were given to the families. A toy and one shilling was sent home for each child. On the first couple of occasions, the ladies were given some tea and sugar and the men a silk tie. By 1918, each household got two bags of coal instead.

There are several reports of wounded soldiers being transported by canal to Gargrave for a day out during the summer of 1917. One group of soldiers from Morton Bank Hospital at Keighley were entertained at the Sanitary Laundry. On another occasion, soldiers disembarked by Fred Green's warehouse and then went for tea and entertainment at Knowles House, courtesy of Fred Garnett. Wounded soldiers from the

Skipton Military Auxiliary Hospital came to the Horticultural Show in August where they were entertained by the Boy Scouts.

CHURCH ACTIVITIES

Most church events carried on as before, but special services were held each year to mark the anniversary of the start of the war. Many patriotic sermons were preached, urging young men to join up and encouraging more people to come to church.

As more of the Gargrave lads were lost in the conflict, a regular feature of worship was that the congregation would stand in silence whilst the organist played the "Dead March" by Handel.

In 1916, when the dreadful losses incurred at the Somme had shocked the nation, the Archbishops of Canterbury and York instigated The National Mission of Repentance and Hope. This would be carried out in October and November of that year and each diocese and its parishes were required to participate.

The reason behind the campaign was that the church felt that the war had come about by a failure of Christian countries to live together, and this country needed to collectively repent from its sinful ways. The war had damaged public morale and weakened their faith, so the idea was also to give people hope of a better future.

There was a lot of inflammatory rhetoric at the time. G. K. Chesterton wrote:

> *"The materialism and ungodliness of the Prussian Empire has brought forth terrible fruit. The atrocious savagery that has characterised the German conduct of the war is the product of debased morality and indifference to religion which has affected the German people. There is a warning for Great Britain in these facts."*

Others stirred up a feeling of collective guilt by switching the focus of attention from German atrocities to the godlessness of the British people as the cause of God's wrath and British military failure.

Gargrave joined in with the mission, and Mr Edward Burlend, the church organist was appointed secretary to the Bishop's Company, to organise the October events.

In September, the way was being prepared. Two itinerant visiting preachers held open-air services, one on a Monday evening at Coronation Square and the other on Low Green on the following evening. The preachers then moved on to Coniston Cold.

The main gathering was at the beginning of October, when a visiting minister preached to a good congregation at the Parish Church. The Rev Blunt (who had been appointed a minister by the Bishop) assisted.

After this, nothing much was heard about the National Mission on a local level. By the end of 1917 it was clear that the Mission had done nothing to restore religious convictions, and the Mission was deemed to be a failure. However, it did serve as a wake-up call to the Church of England that times had changed, and the church would need to adapt.

FOOD SHORTAGES AND PRODUCTION

In 1914, Britain relied heavily on imports of basic commodities. 80% of wheat, 40% of meat and almost all sugar came from abroad. Initially, there was no impact on food supplies other than some hoarding and profiteering. However, the situation worsened in 1917 due to a poor potato harvest and the disruption of the food supply convoys which were being attacked by German U-boats. At first, the government encouraged voluntary

Don't Waste Bread Poster
© IWM (Art.IWM PST 13354)

rationing, urging people to cut waste, eat less of the food in short supply and grow their own fruit and vegetables.

In rural areas, the situation wasn't too bad as there was access to land for food production and chickens and pigs were kept in gardens and allotments. The rivers and countryside provided sources of fish and meat, so there is no mention in Gargrave of the starvation and malnutrition that affected the cities. There were already some allotments off the Marton Road and more were provided between the Settle Road and the canal. Most of the cottages had small gardens that could be put to food production and this was encouraged by the Horticultural Society organising lectures and demonstrations.

Every August, the Horticultural Show was held for growers to exhibit their produce. As the war progressed, the emphasis shifted away from prize flowers to the best fruit and vegetables. The 1917 Show listed an impressive range of crops – potatoes, carrots, cauliflowers, turnips, beetroot, broccoli, celery, peas and beans. Soft fruit included redcurrants, blackcurrants, gooseberries and raspberries. No doubt other fruit was grown, but the strawberries would have been over by August and it was too soon for apples, pears and plums. Prizes were awarded for the best allotments and the Boy Scouts had an inter-patrol allotment competition.

Although the village pulled together to grow their own food, the sugar shortage hit everyone in the country and seriously compromised jam production. A letter to the Yorkshire Post was printed from a reader in Gargrave complaining that it was unfair that so much sugar went to the factories, forcing people to buy mass-produced jam. She suggested that extra sugar rations should be given to cottagers in the countryside so they could make their own (much nicer) preserves.

The government took measures to ration sugar and made provision to ration other items in the future. Local Food Committees were set up and the one for the Skipton Rural area, was based at 16 Gargrave Road, Skipton, which was the address of the Workhouse.

The job of the local committee was to register the suppliers of sugar and then to implement the ration card system. The local paper had extensive publicity campaigns to inform people how to apply for cards and how the system would work. It came into effect at the beginning of 1918, but by then, meat, tea, butter and margarine were also in short supply.

KITCHEN TIPS

As food shortages started to take effect, the Craven Herald ran a regular column of tips and recipes, sent in by readers.

> "A good substitute for coffee can be made from the small ends of parsnips. Wash, clean and bake thoroughly in the oven until a nice dark brown. Crush or grate them fine. Put one teaspoonful into a half a pint of boiling water and boil for one minute. Add boiled milk and a little sugar. I am finding this very good."

> "Runner beans can be left on the plants until the pods are dried. Shell the beans out of the pod and dry them before the fire. Store them in a dry place and use instead of haricot or butter beans."

FARMING

The first effect on farmers at the beginning of the war, was the exodus of young men to the front and the requisition of horses. As more men were needed, the situation got worse. The Women's Land Army was formed to help out, although there is little information about whether they were used in Craven. Possibly there was less of a need, as the farms were mainly raising livestock. There was a reported sighting of women at work.

> "Two women were seen, along with a faithful cur dog driving a flock of sheep through Gargrave High Street in the direction of Skipton. They seemed to take to their duties as to the manner born."

For farmers, the government's food production policies caused local problems. The Corn Production Act of 1917 – usually referred to as the 'ploughing up campaign' – was not popular in Craven. The government wanted farmers to change from grazing to food production, and there were possibilities of providing horses or tractors to help with this initiative.

A meeting of Gargrave farmers and landowners was reported at length in August 1917. It was chaired by William Harrison, a farmer from Skipton, who was there to promote the government policy and met with considerable scepticism and opposition. He claimed to be successfully growing cereal crops on his land, but Charles Airey from Eshton challenged this by inviting him to visit Mr Drinkall's farm where the crop he'd planted was clearly going to fail. Isaac Hitchon from Holme Bridge Farm wanted to know how this would affect his milk production – he got no satisfactory answer.

Eventually, some fields were ploughed up to grow oats. More meetings were held, urging greater crop production and the general impression was that farmers in this area were dragging their feet and not engaging in enough patriotic ploughing.

GERMAN PRISONERS OF WAR IN THE VILLAGE

The first batch of Germans was deployed in Gargrave in September 1918. At the time, it was estimated that about 750 prisoners were working in the West Riding of Yorkshire, based in permanent depots (mostly in the casual wards of the workhouses). As well as these, there were the harvest gangs that had been brought in from other areas. The 20 Germans who arrived in Gargrave would have been one of these gangs, as they had previously been harvesting flax in the Wetherby area. Farmers could employ these men at a fixed Government rate of 15s per week, of which the prisoners received one penny per hour. To prevent the prisoners escaping with a hoard of British money, they were paid with tokens, higher values usually embossed sheet metal with units lower than six pence made of card.

Sketch of money tokens issued at Raikeswood POW Camp in Skipton.
Scanned from
"Kriegsgefangen in skipton" - ("war prisoners in skipton") By captain S. Sachsse and Lieutenant-Colonel Cossmann Munich 1920 - Publisher - Ernst Reinhardt

The prisoners would bring their own food with them, and the farmers only needed to warm the food and provide hot water for coffee. However, some Yorkshire farmers had been giving them extra food, such as milk puddings and roast potatoes, which was against the rules, but probably increased productivity. The Gargrave contingent was housed in the outbuildings at the Grouse Hotel and a further 20 were based at West Marton Institute. Different groups of German prisoners would be working in and around Gargrave even after the end of the war.

John Wallace, who was six at the time, recalled later in his life how he saw the German prisoners in the village. He and the other children stood at the school railings and watched them march past, dressed in overalls with red circles on them. John thought these circles were the places where they could be shot, if they tried to escape.

One Sunday, he was joining his father on his farm work and confided that he felt sorry for the prisoner with a circle on his bottom, as he wouldn't be able to sit down if he got shot. His amused father then had to explain that the circles weren't for shooting at, but only to show that they were prisoners.

New arrivals marching into the Raikeswood POW camp in Skipton
Scanned from
"Kriegsgefangen in Skipton" - ("War Prisoners in Skipton") by Captain Sachsse and Lieutenant-Colonel Cossmann - Munich 1920 - Publisher - Ernst Reinhardt

Armistice 11th November 1918

The news of the end of the war travelled quickly and soon after the official telegram was displayed in the Post Office window, the village was decked out with flags and bunting. An impromptu holiday was declared with the schools, mill and businesses shutting for the afternoon. Residents marched around the village waving flags and singing patriotic songs such as "Tipperary" and "Keep the Home Fires Burning". Apparently, the German prisoners who were returning from their work, saluted the flags – no doubt having a sense of relief that the war was over. In fact, their repatriation didn't come into effect until the following summer, as the Peace Treaty of Versailles had to be ratified before the POWs could go home.

In the evening, Benjamin Walls assembled the Scouts and the Bugle Band, and an organised procession made its way to the Wesleyan Chapel for a service of thanksgiving. This brief service consisted of a hymn, psalm, prayers and a short address by Mr Walls. The procession then reformed and marched to the Parish Church where the vicar said a few words, offered suitable prayers and everyone sang the whole of the National Anthem. The church bells were rung and then there was a free dance at the Victoria Hall. The music was supplied by Mr Deadman, Miss Deadman and Mr Tom Rhodes. After dark, the village didn't really get lit up; there were a few fairy lights and James Mitton displayed an illuminated colour portrait of Lord Kitchener at his house in South Street. The picture had been painted by his son George, an art teacher, who had moved to Morecambe some years earlier.

On the following weekend, the celebrations continued with a fancy dress parade. John Wallace went as Pat-a-Cake, the baker's man. His mother made him an apron and a chef's hat and some cakes to carry on a pastry board. Unfortunately, the other children in the procession helped themselves to the cakes, so there were none left when it came to the judging. John didn't win a prize, but got 3d for taking part, so he could buy some sweets. He said that his favourites were aniseed balls and gobstoppers.

Life didn't return to normal for a while as there were still food shortages, wounded men to look after, and the wait for our soldiers to come back home.

GARGRAVE'S FALLEN

A COSTLY CONFLICT

Britain had the smallest armed force of all the warring nations at the start of the Great War, with just over 247,400 men. Around half of these men were serving overseas scattered throughout the Empire in India, South Africa, and other places that it was felt should be garrisoned. Because of the commitments demanded by the Empire, only 150,000 men were initially available to form the British Expeditionary Force whereas the French had mobilised 1,650,000 men and 62 infantry Divisions by 1914 and the German Army's strength was 1,850,000. By August 1917 the numbers of the British Expeditionary Force had risen to 2,044,627 officers and soldiers in an 'Army Group' of five armies. The armies of the six additional theatres of war have not been included. If we were to include the numbers fighting in all the other 'Theatres of War' the figures rise to a staggering nine million or so officers and men from the United Kingdom and the Empire. This was a force more significant than any in the history of Britain, a force that will probably never be equalled in terms of pure manpower. Despite the strength of the British armies on the Western Front, the British Expeditionary Force and the contingents from the Empire suffered over 2,690,000 casualties during the conflict, including around 677,500 dead or missing in combat. The figures quoted here are debatable, with many sources giving different values. It seems that the real human cost will remain unfathomable.

The men of Gargrave fought in many 'Theatres of War' including the Western Front, the Mediterranean, the Balkans, North Africa and Mesopotamia. Their stories on the following pages are an attempt to paint a picture of not only the men but of where they fought and the conditions that they endured during the war.

In September 1940, an incendiary bomb struck the War Office Record Store in London. About 67% of the 6.5 million records for soldiers of World War 1 were destroyed. The majority of the surviving documents were charred and water damaged, making them unfit for consultation. These remaining papers are now referred to as the 'burnt documents'. Use has been made of digitised copies of the burnt documents available online when researching soldier's details.

1914

14TH SEPTEMBER

Mostyn Eden Cookson
"Craven's Part in the Great War"
Clayton 1919

Major Mostyn Eden Cookson
2nd Battalion
Royal Sussex Regiment
2nd Brigade
1st Division

Mostyn Eden Cookson, the son of Major William and Eleanor Anne Cookson, née Wilson, born on the 1st of January 1867, was probably the first of the men associated with Gargrave to lose his life during this horrific war. As his mother was closely related to the Wilsons, an influential Gargrave family who installed Colonel Cookson's memorial tablet in Saint Andrew's Church Gargrave, he has been included in this chapter.

Mostyn was enrolled in Bedford Grammar School, which he attended from May 1882 for four terms. On 5th February 1887, we find him with a commission and the rank of Second-Lieutenant in the 1st Battalion of the Royal Sussex Regiment. He was promoted to Lieutenant 6th August 1890, to Captain 29th May 1895 and finally to Major on the 24th September 1904.

In August 1914 the Battalion was mobilised and sent to France where they were with the 2nd Brigade in the 1st Division, a Regular Army Division with a long history. The unit was involved in several battles along the Western Front during 1914. September 1914 saw the first of three very bitter battles fought in the Aisne Valley. The Battle of the Aisne took place over four days. In this brief period, the British forces tally of dead or wounded amounted to 13,500. The French and German forces suffered similar numbers. All this devastation took place over a fifteen mile stretch of the River Aisne. This First Battle of the Aisne is where Major Cookson lost his life.

The positions held by the Germans were tactically powerful. They could opt for a delaying action or a defensive encounter. From the high ground on either side, the tops of the plateau on the opposite bank are not visible. The woods on the edges of the slopes provided additional camouflage for the defending force. All the bridges along this stretch of river were vulnerable to either direct or high-angle artillery fire. Field Marshal French in his communiqué to the Secretary of State for War, and published in the London Gazette, stated that the country...

> "... North of the Aisne, is well adapted to concealment and was so skilfully turned to account by the enemy as to render it impossible to judge the real nature of his opposition to our passage of the river, or to accurately gauge his strength"

With many of the permanent bridges having been destroyed by the Germans, most of the British Expeditionary Force (B.E.F.) crossed the Aisne using pontoon bridges on 13th September. However, the 1st Division in I Corps reached the Aisne opposite Bourg on 13th September where they surprised a party of Germans attempting to blow up a bridge and crossed without difficulty, moving on to the Chemin des Dames ridge to reach the German lines at Vendresse and Moulins.

On 14th September 1914, Major Cookson advanced with his Battalion to Vendresse in support of an attack on the German positions on high ground above the village of Troyon. The first objective was the sugar factory standing on the Chemin des Dames surrounded by sugar beet fields and held by the Germans who were using the site for their guns.

At approximately 05.15 hours, the 2nd Battalion of the Royal Sussex Regiment advanced. They took a challenging route over the sugar beet crops wading through the extremely wet clay soil, with heavy rain driving into their faces. They eventually reached a defensive position in a sunken lane where they could open fire on the German trenches to the left of the sugar factory. Shortly afterwards, several hundred Germans showed themselves, holding up their hands as if to surrender and waving white flags. The senior officer, Colonel Montresor assumed that they were yielding and took steps to take the enemy troops prisoners of war. At some point during the attempt to take the surrendering troops into custody, German machine gunners to the right and left flanks of the British forces opened fire. In the space of two minutes, the British Battalion strength was reduced by a third. This apparent false surrender is not substantiated, but there are reports of large numbers of Germans approaching the British lines under the white flag on subsequent occasions. Conflicting reports on the cause of Major Cookson's death include sniper fire, machine gun fire and shrapnel. It was impossible to recover any injured or dead because of efficient German sniper fire.

Between the 12th September and the 18th September, the total of killed, wounded and missing numbers from the Division reached 561 officers and 12,980 men.

Major Cookson is remembered on the English Memorial at La Ferte sous Jouarre, a small town 66 kilometres to the east of Paris, located on the main road (N3) running east from Paris. The Memorial is situated in a small park on the south-western edge of the town, on the south bank of the River Marne, just off the main road to Paris, The Memorial Register is kept at the Town Hall.

*The English Memorial at
La Ferte sous Jouarre*
Photograph by Ray Jones 2014

 A marble memorial plaque honouring Major Cookson can be seen in the St. Andrew's Church at Gargrave.

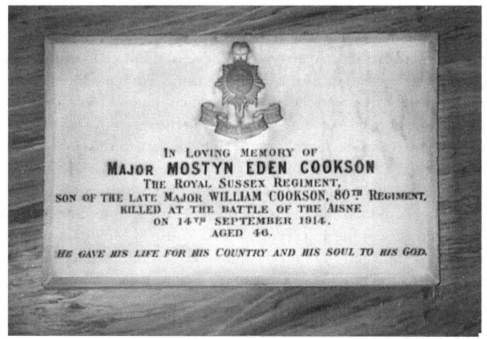

IN LOVING MEMORY OF
MAJOR MOSTYN EDEN COOKSON
THE ROYAL SUSSEX REGIMENT,
SON OF THE LATE MAJOR WILLIAM COOKSON, 80TH REGIMENT,
KILLED AT THE BATTLE OF THE AISNE
ON 14TH SEPTEMBER 1914.
AGED 46.
HE GAVE HIS LIFE FOR HIS COUNTRY AND HIS SOUL TO HIS GOD.

Memorial tablet for Major Cookson St. Andrew's Church Gargrave
Photograph by Don Slaven 2014

1915

17TH MARCH

Charles Oswald Sewell
"Craven's Part in the Great War"
Clayton 1919

z/74 Rifleman Charles O. Sewell,
Rifle Brigade (The Prince Consorts Own)
A Coy
3rd Battalion
24th Division

Charles Oswald Sewell was the son of George Walter and Emma Sewell née Siswick. George was born at Bramley and Emma in Holmfirth, Yorkshire. The family moved, and in 1881, they were living in Heckmondwike where Charles was born. The year 1891 found the family in Gargrave, Yorkshire residing at 2, River Place. Charles, now 20, was working as a limestone quarryman. Charles married Annie Thistlethwaite on 6th July 1907 at Addingham Parish Church. In 1911, the couple, with their two-year-old daughter, Sybil Irene, resided in West Witton where Charles continued work as a limestone quarryman.

Charles enlisted with the Rifle Brigade, a unit renowned for its marksmanship and often referred to as the Sharpshooters, and after training found himself at the Western Front in February 1915.

Most of his service records are 'burnt documents'. There are scant details of his last movements. However, it appears that the penultimate action he took an active part in was the Battle of Neuve-Chapelle, 10-13 March 1915. Although fought with a force of 60,000 men, supported by 500 artillery guns this battle was deemed later to be on a small scale. It was designed to weaken the German hold to the south of Ypres.

Although the battle ended on the 13th March 1915 with the village under the control of the British, Auber's Ridge continued to be firmly held by the Germans. The opposing forces did not stop action entirely, and on the 17th Charles Sewell came under deadly enfilading machine gun fire during a sortie on Layes Bridge, a German stronghold southeast of Neuve Chapelle. He did not survive his injuries.

The Craven Herald published the following report on 23 April 1915

> *"A HORTON-IN-RIBBLESDALE HERO*
>
> *Mrs. Annie Sewell, of Fourdale Cottages, Helwith Bridge, Horton-in-Ribblesdale, writes informing us of the death of her husband, Pte. Sewell, of 'A' Company, 3rd Battalion Rifle Brigade, with the Expeditionary Force, whom she was expecting home in May. In a letter received from Corp. W. J. Gayton, of the same Company, and dated March 28th, it appears that Pte. Sewell was shot while doing duty in the trenches. The communication adds:–*
>
> *"His death is greatly regretted by his comrades. Having command of the section in which he served, I can say that he was one of the best men in it, quiet, hard-working, shirking nothing. Whatever duty was entrusted to him was faithfully carried out, and although an enemy bullet cut short his career, he died as a soldier should, in the execution of his duty. Not only the section and myself, but all the NCOs and men who knew him join in forwarding their condolences in the bereavement that has unfortunately fallen on you and family."*
>
> *The widow of the deceased soldier has four children-ranging from one to six years old, and the heartfelt sympathy of the district will be extended to her in her sorrow".*

Annie, Charle's widow, now living in Giggleswick, was left with four young children, Sybil Irene 6, Alfred Arnold 4, Katharine Marie 3 and Margaret Agnes 18 months old. Her widow's allowance of 25 shillings a week would buy goods to the value of £121 in 1917. Even today, this is not a lot to feed and clothe four children.

Charles is interred in the Ration Farm Military Cemetery, La Chapelle d' Armentières in row VIII, Plot A, Grave 20 and remembered on the War Memorials at Gargrave, Horton-in-Ribblesdale and Spennithorne. His name is also recorded in the Rolls of Honour held at St Oswald's Church, Horton-In-Ribblesdale and the Gargrave Wesleyan Chapel Roll of Honour Bronze plaque now housed in St. Andrew's Church, Gargrave.

Ration Farm Military Cemetery
Photograph by Ray Jones 2014

Charles Oswald Sewell's Gravestone at Ration Farm Military
Cemetery

4TH MAY

Godfrey H. Ermen
Public Domain
"Craven's Part in the Great War" - Clayton 1919

Captain Godfrey Henry Ermen

Duke of Wellington's (West Riding Regiment)
2/6th Battalion
62nd (2nd West Riding) Division

Born in 1878 at Dumplington, Barton-upon Irwell, Lancashire to German-born parents Francis and Johanne Ermen. Francis was a Cotton Manufacturer with his own company, Ermen Roby Ltd. Godfrey's grandfather, also named Francis, was a partner in the company Ermen and Engels based in Manchester. He was the fifth Ermen brother to join the company.

Godfrey was educated at Rossall School, Fleetwood Lancashire. During the years 1907 to 1908, he worked at his father's company, and it was during this time he enrolled in a sewing cotton course, at the Manchester Municipal College of Technology. At the onset of the Great War, Godfrey was the general manager of the English Sewing Company based at Belle Vue Mills in Skipton. Known locally as Dewhurst's Mill, the company produced a range of sewing cotton yarns known as 'Sylko'. Godfrey lived with his wife Nora at Milton House in Gargrave.

The company, Ermen and Engels, was prominent in cotton and had mills both in Bergisches Land and in Manchester and Oldham. It was to Victoria Mill, in Weaste that Friedrich Engels (the father) sent his son Friedrich in 1842. While working for the firm, Friedrich wrote his influential book "The Condition of the Working Class in England".

Friedrich Engels author of
"The Condition of the
Working Class in England"
Image Author Unknown

Godfrey Ermen, together with Norman England, a fellow territorial army officer and Gargravian, was actively involved in the recruiting and training of the young men who joined the 6th (Reserve) Battalion of the Duke of Wellington's (West Riding) Regiment (TF). The Skipton based 6th Reserve Battalion used the Drill Hall in Otley

Street Skipton as their headquarters to administer seven Companies. Only two companies, A Coy and B Coy, were billeted in Skipton. C Coy was in Guiseley with D and E Coy in Keighley, F Coy was in Settle and Ingleton. Haworth was the home of G Coy, and H Coy was in Bingley.

On the 8th February 1915, C Company was attached to form part of the coastal defence force based at Withernsea joining other units of the West Riding Regiment. They were given minimal training and armed with a mix of antiquated Charger Loading Lee-Enfield's (CLLE) or Lee-Metford rifles. This would have been a difficult first deployment.

The rest of the Battalion remained billeted in Skipton and the immediate neighbourhood and carried on with initial training familiarising them with the 200 'new' charger loading Lee Enfield's and arranging for their next move. They then moved to Derby joining the 2/2nd West Riding Infantry Brigade for further training. Capt. Ermen was appointed adjutant on the 3rd April. The 12th of April saw the unit move to Doncaster. Their accommodation was a tented camp on the race course recently vacated by the first line units who had been sent on active service to the Western Front.

The unit was now issued with 860 Japanese Arisaka type 38 rifles. More training in the use of these 'novel' weapons was needed. Initially obtained for use by the Royal Navy to free up the Lee-Enfield rifles for the British Army, these weapons were also used by training Battalions. To complete the kitting out of the unit 100 sets of 1914 pattern equipment was issued to the men. Although fully kitted for action, they were not yet fully trained. Captain Ermen's job was difficult enough without the added workload of training on unfamiliar weapons.

Capt. Ermen was taken ill before he could take part in any action and repatriated from Doncaster to Gargrave. He died at home on the 4th May 1915 while on sick leave. The illness was diagnosed as influenza.

Captain Ermen's Grave
St. Andrew's Church, Gargrave
Photograph by Ray Jones 2014

He is at rest in St. Andrew's Church Graveyard and remembered on the Roll of Honour in the Church, Gargrave War Memorial, a Brass Plaque in Dewhurst's Belle Vue Mill, Skipton and on the Manchester Municipal College of Technology Memorial in the Sackville Building, University of Manchester.

13TH MAY

Walter Scott
"Craven's Part in the Great War"
Clayton 1919

6465 Private Walter Scott,

18th Hussars (Queen Mary's Own)
2nd Cavalry Brigade
1st Cavalry Division

Walter Scott, born in Gargrave in 1893, son of Richard Walker and Margaret Scott. The 1901 census finds the family living in Holme, Lancashire.

1911 sees Walter, now 18, already a serving member of the Armed Forces at Tidworth, Hampshire as a Private in the 18th Hussars (Queen Mary's Own), at Aliwal Military Barracks.

On 15 August 1914, Walter's unit was sent to the Western Front, landing at Boulogne-sur-Mer on the 16th August as part of the 2nd Cavalry Brigade in the Cavalry Division. The Division was renamed as the 1st Cavalry Division in September 1914.

Walter fought through several battles during his service at the Western Front, the last being the Battle of Frezenberg Ridge which took place from the 8th to the 13th May 1915. This was one of a number of actions which took place during the campaign termed the 'Second Battle of Ypres'.

The German forces moved their field artillery to oppose the British 27th and 28th Divisions, and on the 8th of May, the three German armies began their attack. They opened their offensive with a bombardment on the trenches situated on the slope of Frezenberg Ridge, followed by two infantry assaults on the trenches. These were successfully repulsed by the survivors of the bombardment. The third attack by the Germans on the trenches followed closely that morning, and the defending force was pushed back. While the 80th Brigade managed to hold fast; its neighbour the 84th Brigade was pushed back. This left a significant gap in the defences of around 2 miles through which the enemy might have passed. However, counterattacks by the Princess Patricia's Canadian Light Infantry together with a night assault by the 10th brigade stopped the German army from gaining any further advantage.

This was at a terrible cost to the Canadians who lost 550 men from their force of 700. Their motto, coined that day and which is still in use is

"Holding up the whole damn line!".

According to a report of the 9th of May dispatched to the War Office, there was a critical shortage of ammunition for the 4.5-inch howitzer field guns despite a repeated request to replenish the depleted stocks. Shortages of ammunition also existed for other heavy weapons, and machine guns. Ammunition for rifles was down to 93 rounds a weapon. The rifles themselves were in such short supply at home that it was proposed that new draftees should proceed to the Theatre of War without them.

At 3.30 am, on the 13th of May 1915, the German forces commenced bombarding the British trenches and back areas with an incessant barrage of heavy gunfire. Shells fell continuously throughout the morning until 1.00 p.m. The shells fell intermittently during the rest of the day well until nightfall.

The trenches the troops occupied, built by the previous tenants while under fire, were poorly constructed, had no communication trenches, and practically no wire for protection. There was little time to repair and improve the trenches. As much as possible was done under cover of darkness, but the defences were still inadequate. To add to the confusion parties of the engineers and other infantry units sent to help foundered in the dark and missed their intended locations. The state of the trenches gave the soldiers little protection. The most substantial bombardment, using shrapnel and high-explosive, fell on the front between Hooge and a small village called Wieltje on the road leading to St. Julien. This sector was held by the 80th Brigade (27th Division) and the Cavalry Force.

The heavy shelling together with the equally incessant rain turned the area into a sea of mud, which made any movement an onerous task and the use of rifles extremely difficult. It was around 8 am. when the German forces drove through the defence line in on the front of the 7th Cavalry Brigade the Leicestershire Yeomanry, 2nd and 1st Life Guards. This line situated on a long gentle forward slope and due to the fact it was very exposed, was difficult to defend. Once in position, the incoming force continued to attack the defenders with stick grenades. As the British were without hand-grenades with which to reply, the two squadrons of the Leicestershire Yeomanry were driven southwards into the sector of the 6th Cavalry Brigade. The third squadron, ensconced in support trenches three hundred yards behind, halted any further enemy advance by continuous and effectual rifle fire. The advancing Germans created a firing line opposite and attempted to continue their onslaught. The 5th Dragoon Guards (1st Cavalry Brigade) and a squadron of the 18th Hussars (2nd Cavalry Brigade) were heavily shelled in their frontline positions losing many men. It is during this conflict that Private Walter Scott lost his life.

The following notice was published in the Craven Herald on the 18th June 1915

"A GARGRAVIAN KILLED IN ACTION

News has reached his Gargrave relatives that Private Walter Scott, of the 18th Hussars (Queen Mary's Own) second son of Mr. Richard Scott, late of Gargrave, was killed in action on the 13th of May. Scott, who was aged 21 years, was a native of Gargrave, having joined the forces in Lancashire."

Walters name is on the Ypres (Menin Gate) Memorial - Panel 5. and Gargrave War Memorial.

Menin Gate Memorial
Photograph by Ray Jones 2014

25th May

Henry Ormerod Eastwood
"Craven's Part in the Great War"
Clayton 1919

2017 A/Corporal Henry Ormerod Eastwood

18th (Queen Mary's Own Royal) Hussars
2nd Cavalry Brigade
1st Cavalry Division

Born in Gargrave on 23rd December 1889, Henry Ormerod Eastwood was the son of Anthony Summersgill and Elizabeth Eastwood. His brother, Private John Eastwood also served during the Great War. He was baptised at the church of St Andrew in Gargrave on the 8th February 1890.

In 1891 the family resided on High Street in Gargrave. By 1901 they had moved to Trees Terrace. The family then moved to Midland Street, Skipton in the early part of the 1900s. For a short time, Henry was employed as a fitter by the Midland Railway Company. At that time, the railway company in Skipton was a significant employer, second only to the English Sewing Cotton Company at Belle Vue mill and dye house.

Sometime before the 1911 Census in Great Britain, Henry joined the Armed Forces and began his travels abroad. The 1911 Indian Census shows Henry as a private in the 10th Hussars stationed at Lucknow in Punjab. The Hussars not only served in India but South Africa, and Egypt. From Egypt, Henry went with his unit to France and Flanders on the 15th of August 1914. Henry was wounded on active service more than once. His first injury occurred in September 1914. He recovered from this early injury quickly at a field hospital near the front. In a letter home, dated the 8th December 1914, Henry wrote the following

> *"I have been all over France since I was wounded, and I am in the best of health. I am now back in the firing line with my regiment, but I am expecting 72 hours' leave in England, so I will be able to come and see you. What I have seen and been through would turn you grey. I am hoping to come to England, for I have not been for six years."*

Unfortunately, the 72-hour leave was never granted. Henry did not see his family again. Between the writing of the letter seen above and his next message to home, Henry was injured once more, this time a gunshot to his back while he attempted to carry his fatally wounded commanding officer to safety. He lay for twenty-four hours in the mud and then tried to crawl back to his lines. Henry then got a further shot in the leg. He eventually reached the relative safety of the trenches and received treatment for his wounds. On the 12th December, he wrote home describing his ordeal. An extract of this letter is reproduced below

"I have been made Corporal since I came back, and I am getting on A1. I got wounded at a place called Vendrassy in Belgium. My troop officer got shot through the head, and while I was carrying him, I got shot through the back. I laid there for 24 hours and when I tried to crawl away I got shot again in the leg, but I thank God I have pulled round, and I expect to kill a few more Germans before the war ends."

The 2nd Cavalry Brigade, comprising the 4th Dragoon Guards, the 9th Lancers and the 18th Hussars, under the command of Brigadier General R.L. Mullens, was involved in the Second Battle of Ypres, notably the Battle of Bellewaarde Ridge in the period 24th and 25th May.

- Imperial Russian Medal of St George 4th Class
Public Domain

The 24th May 1915 saw the first mass use of gas as a weapon of war by the German forces. The attack resulted in about 7,000 casualties who were treated at casualty clearance stations before being returned to duty or admitted as patients to a field hospital. Henry suffered further injuries during this encounter. On the 25th of May 1915, he died of his wounds.

A/Corporal Henry Ormerod Eastwood was awarded the Russian Medal of St George, 4th Class with Clasp. This military decoration is awarded for meritorious service in combat. Henry's decoration is mentioned in the Second Supplement to The London Gazette dated Tuesday, the 24th of August 1915. page 8515. However, his parents were not aware of this award until the following year when a letter from the War Office arrived for Anthony, his father, now residing in Skipton, notifying him of the award to his son, Henry.

The text of the award notice is reproduced below

"WAR OFFICE, LONDON S.W.

7th April 1916

"Sir – I am delighted to inform you that His Imperial Majesty the Emperor of Russian has been graciously pleased to confer, with the approval of His Majesty the King, the Medal of St. George with Clasp upon your son, the late No. 2017 Lance Corporal H.O. Eastwood, 18th Hussars, in recognition of his gallant conduct in the field.

I am accordingly to forward the decoration herewith, to be retained as a memorial of the deceased non-commissioned officer's distinguished service, and to request that you will be so good as to acknowledge its receipt.

I am Sir, Your obedient servant,

Signed H. H. HARRINGTON, Capt.,

   for Director of Organisation."

Henry is interred at Bailleul Communal Cemetery Extension Plot I, Row F, Grave 106, in the Nord region of France. Bailleul is near the Belgian border in France. The town lies 14.5 Km south-west of Ieper (Ypres). Henry is commemorated on Skipton War Memorial.

13TH OCTOBER

Philip Chamberlayne
"Craven's Part in the Great War" - Clayton 1919

Captain Philip Chamberlayne Preston

Norfolk Regiment
7th (Service) Battalion
12th (Eastern) Division

Captain Philip Chamberlayne Preston came from a long-established family in Gargrave. The presence of the Preston family at Flasby can be traced back to Christopher Preston, a merchant of Leeds who died in 1639. Christopher's great-grandson, William, the son of John Preston, Mayor of Leeds in 1692, bought Flasby early in the 1700s. The manor was rebuilt in the 19th century and brought up-to-date. Having gained armorial rights, they built a folly in the grounds representing their crest which depicts a ruined tower with a falcon rising.

The tower, overlooking an ornamental lake, is still in existence and has in the past been used as a dovecote and later a summer house.

Philip Preston was born on 19th February 1879, to John Norcliffe J.P., late Captain of the 3rd Light Dragoon Guards and Thermuthes Fauquier Preston née Chamberlayne youngest daughter of Henry Thomas Chamberlayne.

When in 1873 Levi Strauss introduced his blue denim work wear using Indigo as the colourant he unwittingly created a worldwide demand for this dye. Indigo plantations multiplied throughout the tropical regions of the world to provide the clothing industry's needs. Philip was sent by his family to manage an Indigo Plantation near Purnea (Purnia in the Indian state of Behar).

While he was there, he heard the call to join a fighting force which was raised by a Colonel Lumsden. Named the Indian Mounted Infantry Corps, but popularly known as 'Lumsden's Horse', the force was raised by Lumsden to be used to help break the siege of Ladysmith in South Africa. With initial finances of 15,000 rupees, provided by Lieutenant-Colonel Dugald Mc Tavish Lumsden himself,

Trooper Philip Preston ca. 1900
From "A History of Lumsden's Horse"

Lumsden's Horse was officially formed by the Government of India with the approval of the Government in the United Kingdom. A payment of 1 shilling and 2 pence (1s / 2d), in today's money around six new pence but with a present-day value of around £6.83, a day for each trooper, a sea passage to South Africa, weapons, ammunition and a basic food ration were authorised. However, the most vital components for a mounted troop, horses, were not. Many of the troopers volunteered their mounts, the shortfall being found through public subscription.

It was during Philip's service with Lumsden's Horse that he gained his Distinguished Conduct Medal (DCM). Philip and seven members of Lumsden's Horse, were sent out on patrol from Germiston with orders to take Johannesburg Waterworks. The mission ended successfully and Philip returned. Taking the shortest route and riding at speed he delivered the news to Germiston the waterworks had been taken.

During his return, English-speaking tribesmen warned Philip of an armed Boer waiting in ambush on a small-rocky hill on the left of the road ahead. On hearing this he dismounted and with his rifle at the ready walked cautiously toward the hill.

The Boer remained under cover until Philip, with his rifle aimed at the largest rock he could see, shouted "Hands up, or I fire!". Two hands appeared above the rock. A further order of "Hold up your rifle!". Obeying immediately the Boer was disarmed and captured. The prisoner was handed over to an Australian unit, and he continued his journey to deliver the news of the waterworks capture.

Philip returned home after his adventure in South Africa and stayed at Flasby for a short time before joining the trading company, Chamberlayne & Co. in Swaffham, Norfolk in 1908. The company dealt with corn, coal, seed and wine and spirits.

In 1914 Philip went on to serve in the Dorsetshire Regiment, 7th (Service) Battalion as a Temporary Lieutenant for a short time. Formed on 5th December 1914 as part of the 13th Division, the unit was based at Kinmel Camp, Rhyl to provide the trained infantry and artillery needed for Kitchener's New Army. On 10th April 1915, the unit disbanded, and the serving members dispersed to active units at the front and 2nd line training Battalions. Philip found himself in the Norfolk Regiment, 7th (Service) Battalion as a Temporary Captain.

By the 4th June 1915, all the Division had reached Saint-Omer. On 5th June the Division advanced and joined III Corps reaching Haisnes to join the Battle of Loos.

The Battle of Loos took place between 25th September and 19th October 1915. It was in a particular phase of this battle which took place on the 13th October 1915 that Captain Preston met his death. There was much action South of Ypres and near the border with France at around this time and Loos en Gohelle was on the British front line near Lens. Shelling and attacks to test each side's lines and defences were everyday events, and men died in all such actions. Using tactics previously used with little success at Auber's Ridge, the battle started with a preliminary artillery bombardment. The 7th (Service) Battalion took part in the action at the Hulluch Quarry.

The following extracts from an eyewitness account of the action on that day which appeared in the 'Lynn Advertiser',

> *"Private Spooner of the Norfolk Regiment, home from the War Front on leave in Swaffham, described in some detail the events in which he was involved. The communication trench being navigated by Pte. Spooner's Company led down to a German trench".*

> *"...Captain Preston was seen in the German trenches with a wound in his thigh, but he had a rifle and bayonet and was shooting the Germans and forcing them past the communication trench. Later, after the trench to the right had been cleared, they went back past the communication trench to the right to finish clearing it, and Captain Preston was seen in the same position, but dead, having received a bullet wound in the left temple. It is quite clear that Captain Preston, after getting into the German trenches, took one of his men's rifles and sold his life dearly. The fighting continued from 2 o'clock to 8 p. m., the Germans, when they lost the trenches, shelling them with great effect. The Norfolks were relieved at 8 p. m. by the Berks. Regiment The next day they tried to recover Captain Preston's body, but the shells had worked havoc with the trench, and he was apparently buried,"*

Captain Preston is commemorated on the Loos Memorial just outside the village of Loos en Gohelle which is alongside the D943, Bethune to Lens road. His name is inscribed on panels 30 and 31. He is also recorded on the Gargrave War Memorial, Gargrave Roll of Honour, Swaffham Memorial and in the Regimental Church of St. Mary, Bury St Edmunds, Norfolk.

Loos Memorial Graveyard
Photograph by Ray Jones 2014

7TH NOVEMBER

Williamson Austin

122899 Pioneer Williamson Austin

Royal Engineers
9th Labour Battalion

Williamson Austin was born on the 26th August 1862 at Broughton, Yorkshire, to Alice Austin (born Broughton, Yorkshire, c. 1826), daughter of William and Ellen Austin. In 1871 he was living in Gargrave with his grandmother, Flora M. Stockdale. Williamson married Elizabeth Cain in 1882. He and his wife and moved several times while living in Skipton. His addresses were 21 Quakers Place, 16 Triangle Union and 9 Alexandra Buildings, Keighley Road. Williamson moved between jobs from coal carter to railway labourer and then boatman before enlisting.

He joined up while in London in September 1915. His short military career lasted just two months. He was killed by a light engine on the railway line he was crossing. The Craven Herald article from the 12th November 1915, reproduced below details the accident.

"A SKIPTON MAN'S FATE - ACCIDENTALLY KILLED IN FRANCE

Mrs. Austin, 9, Keighley Road, Skipton, has received official information that her husband, Pte. Williamson Austin, 9th Labourers Battalion, Royal Engineers, has been accidentally killed while serving with the British Expeditionary Force in France. The sad intelligence was contained in the following letter from Lieut.-Col. R. B. Haywood, R.E., Commanding 9th Battalion:-

"Dear Mrs. Austin, - It is my painful duty to write and let you know that your husband has suffered a sad accident, which, I regret to say, has cost him his life. He was returning to his billet from a neighbouring village yesterday evening about 8-30, and when crossing the light railway which passes across the road, he evidently failed to notice an engine and train. The former whistled, but failed to attract his attention, so that he was knocked down. The doctor was in attendance shortly after and pronounced life extinct, expressing the opinion that death has been instantaneous.

"Let me assure you of my profound sympathy in this shocking blow. You may rest assured that everything possible will be done to mark the presence of his resting

place. The Church of England Chaplain will conduct the burial service this evening, and he will be laid to rest close to where the sad accident occurred. It will be my privilege to attend the service and offer reverence to one who lost his life for his country's cause, for, though not actually fighting, he was doing his duty."

Pte. Austin was 52 years of age and only joined the Labourers Battalion about two months ago. He enlisted on the Monday and went to France on the Friday following. He leaves a grown-up family, one of his sons being Corpl. Instructor Austin, who is attached to the 3/6 Battalion Duke of Wellington's Regiment, now at Clipston Camp. Prior to joining the Army, deceased was a boatman."

Williamson Austin is interred at St Hilaire Cemetery Extension, Row J, Grave 1, Frévent in France and remembered on the Skipton War Memorial.

1916

7TH JANUARY

George Naylor
"Craven's Part in the Great War" - Clayton 1919

514474 *Corporal George Naylor*

West Riding Regiment
8th Battalion
11th (Northern) Division

George Naylor was born in 1889 to George Arthur and Jane Hannah Naylor, née Atkinson and brother of Private Sam Naylor. (Sam was lost during the Campaign to relieve the Siege of Kut.) George's father was born at Gargrave and his mother Jane at Lancaster. In 1891, the Naylor family were living in Low Warehouse in Gargrave.

In 1901 the Gargrave Census showed they had moved to 7, South Street. The family shortly left Gargrave to live in Keighley, and in 1911 their home address was at Low Mill Cottage, Ingrow.

Issued on 21st August 1914, Army Order 324 authorised the formation of a 'New Army' of six Divisions as suggested by Lord Kitchener. The new force was known as Kitchener's First Army, shortened to K1 in army records. The six Division completed their 'basic training' at the regimental depots. After which the units dispersed to their base camps in Britain. The infantry was based at Grantham in Lincolnshire. On 14th October 1914, George enlisted in the newly formed infantry unit. Still desperately short of uniform and equipment, the infantry of the Division was inspected by Lord Kitchener at Belton Park. On 4 April 1915, the Division assembled at Witley and Frensham, where training was completed. King George V inspected the Division on Hankley Common on 31 May 1915.

On 12 June 1915, the Division received orders to prepare for service at Gallipoli. On the 30th of June 1915, they were at Liverpool to embark on a journey to the shores of Turkey. Most of the Division sailed on the ships RMS Aquitania and RMS Empress of Britain. The Division reached Lala Baba at Suvla Bay between the 6th and 7th August 1915. George survived the horrors of Gallipoli and went with the Division when it withdrew on the 19th and 20th December 1915 to reach relative safety on the Turkish island of Imbros, now renamed to Gökçeada. It is here on Imbros toward the end of December 1915 that George became ill. He was admitted to the Field Hospital, where the illness was diagnosed as pneumonia. Within ten days George succumbed to the then deadly disease. On the 14th of January 1916, the Craven Herald published the following,

"FORMER GARGRAVE MAN DIES IN HOSPITAL

Following a telegram from the War Office last week, news has been received by Mr. Geo. Naylor, of 293, Beech Grove, Ingrow (and for many years a resident of Gargrave), of the death in hospital from pneumonia of his son, Corpl. George Naylor, of the 8th Duke of Wellington's West Riding Regiment, aged 27 years.

Corpl. Naylor, who was a single man, and who, like his father, worked at Broughton Quarries up to leaving Gargrave, died on January 7th after going through the Dardanelles campaign.

He enlisted October 14th, 1914, and, judging from letters home, had been in the thick of that disastrous campaign. Out of a thousand "of the old lot," he wrote early in December, "only 70 or so are left. I have not been stripped for four months."

The deceased has two brothers serving his King and Country, viz:– Lance Corporal Sam Naylor of the 2nd East Lancashire Regiment, aged 39 years, who is in Serbia, (and who has a son, aged 18, Lance-Corpl. Albert Naylor of the 11th East Lancs., serving in Serbia); and Pte. John Naylor, 29 years old, with the Canadian Contingent.

Sincere sympathy will be extended to the family in their trouble.

Their Majesties the King and Queen have forwarded an expression of regret."

An extract from a further announcement by the Craven Herald on 11 February 1916 is reproduced below.

"THE FATE OF A FORMER GARGRAVE SOLDIER...... Second-Lieut. J. E. Troughton, who had charge of Corpl. Naylor's platoon, writing on the 9th of January, offers the deepest condolences of the officers and men, and adds:–

He was very popular with the men, N.C.O.s and officers, and had done very good work both on the Peninsula and here. Had he lived, he would have been promoted to the rank of sergeant. He was taken ill about ten days ago and was removed to hospital two or three days later, suffering from pneumonia. He died on Thursday, the 6th of January, and was laid to rest on the 7th on the Island of Imbros. Our

Company Quarter-Master-Sergt. and Sergt. Regan, together with several N.C.O.s and men from his platoon, attended his funeral. Drummer Grady sounded the Last Post."

George is interred at the Lancashire Landing Cemetery in Turkey. The Helles Cemetery is located near Sedd el Bahr, at the tip of the Gallipoli peninsula. His name is inscribed on the Gargrave War Memorial.

18TH APRIL

Sam Naylor
"Craven's Part in the Great War"
Clayton 1919

6769 Private Sam Naylor

East Lancashire Regiment
6th (Service) Battalion
13th (Western) Division

Sam Naylor was a volunteer in the 6th (Service) Battalion, East Lancashire Regiment. The unit was part of the 13th (Western) Division, one of the Army Divisions formed on Salisbury Plain by the New Army in August 1914. Born in Haslingden, Accrington, Lancashire in 1877, Sam moved with the family to Gargrave when he was very young. At the age of four, he was living with his family at High Mill. In 1889, they are still shown residing in Gargrave but now living in Low Warehouse, Water Street. Sam now at the age of 14 was working as a sawmill labourer.

On the 1st of January 1896, Sam married Christina Elliott, born 1876 in Ulverston, Lancashire. The marriage took place in St. Andrew's Church, Gargrave.

The 1901 Census shows Sam living at 16 Cedar Street, Accrington with his three children, Albert aged 3, Sam aged 2, and Christina aged one. Sam (senior) was working as an iron plate moulder. Serving for a short spell in France, Sam suffered from frostbite of hands and feet and spent some time back in the United Kingdom.

On returning he was sent, with his unit, to Gallipoli in July 1915 to reinforce the Anglo-French expedition there. They arrived at Anzac ready to prepare for the 'August Offensive' along with the rest of the infantry Battalions that composed the Divisions. The supporting artillery for the Division did not arrive until several months later. This caused the planned attack to be stalled, and consequently, the 38th and 39th brigades of the New Zealand and Australian Division were sent in as reinforcements.

They were eventually to leave the Gallipoli battle zone to regroup in Egypt with the intention of building up their strength and to re-equip ready for the next phase. The respite was short lived as the troops, despite not being battle ready, were required urgently elsewhere.

Higher command identified the next job of the Division, to reinforce the Anglo-Indian forces attempting the relief of the Siege of Kut Al Amara in Mesopotamia, now known as Iraq. The journey from Egypt to Basra and further to the Tigris to join the rest of the Tigris Corps took until the end of March 1916.

They started their journey by boarding the H.M.T Corsican at 2 pm on February 13th. The following morning, February 19th they set sail and travelled through the Red Sea passing Aden, Masirah and along the coast into the Persian Gulf. Once in the Gulf, they moved North to Koweit (Kuwait) which they reached on the 26th of February. They waited until the 3rd of March before being trans-shipped to their next transport, a shallow draft steamer designed for river work called the Thongwa.

They travelled up the river Tigris towards the base camp of the Mesopotamia Expeditionary Force, reaching Basrah on the 6th of March.

The 13th Division soon found that the logistical situation in Mesopotamia did not meet the requirements needed to provide the necessary support. The port facilities at Basrah were inadequate. With no roads suitable for heavy traffic or a fully functioning railway, virtually everything travelled by river. Unfortunately, there were insufficient numbers of boats to keep the Anglo-Indian force, which the 13th Division was joining, adequately supplied. What the 13th Division did have were the new heavy artillery field guns and howitzers.

The 13th Division, as the strongest unit available, became the spearhead of the Tigris Corps' attempt to relieve the Kut garrison beginning on 6 April 1916. The Division fought at Hanna, Fallahiya, and Sanniyat. After taking the first two, the 13th Division was stopped by the Turkish forces at the Battle of the Sanniyat on 9 April 1916.

After three more days of fighting, the Division was given a respite being placed as a reserve for the Tigris Corps during the next phase of the operation. On 16 April 1916, it joined with the 7th (Lahore) Division on the right bank of the Tigris, to assist in the capture of the Bait Isa line, part of the Es Sinn defences. Taking the Bait Isa line exposed the Sanniyat position to enfilading artillery and machine-gun fire, essentially this meant the defending force could be fired upon down the line instead of across which was much more effective.

Unfortunately, on the night of 16–17 April 1916, the Ottoman reserve forces, under the command of Khalil Pasha, launched a counter-attack in a bid to retake Bait Isa. The 13th Division was struck while preparing to storm the Turk's next defensive position. The trenches that the 13th Division and 7th (Lahore) Division had taken now came under deadly machine gun fire down the line causing many casualties. On the 18th of April, Sam Naylor died from wounds sustained during this engagement.

Sam's name is inscribed on the Gargrave War Memorial, and he is also remembered on the Basrah Memorial, Iraq. Due to difficulties in visiting this region, a two-volume Roll of Honour listing all casualties buried and commemorated in Iraq is now on display at the Commonwealth War Graves Commission's Head Office in Maidenhead for the public to view.

26TH APRIL

Charles William Luff
"Craven's Part in the Great War - Clayton 1919"

3/11672 Corporal Charles William Luff

West Riding Regiment
9th (Service) Battalion
17th (Northern) Division

Born in 1893, Charles William Luff was the son of Elizabeth Luff, daughter of Charles and Emma Luff. Elizabeth was born in Eaton Socon, Bedfordshire. Charles' mother Elizabeth, known as Lizzie, remarried John Robert Barker and in 1911 was living in Barnoldswick with her new family, John, one-year-old Kate Winifred and 17-year-old Charles. Charles was working as a cotton weaver at a local mill. Charles' future bride, Phyllis Jones, was born in 1895 at a district of Derby. At the age of six, Phyllis was living in High Street, Gargrave as the adopted daughter of an 81-year-old retired shoemaker, John Maudsley together with John's daughter, Ada, aged 44. In 1913 Charles married Phyllis.

Charles served with the 6th Battalion, Duke of Wellington's West Riding Regiment Territorial Force from 10th November 1909 until the 19th November 1913. In September 1914 he enlisted with the regular army in response to recruitment drives for K2, the second of Kitchener's New Armies. His unit, the West Riding Regiment, 9th (Service) Battalion was formed in Halifax in September 1914 as part of 52nd Brigade within the 17th (Northern) Division.

Charles Luff was in action with his unit during the period of the Second Battle of Ypres. The 9th (Service) Battalion, a unit of the 17th Division, was involved in several actions.

An extract from a letter received from his superior officers follows: -

> "He was killed doing his duty in a willing and cheerful manner under most trying conditions, he having always proved himself to be a good soldier and an energetic and capable N.C.O. He died as he lived, doing his duty, and leaves a good name and a fine example behind him."

Charles is interred in the Cite Bonjean Military Cemetery, Armentieres, Plot IX, Row G, Grave 8. His name is inscribed on the Gargrave Roll of Honour, Gargrave War Memorial and Barnoldswick War Memorial.

Cite Bonjean Military Cemetery, Armentieres
Photograph by Ray Jones 2014

26TH APRIL

John Edward Heyes

4607 Private John Edward Heyes

West Riding Regiment
1/6th Battalion
49th (West Riding) Division

Born during 1878 at Accrington in Lancashire, John Edward Heyes was the second son of Richard and Sarah Heyes. In 1881 the family of Richard Heyes (33) and Sarah Heyes (32) - James Thomas aged 5 and John Edward now 3, were living at 30, Royds Street in Accrington. Ten years later, John is found living with his father Richard and brother James Thomas at 20 Royd Street with a stepmother Chaterina and a new brother aged 9. John, now thirteen, was working in the local mill as a cotton creeler.

In 1898, twenty-year-old John married Abigail Mary Riley. They set up home at 130 Henry Street in the village of Church about a mile west of Accrington. Together they had two children. The first to arrive in 1905 on the 5th of July, was a boy named Edward after his father. Catherine, his sister, was born on the 21st of January 1907. Sadly Abigail died, two years after the birth of her daughter, on the 22nd of August 1909. She was just 32.

John enlisted with the 6th Battalion Duke of Wellington's West Riding Regiment in Skipton on the 11th August 1915. After training, John was sent to Le Havre on the 13th June 1916. From there he joined his base unit on the 28th June. He was with the 49th Division at a location overlooking the Ancre River, north of Albert near Thiepval, in Northern France. The 49th Division became part X Corps under the command of Lieutenant General Thomas Morland. On the 7th of July, X Corps was to launch an attack on Ovillers-la-Boisselle. However, a massive artillery bombardment by the Germans, which fell on the 49th Division, followed by an attack on the British positions halted the planned offensive. John's active service was brief; his life ended just 9 days after landing in France on the 7th of July.

He is buried at Plot VII, Row E. Grave 1 in Lonsdale Cemetery near Authuille, a village 5 kilometres north of the town of Albert on the D151 road to Grandcourt. He is remembered on the Gargrave War Memorial.

14TH JULY

George Platt
"Craven's Part in the Great War" -
Clayton 1919

A/Corporal George Platt

Leicestershire Regiment
9th (Service) Battalion
21st Division

Born in Castleton, Lancashire in 1889, George Platt was the son of Samuel James and Maria Jane Platt, née Rawling. Samuel was born at Oundle, Northamptonshire and Maria at Bramley, Yorkshire. Two years later, the 1891 census shows that Samuel is no longer with the family and Maria is shown as the family head supported by her 14-year-old daughter, Elizabeth who works as a cotton card box tenter, and her son James aged 12 who is a cotton plaiter.

The family is completed with Henry, 9; Samuel, 4; George, 2 and the newly arrived Rawling.

The 1901 Census records the family living in a house at High Mill. The eldest daughter Elizabeth has left the family home, and Rawling is not here. Son James aged 22 is working as a skinner and fellmonger; Henry 19, a domestic labourer and Samuel, 14 was also working as a labourer in the sawmill. George now 12 years old was still a student as was his sister Mary, 7 and Herbert just four, who was later to fight in the same war as his brother, George.

George enlisted in the Leicester Regiment. The Regiment formed a significant part of the 110th Brigade, also known as the Leicester Tigers Brigade, which was raised in September 1914 as the first of six brigades formed for Kitchener's Third New Army. The Brigade was made up of four Battalions, the 6th, 7th, 8th and 9th together with the 110th Machine Gun Company and the 110th Trench Mortar Battery. The brigade was under the control of the Commanding officer of the 21st Division.

George was sent with his unit to France arriving on the 29th July 1915. In March 1916 he was admitted to No. 2 General Hospital at Le Havre where he spent four days being treated for an injury to his leg. He was discharged back to duty on the 10th March.

Cpl Platt was involved in many actions during his time in France. He survived the First Phase of the Battle of the Somme, the Battle of Albert, which had been a failure on behalf of the British Forces. The commanders did not fully achieve any of their aims. However, they did manage to reach the German second line of defence on Bazentin Ridge. It had taken from the 1st until the 13th July to advance a very short distance.

The beginning of the second Phase of the Battle of the Somme was the attack on Bazentin Ridge. The action began at dawn on the 14th July with a five-minute bombardment on the German lines. Immediately after the bombing at 3.25 a.m. the infantry advanced. The dawn attack took the Germans by surprise.

During General Douglas Haigh's tenure in command, he was reluctant to commit his inexperienced troops who he thought were not able to carry out the tricky manoeuvres required to prepare for a dawn raid. General Rawlinson, now in command of the 4th Army, had no such misgivings and committed his troops. The military operation was a success, and the objectives were achieved, but at a terrible cost.

The British force suffered a staggering total of 9,194 casualties on that single day, George Platt was just one of the many fatalities.

George has his name inscribed on Pier and Face 2C and 3A of the Thiepval Memorial and on the Wesleyan Chapel Roll of Honour Bronze plaque which can now be seen in St. Andrew's Church, Gargrave.

Theipval Memorial
Photograph by Ray Jones 2014

14TH AUGUST

John Eastwood
"Craven's Part in the Great War"
Clayton 1919

3/6316 Private John Eastwood

East Yorkshire Regiment
8th (Service) Battalion
3rd Division

The ninth child in the family of Anthony Summersgill and Elizabeth Eastwood, John Eastwood was born in 1898 at Trees Terrace in Gargrave. His brother, A/Corporal Henry Ormerod Eastwood also served and lost his life serving his country.

The Eastwood family moved to Skipton, and the 1911 census shows them living at 22, Greenfield Street, Broughton Road. John was now 13 years old. It appears that his mother, Elizabeth, had died some time ago as he is described as the son of Anthony and stepson of Margaret A. Eastwood. Anthony married Margaret Ann Beck in 1907. Both Anthony and Margaret had married twice.

John married and set up his family home in Witty Street, Hessle Road, Hull. However, the Army Registers of Soldiers Effects show his sister, Mary E. Nunns, as next of kin and sole legatee.

John enlisted in Hull with the East Riding Regiment. Records indicate that John was involved in several battles, being injured on the 28th of April 1916, just eighteen days after his arrival in France. It appears from accounts of the time that his unit, with the 3rd Division, was involved in a number of battles during the Somme Offensive. The Battle of Bazentin Ridge, which took place on the 14th July 1916 and is considered to mark the beginning of the second phase of the Somme Offensive, is probably the battle where John met his death.

A French commander was scathing of this action taken on by the British Territorial Force and described it as

> '... an attack organised for amateurs by amateurs...'

How wrong he was. The battle proved to be a hugely successful British action.

Two corps of the Fourth Army, the XV Corps and several Divisions of the XIII Corps were tasked with an attack on the German second line of defence held by the 3rd Guard Division of the German Second Army. The XV Corps was deployed to the left to take Bazentin le Petit and Bazentin le Grand The XIII Corps units were to work between Bazentin le Grand and Longueval. However, the attack by the 3rd Division from Montauban against Bazentin le Grand did not go as planned. The wire tangles before them remained uncut which held up operations, exposing the troops to extensive machine gun fire.

In securing all their objectives during the Battle of Bazentin Ridge and subsequent actions on the following days the 3rd Division suffered 2322 casualties.

John died on July 15th 1916 and is remembered on Pier and Face 2 C of the Thiepval Memorial, Kingston upon Hull Guildhall, the Hull Golden Book of Remembrance and Skipton War Memorial.

3RD SEPTEMBER

Percy Wharton
"Craven's Part in the Great War" -
Clayton 1919

7070 Private Percy Wharton

West Riding Regiment
1/6th Battalion
49th (West Riding) Division

Percy, born at Water Street, Gargrave on the 5th of October 1895. joined the Wharton family headed by Michael, a groom and his wife Elizabeth, as the youngest member of the family. His eldest brother, Fred aged 20, worked as a domestic gardener, the eldest sister, Mary 19, was a winder in the local cotton factory with George, 12 years old, working as a creeler in the same factory. Harry 12, Alan 8, and Mary a five-year-old and Richard 2 completed the family. By the time of the 1901 census, the family had moved to Thornton-in-Craven in the Urban District of Earby.

Percy's father was still employed as a groom, Fred and the eldest sister, Mary, had left the family home. George, Harry and Alan were working as cotton weavers. Richard, Mary, the younger sister, and Percy were still in education. According to the 1911 Census, George and Harry had left the family home, now at 8 George Street in Earby, leaving Alan, Mary, Richard and Percy – all now working as Cotton Weavers.

It is more than likely that Percy was killed during the disastrous Battle of Pozieres Ridge which commenced on the 27th August 1916 with the final attack taking place on the 3rd of September 1916. The result of all the fighting was a resounding German defensive victory. The 49th (West Riding) Division, were instructed to prepare with 39th Division, for a joint attack on the ruins of Thiepval village.

Attacking from the North, 146th Infantry Brigade was on the left, 6th West Yorkshire Regiment and 8th West Yorkshire Regiment the attacking Battalions, with their objectives to capture the German lines from the Pope's Nose to Peterhead Sap. Support for the leading Battalions would be provided by 5th West Yorkshire Regiment.

147th Infantry Brigade on the right had 4th Duke of Wellington's Regiment and 5th Duke of Wellington's Regiment as their attacking Battalions. Initially timetabled for 30th August, the attack finally took place on 3rd September.

Both arms of the attack did initially gain some foothold in the trenches, but the failure of 4th Duke of Wellington's Regiment to capture the machine-gun position at the Pope's Nose, left both sides open to enfilading machine-gun fire, and they were eventually pushed back by German counter-attacks. Although 49th Division was unable to remain in possession of the German trenches, they held them for as long as they were able, in some instances to the last round of ammunition and last Mills bomb.

Divisional Head Quarters were unable to keep in contact with the attacking Battalions because the signallers were all killed or wounded, several runners were sent back but failed to gain the British lines. As the numbers of British soldiers still fighting fell, an officer from another unit (who had become mixed up with the Duke of Wellington's Regiment) gave the order to withdraw.

Initially, Percy was presumed to be missing after the disastrous result of this military action, and on the 3rd of November 1916 the Craven Herald announced

> *"EARBY MAN MISSING*
>
> *Pte. Percy Wharton, Duke of Wellington's (7070), has been officially reported missing since September 3rd. Any news of him will be gratefully received by his parents, 8, George Street, Earby. Mr. and Mrs. Wharton have three other sons in the Army – Sergt. Allen Wharton, in the 10th Duke of Wellington's, and Lance-Corporal Richard Wharton, in the 9th, and another on home service. The two first mentioned have been in France during the greater part of the conflict. A son-in-law, Gunner Frank Whitehead, is serving in India"*

It wasn't until the 17th of August in 1917 that the following article was published,

> *"EARBY – MISSING MAN'S DEATH PRESUMED*
>
> *The Army Council have sent to Mr. and Mrs. M. Wharton, 8, George Street, Earby, an official intimation presuming the death in France of their youngest son, Private Percy Wharton, Duke of Wellington's Regiment, who had been missing since September 3rd of last year. He was 22 years of age and unmarried. Before enlisting he was employed at Messrs A. J. Birley's Ltd. as a weaver. Mr. and Mrs. Wharton have two sons still in France who have been there two years, and two in training in England. A son-in-law (Rifleman Robert Duxbury) has been missing since May 12th, and another son-in-law is serving in India."*

The family's losses were not yet over. Richard, the younger son, was soon to join the armed conflict.

Percy is remembered on the Gargrave War Memorial, Earby War Memorial and the Thiepval Memorial Pier and Face 6A and 6B.

3RD DECEMBER

Richard Wiseman
"Craven's Part in the Great War" -
Clayton 1919

59715 Gunner Richard Wiseman

Royal Field Artillery
82nd Battery, 10th Brigade
6th (Poona) Indian Division

Richard Wiseman was a regular soldier serving in the Royal Field Artillery, 82nd Battery, 10th Brigade 6th (Poonah) Indian Division. Born in 1886, Richard spent his early years living at New Brighton and Water Street in Gargrave. His parents were the Craven Harriers groom and kennel-man, Robert and his wife, Mary Wiseman. The family, recorded in the 1901 census, included Robert and Mary and their five children Janet aged 20, Richard now 17 and working as a shirt collar cutter, James ages 12, William 9 and the youngest member just three years old, Herbert. The census also records four lodgers at the same address in Water Street.

He had served with the British Armed forces for four years before the outbreak of the Great War. His attestation took place in Keighley on the 18th October 1909. Although apparently living in Keighley at the time, his parents and two brothers still resided in Gargrave with homes in Riverplace and South Street. Richard's first overseas posting was with the Royal Field Artillery 82nd Battery Kirkee (now Khadki) near Pune (Poonah) a sizeable military cantonment set up around 1817-1818 which was the home of the Royal Regiment of Artillery's base for nearly a century.

Richard Wiseman was with the 6th (Poona) Division, whose headquarters were at Poona in the Bombay Presidency when the force was deployed with the Indian Expeditionary Force D in Mesopotamia. Under the command of Lieutenant-General Sir Arthur A. Barrett, K.C.B., the Division was sent in November 1914 and was tasked with guarding the British oil installations in and around Basrah. All that was needed at this time was to secure the area around the terminus of the Anglo-Persian Oil pipeline, the source of the Royal Navy's fuel supply. A commentator of the time suggested that

"If the English had been satisfied with that, the misfortune which was to come to them might never have occurred, but the whole expedition was essentially political rather than military in its nature."

It seems that both the British and the Indian governments agreed that after the disastrous year full of military 'cock-ups' a success story was needed. The most recent fiasco was Gallipoli. With the British preparing to pull out of the region, the idea of pushing beyond Basrah to take Baghdad was put forward and approved. General Nixon, commander of the Mesopotamian Expeditionary Force, ordered General Townshend to take his force upriver to secure Baghdad. His move forward toward Baghdad was marked by a series of early successes and by September Townshend's Anglo-Indian troops had captured the town of Kut Al Amarat.

At this point, Townshend decided that his troops had need of rest and argued against stretching his supply line any further without strengthening the weak supply lines from Basra. He also specified the need for further transport and trench warfare equipment.

The British government disagreed with the decision to advance on Baghdad, but the Indian government enthusiastically endorsed it. The extent of India's support overcame the reluctance of the British government, and the go-ahead was given to march to Baghdad.

In the intervening time between the occupation of Kut and the move forward toward Baghdad, the Turks defeated at Kut had retired to Ctesiphon an ancient city on the banks of the Tigris and taken up position in carefully prepared defence positions amid the ruins of the old city. Here they created the forward defence of Baghdad using two lines of deep trenches on either side of the river. Some 1,800 experienced troops manned the positions. The Turks also had the opportunity of calling for rapid and substantial reinforcements from Baghdad, just 25 kilometres away.

The army that advanced toward Ctesiphon was much smaller, 11,000 Anglo-Indian troops, and a force that was unlikely to be further strengthened due to the distance from the base at Basra and the lack of suitable transport. They were also faced with the dilemma of the two banks of defences. An attack on both sides was impractical due not only to the number of men available but the poor ground conditions on the Western bank. To add further to his problem, Townshend could not call on the Royal Navy as he had done previously. The extensive deployment of mines and artillery prohibited any Naval craft's success in reaching its target. He, therefore, decided to concentrate his attack on the East bank. He marched toward Ctesiphon at night; a tactic used successfully at Kut al Amara. aiming to surprise the Turks with a flanking movement.

However, the element of surprise was lost due to many of his troops getting lost in the dark during the negotiation of the Turks second line defence.

The Turks launched a counter-attack on 23rd November during which 40% of Townshend's fighting men were killed or injured. Despite these alarming losses, the counter-attack was a failure. The Turkish military lost 9,600 men. The Turkish commander, Nur-Ud-Din, under the impression that British reserve forces were due, ordered a retreat, despite the fact that he could readily call for backup from Baghdad. The retreat was short lived. When the realisation that no British reinforcement was due he turned and took a stance. The single reconnaissance aircraft at the disposal of Townshend reported this change causing Townshend himself to retreat.

They retreated to the town of Kut being harried relentlessly by Marsh Arabs and the Turks. The retreat cost the force its warships which were sunk by Turkish batteries on the shores of the Tigris although it appears that the makeshift hospital craft which preceded the withdrawal made it through. The retreating force reached Kut Al Amara on 3rd December 1915.

Protected on two sides by a loop of the great river Tigris Kut offered an excellent defensive position. Kut, situated 387 km from Basrah, the principal city and port captured and held by the British in 1914 which was the primary source of supplies. Logistical difficulties prevented the rapid replenishment of supplies or reinforcements. Although the defence position was right, it also was in a prime location for a successful siege. The force within the defence position could be contained without too much difficulty on behalf of the besieging army.

The Ottoman forces, commanded by the Prussian General Baron Colmar Von Der Goltz, arrived on the 7th December with enough fighting men to lay effective siege to the British garrison. He successfully held the blockade and repelled several relief expeditions which were launched without success, including the final failed attempt by the British 13th Division on 5th of April 1916.

The 23rd of April found General Townshend attempting a way of extricating himself and his troops from the desperate situation in which they found themselves. He sent a wire to Headquarters containing the following message

> "We must face the situation, namely that Gorringe with 30,000 men and 133 guns has been repulsed a second time, and I must suppose with heavy loss. We are now at 23rd April, my extreme limit of resistance is 29th, and Gorringe is not even at Sannaiyat. Therefore, short of a miracle, he cannot relieve me."

On the 26th April 1916, a cease-fire was negotiated, and on the 29th the garrison commander General Townshend surrendered. General Goltz was not to see the triumphant ending to his siege. He died in Baghdad on 19th April 1916, only two weeks before the surrender of the British garrison in Kut al Amara. Officially the cause of his death was typhus. It was rumoured that the actual cause of his death was poisoning by Turkish officers, although there was never anything to substantiate this. The siege lasted 147 days, and the surviving 13,000 Allied soldiers and ancillaries were marched over 1,000 km to Aleppo, in modern-day Syria, and further into Turkey.

General Townshend did not need to march anywhere. He was taken by various transports including road, rail, and horseback to the island of Halki (also known as Heybeli Ada) on the Sea of Marmara where he spent the rest of the war under house arrest in a luxury villa. In 'captivity' he was treated as an honoured guest, and he enjoyed the services of his Portuguese cook, two orderlies and an aide-de-camp. He was even furnished with transport in the form of a launch and a car. He was allowed much freedom and could take daily swims in the Sea of Marmara, travel without hinder to Constantinople, visits the British and American Embassies, and it seems he may even have indulged in some sightseeing.

A far different fate was suffered by his unfortunate men. The road from Kut to their final destinations was not an easy one to travel. Many of the Allied soldiers, 70% of the British and 50% of the Indian, died of disease or at the hands of their captors during the long march or captivity.

The expeditions to relieve Kut al Amara were costly regarding lives wasted. Around 23,000 allied killed or wounded with the Ottoman casualties thought to be about 10,000. On the 29th April, the strength of the besieged Kut garrison amounted to 13,309 of whom 3,248 were Indian non-combatant followers. During the siege their total casualties had been 3,776, of whom 1,025 had been killed or died of wounds, 721 had died of disease, 2,446 had been wounded (including 488 who died of their injuries), and 72 were missing.

A substantial proportion of the missing were men of the 67th Punjabis, killed or wounded. Among the civil population of the town 247 had been killed or died of wounds and 663 more had been wounded. Lives lost to a desire to counter the bad press that the British forces had been receiving over past blunders. Approximately 12,000 people went into captivity, where over 4000 died, amongst them Gunner Richard Wiseman.

The release from Kut al Amara's siege conditions was not one that the troops could rely on to bring better conditions, the promised transport that was to take them on the journey to imprisonment did not materialise. A few mules and horses were provided, but only for the officers. Not one of the surviving members of the besieged force was in any condition to complete the march to their final destinations nearly 1,300 miles from Kut al Amara.

In general, the Turkish troops did not follow the conventions applied to Prisoners of War by the Western Allies.

The troops were herded, rather than marched, by mounted Arab soldiers and Turkish guards using whips and sticks to keep the column moving through villages, towns and cities along the way where the inhabitants were encouraged to revile the prisoners. With the very minimum of food available and scant access to fresh drinking water, the desert conditions had a terrible effect on the health of the P.O.W.'s. With the Turkish officers exercising little control over their men, there are reports of the Guards and Turkish troops taking the captives water bottles, clothing and footwear further adding to their plight in the hot, dry and dusty conditions that prevailed during most of the journey. Those prisoners that fell due to illness, injury or pure exhaustion were often left to fend for themselves in mud-walled shelters abandoned by the local population. These were usually in an impoverished state, filled with vermin. These poor souls were reduced to begging for food from passing Arabs. Many were robbed of their last possessions and left to die; others were murdered for what little they had.

On reaching their destination, the remaining P.O.W.'s were imprisoned in a variety of ways. Some were placed in regular prison establishment; others deemed fit to work were sent to work camps to labour on railway construction sites. Records indicate that Richard Wiseman ended up at a place called Bagtche (Bahçe), in Turkey for imprisonment and forced labour.

At Bahçe the workforce was driving a rail tunnel a distance of twelve miles through the Amanus mountains to link Bahçe to Entilli. The hours of work were in two shifts, the first from around 04.30 in the morning until 11.00 am followed by a second between 13.00 hours until 18.00 hours. Food was meagre and consisted of black bread, beans, rice and if they were lucky, a little meat. The workforce was not entirely from British P.O.W.'s but had many Armenian prisoners who were dismayed at the appalling condition of the newly arrived workforce. Grigoris Balakian, an Armenian cleric and author of "Armenian Golgotha", who was at Bahçe when the British arrived, wrote in his book of his first encounter with the British and Commonwealth prisoners of war stating;

> "...when the caravan arrived at the Bahçe railway station, we were surprised to see British and Indian soldiers emerge. humpbacked, in tatters, covered in dust and reduced to skeletons.

... we had attentively waited for our saviours, the victorious troops of our Powerful friends, the Allies... but we were now witnessing with our own eyes, their emaciated living ghosts."

Their guards were a mix of German and Turkish troops, and work was carried out under the supervision of the German civilian railway engineers. Workers were paid up to six piastres (or kuruş – pronounced kooroosh), a coin valued at 1/100th of an Ottoman 'pound' or Lira, a day. This was less than six old pence a day, (buying about £3:40 worth of goods in today's money) but from this small amount of money, the cost of their meals was taken.

It is very probable that Richard did work for a brief time in Bahçe but succumbed to enteric fever, possibly typhoid, and died on the 3rd September 1916.

He was buried in the P.O.W. cemetery North East of the railway station at Bahçe. After hostilities ceased, he was later re-interred at Baghdad North Gate War Cemetery. North Gate Cemetery was destroyed during the Iraq War. The Commonwealth War Graves Commission will rebuild when conditions allow. Due to difficulties in visiting this region, a two-volume Roll of Honour listing all casualties buried and commemorated in Iraq has been produced and is on display at the Commission's Head Office in Maidenhead and are available for the public to view. He is remembered on the Gargrave Roll of Honour, Gargrave War Memorial and the Gargrave Wesleyan Chapel Memorial plaque.

1917

17TH JANUARY

Thomas Wilfred Chester
"Craven's Part in the Great War"
Clayton 1919

24009 Private Thomas Wilfred Chester

Duke of Wellington's (West Riding Regiment)
8th (Service) Battalion
11th (Northern) Division

Born in 1896, Thomas Wilfred Chester was the son of a fifty-year-old journeyman carpenter, William Chester and his second wife, Emma, aged 37.

William's first wife Hannah appears to have died at the age of 35 during 1882. Their family, who lived at Mill Hill in Gargrave, included Annie born in 1873, Grace Elizabeth b. 1873, Richard b. 1877, Nancy b. 1879, James 1880, and Henry b. 1881.

In the period between the 1881 and the 1891 census, William married Emma. In the census of 1891, the two elder daughters have left home. Grace seems to have been employed by a family as a cook at the Manor in Thornton in Craven. There were three additions to the family, Edward Oliver three-years-old, Lilian 2, and Ida a newcomer aged just eight months. In 1901, the parents and their six children, Edward Oliver 13, Lilian 12, Ida 10, Harold 8, Thomas 5, and Charles 2, still lived at the same address, Mill Hill in Gargrave. Sadly, Emma Chester passed away in 1904. By 1911, the family had reduced to the father, his daughters Lilian and Ida, and his sons, Thomas Wilfred, and Charles Sydney. Thomas at this time was employed as an office boy at the Canal Office in Gargrave. He later progressed to work in the Midland Railway Collectors Office in Skipton.

Thomas Chester joined the Duke of Wellington's Regiment on June 18th 1915. His unit, the 8th (Service) Battalion was with 32nd Brigade of the 11th (Northern) Division of the 5th Army. Shortly after his enlistment, the Division was sent to the Mediterranean to become part of the Suvla Bay landing force, Gallipoli on the 7th of August. The 8th Battalion had formerly been with the 34th Brigade until January 1915. The 32nd Division served at Gallipoli until December 1915 when the forces in Suvla were evacuated. The unit spent a brief time guarding the Suez Canal in Egypt, before being transferred to the

Western Front. The Division was to remain here taking part in the final throes of the Somme offensive as British sought tactical advantage on the heights above the River Ancre valley.

These actions took place during the final phase of the Somme Offensive. The Battle of the Ancre in November 1916 saw the British taking German positions on Beaumont Hamel spur and the village of Beaucourt before the weather conditions drew the advance to a halt. Constant rain softened the ground which was churned by shellfire becacoming a quagmire of thick mud. Even though the push forward was at a standstill, operations did not stop entirely.

Although the ground was still sodden from the soaking it had been given and was extremely difficult to traverse; the weather improved sufficiently for actions to be taken against the enemy troops. It was decided that the forces could advance with the use of duckboards. In the early hours of 10 January, an 18-hour bombardment and a standing barrage on the objective began. Following the artillery bombardment, infantry from the 7th Division, advanced, carrying their duckboards, on the trenches either side, including Muck Trench about 1,000 yards (910 metres) east of Beaumont Hamel. They had 20 minutes to cross the 200–300 yards (180–270 metres) of no-man's-land, a difficult task even without the added burden of carrying and laying duckboards.

On the 11th, positions of Munich Trench, from "The Triangle" to the Beaumont Hamel–Serre road were subjected to a major action. A secondary attack by the 11th Division, against German defences east of Muck Trench was carried out without success. A hidden German dugout was overrun in the fog. German troops came out of the dugout and attacked the British troops from behind, at the same time that German counter-attacks from further east began, pushing the British back.

German resistance was slight, except at one post where the garrison held on until 8:00 a.m. After the fog cleared at 10:30 a.m., the ground was consolidated, most of it being free from observation by the Germans.

V Corps took over from XIII Corps, with the 32nd Division and 19th Division by 11 January, with II Corps on the south bank facing north, with the 2nd Division and 18th Division. The 11th Division stayed in the line, for another attack on the slope west of the Beaucourt–Puisieux road.

The bunker overrun in the previous attack was found empty, but German artillery caused many casualties before a British bombardment stopped a German counter-attack as it was forming up at 10:00 a.m. The Division was relieved on 20 January. It is during this operation that Private Chester went missing. He escorted an officer from the front line to a rear-ward position safely, he never made it back to the front line. He was presumed dead almost a year later. A Craven Herald report 18 January 1918 reads

"GARGRAVE - REPORTED 'MISSING,' NOW DEAD

Official news reached Mr. William Chester, Mill Hill, Gargrave, last Thursday, that his son Wilfred, aged 22, who was reported missing nearly twelve months ago, is now considered as dead. When reported as missing he had been escorting an officer to a rear position after an engagement, and started back on his return journey. He was never seen afterwards."

Thomas is commemorated on the Midland Railway War Memorial at Derby, Pier and Face 6 A and 6 B of the Thiepval Memorial, Gargrave's Roll of Honour and Gargrave War Memorial.

Midland Railway War Memorial, Derby
Harry Mitchell [CC BY-SA 3.0 (https://creativecommons.org/licenses/by-sa/3.0)]

26TH FEBRUARY

Arthur Bradley
"Craven's Part in the Great War" -
Clayton 1919

46502 Private Arthur Bradley

Northumberland Fusiliers
13th (Service) Battalion
21st Division

Arthur Bradley was born at Gargrave on the 9th of February 1897, the son of Edward and his wife Sarah Ann Bradley, née Bolland. In 1901, the family, Edward and Sarah Bradley and their children Martha 18, John 17, George 16, James 10, Fred 5 and Arthur 4 were living at 20, River Place. Edward was working as a roller coverer at a local cotton mill, Martha was a card room hand, and George was a mule spinner at the same factory.

The 1911 census shows the family now living at Old Hall Gardens in Gargrave. Martha, John and George have left the family home. Edward is still working as a roller coverer, James and Fred have found jobs as carters and Arthur has started as a cotton cop packer. All are working in the same cotton factory. Trimmer Bruce Bradley, included in this chapter, was a cousin of Arthur.

Arthur enlisted in the British Army at Halifax on 11th May 1916. He was sent to train with the 1st Training Reserve Battalion at Rugeley in Staffordshire. On completion of his training, he was allocated to the 13th (Service) Battalion of the Northumberland Fusiliers. This movement between regiments, which was quite common during this time, can cause considerable confusion. This explains the Durham Light Infantry cap badge Arthur is wearing despite being described as a member of the Northumberland Fusiliers.

On December 19th his unit was sent to France to join the 13th (Service) Battalion during the latter days of the Operations on the Ancre. The Operations consisted of several battles during the final stages of the Somme Offensive. The objective was to gain a tactical advantage over the enemy by occupying strategic positions on the high ground following the River Ancre valley. It was during one of these battles on 26th of February that Arthur's life was taken, just sixty-three days after he arrived in France.

Arthur is in interred at Vermelles British Cemetery in Area V, Row B, Plot 32. His name is inscribed on the Gargrave Roll of Honour, the Gargrave War Memorial and the

Gargrave Wesleyan Chapel Remembrance Plaque now on display in the St. Andrew's Church, Gargrave.

Left
Headstone for Arthur Bradley

Below
View of Vermelles British Cemetery
Photograph by Ray Jones 2014

7TH MARCH

Thomas W. Davis
"Craven's Part in the Great War" -
Clayton 1919

41551 Private Thomas William Davis

Prince of Wales Own (West Yorkshire Regiment)
17th (Service) Battalion. (2nd Leeds)
35th Division

Thomas William Davis, born Duffield, Derbyshire, in 1860, was the son of William and Mary Hannah Davis. Mary was widowed at an early age. On the 28th of December 1886, Mary married Richard Black at the St. Andrew's Church in Gargrave. They are shown as living in Church Lane on the 1891 Census, and in 1901 the family had moved to 4, East Street in Gargrave. Thomas, now 17 is working as a cotton spinner.

By 1911 the family had moved to South Street, Thomas William Davis, aged 26, had a younger brother Dick, 12 years old. Mary Hannah Black was once again a widow, and it seems that her two sons were supporting her as much as possible. Thomas was now a cotton mule minder while his young half-brother was attending school half time and working as a cotton ring doffer.

Thomas enlisted with the 17th (Service) Battalion Prince of Wales's Own (West Yorkshire Regiment) (2nd Leeds). The unit became a part of the 4th Army of the British Expeditionary Force on the Western Front. The enemy forces began their gradual withdrawal into their defensive position in February 1917. It was during a battle in the precursory stages of the German withdrawal that Thomas met his maker.

His death was reported in the Craven Herald on the 23rd March 1917

> *"GARGRAVE SOLDIER KILLED IN DUG-OUT*
>
> *Private Thomas William Davis News came to hand on Sunday of the death in France of Pte. Wm. Thos. Davis, West Yorkshire Regiment, who was killed by a shell on the 7th inst.*
>
> *Deceased, who was 34 years of age and unmarried, was for many years employed by the Midland Railway Company as a member of the permanent way staff at*

Gargrave. He joined the Army about six month ago and had only been in France eight weeks.

In a letter announcing the sad event to deceased's mother (who now resides at 8, Railway Street, Barnoldswick) Second-Lieutenant Jno. Marshall, of the same regiment, writes:–

"He was standing at the door of his dug-out during a heavy bombardment by the enemy when a shell dropped on top of the dugout, killing and burying him in a moment. His death is a distinct loss to my platoon. He formed one of a cheery section of whom I had great hopes, despite the fact that they had only been in France a short time."

Pte. Rd. Black, 1st Surrey Rifles, a half-brother of the above, who has been twice wounded, is now at Winchester awaiting a return to the Front. Both are on the Gargrave Parish Church Roll of Honour.

Richard Black, the half-brother of Thomas, mentioned in the newspaper article above, returned from the war.

Thomas is remembered on Gargrave War Memorial, Barnoldswick War Memorial and The Great Memorial at Thiepval - Pier and Face 2 A 2 C and 2 D. His name is also inscribed on the Gargrave Roll of Honour and the Gargrave Wesleyan Chapel Bronze Memorial Plaque, both of which can be seen in St. Andrew's Church, Gargrave.

28TH APRIL

Edward Fawcett
"Craven's Part in the Great War" -
Clayton 1919

240442 Private Edward Fawcett

Northumberland Fusiliers
27th (Service) Battalion.
(4th Tyneside Irish)
34th Division

Edward Fawcett born in Gargrave on the 22nd July 1888, son of Joseph and Margaret Fawcett, nee Langstroth. Joseph was born at Settle and Margaret in Coniston Cold, Yorkshire. Edward and his parents were living with his mother's parents, John and Ellen Langstroth at 1, River Place in Gargrave.

Edward was a cousin of Robert Thompson. Sarah Elizabeth Langstroth, a cousin of Edward and Robert Thompson, was married to William Edward Parrott.

Edward enlisted with the Northumberland Fusiliers, 27th (Service) Battalion, (4th Tyneside Irish) Formed in Kirkby Malzeard near Harrogate on the 27th April 1915 as part of the 4th New Army's 34th Division. The Division moved to Salisbury Plain for more intensive training. The training continued Until the 3rd of January 1916 when the Division was mobilized and prepared to move into the Western Front. The movement of troops started Friday the 7th of January, and by Saturday the 15th of January 1916 the Division had completed the move to La Crosse. The Division spent the rest of the War fighting on the Western Front with the 27th (Service) Battalion (4th Tyneside Irish) until disbanded in France on the 26th of February 1918.

Edward's unit took part in several battles during the Somme Offensive including the Battle Of Albert on the 1st of July 1916, the Battle of Albert 10th July 1916, the Battle of Bazentin Ridge 14th July 1916, the Battle of Pozieres Ridge 31st July 1916, the Battle of Flers-Courcelette on the 15th of September 1916. The Battles of Arras loom largely in the battle list of the unit. The Battle of Arleux on the 28th April 1917 was Edwards final action.

His death was reported in the Craven Herald on the 1st of June 1917

ANOTHER GARGRAVE SOLDIER KILLED

As briefly announced in our last issue, Private Edward Fawcett, of the Machine-Gun Section of the Northumberland Fusiliers, met with his death instantly in action on April 28th last, aged 28 years. His parents have not as yet had any official intimation of the event, but an Earby youth named Alan Wharton, who formerly lived in Gargrave, sent the news to his mother, who has passed it on here. Wharton is in the same regiment as deceased. Prior to enlisting at Keighley on May 6th 1916, Private Fawcett was manager of Messrs Fred Green and Sons' Warehouse at Clapham, and was a member of the Gargrave Mechanics' Institute and of the local Oddfellows Friendly Society.

The Rev. A.C. Blunt, vicar, feelingly referred to his death at the evening service on Sunday last, and the congregation stood while Mr. E. Burlend (organist) played the Dead March.

Edward is remembered on panels in Bay 2 and 3 of the Arras Memorial, and his name is inscribed on the Gargrave War Memorial.

Arrass Memorial
Photograph by Ray Jones 2014

28TH APRIL

William Stockdale
"Craven's Part in the Great War" -
Clayton 1919

36979 Private William Stockdale

East Lancashire Regiment
8th (Service) Battalion
37th Division

William Stockdale, the son of Albert and Nancy Stockdale, née Thompson was born at Gargrave in 1898. Both of William's parents were Gargravians. The family moved to Brierfield in Lancashire shortly after his birth.

William enlisted with the East Lancashire Regiment and soon found himself at the Western Front in France. He was to be one of the combatants in action within the Second Battle of Arras which took place between the 9th of April and the 15th of May 1917.

The Battle of Arras was conceived as a diversionary tactic to draw German troops away from the Aisne to allow the French offensive in that sector to succeed. This was at the expense of approximately 158,000 casualties, around 130,000 of which were fatalities.

Phase two of the Battle of Arras included an assault on an enemy position near the village of Arleux-en-Gohelle known as Greenland Hill. During the advance, the troops were subjected to fire from the right flank. William Stockdale was one of the casualties of the gunfire.

William's death was announced in the Burnley Express on 9th March 1918

"BRIERFIELD SOLDIER'S FATE

Death Now Presumed

As briefly stated in Wednesday's issue, the death in action is now presumed of Pte. Wm. Stockdale, 36979, of the 8th East Lancashire Regiment, and son of Mr and Mrs Albert Stockdale 4, Mount-street, Brierfield. Pte. Stockdale joined up on October 30, 1916, and after training at Southport, he went out to France in January 1917. He was in action on several occasions round Arras. Then he was reported missing on April 28, 1917, by the War Office, and the authorities sent a letter last week stating that they presumed he was killed on that date or since. Letters from comrades who went into action with him said they had not seen him since that day. There are two other brothers on active service – one, Albert E. Stockdale, is a sergeant in the Flying Corps, and the other, Percy, is in the Navy, serving at present on a drifter and mine-sweeper."

William is remembered on the Brierfield War Memorial and the Arras Memorial on Bay 6.

Arras Memorial
Photograph by Ray Jones 2014

3RD MAY

Robert Thompson

29461 Private Robert Thompson

Duke of Wellington's
(West Riding Regiment)
2nd Battalion
10th Brigade
4th Infantry Division

Robert Thompson, born at Gargrave on the 5th of September 1898, was the son of Robert and Hannah Thompson, nee Langstroth. Initially the family, Robert senior, Hannah, three-year-old Robert junior and one-year-old Ellen lived at Broughton Quarries where- Robert Thompson senior worked as a quarry engine driver. Baby Ellen sadly died, and the family moved from the quarry accommodation to 19, River Place. Robert was a cousin of Edward Fawcett. Sarah Elizabeth, married to William Edward Parrott Langstroth, was a cousin of Robert Thompson and Edward Fawcett.

Robert enlisted for general service in Halifax, Yorkshire on the 20th May 1916. The following day, 21st May, he was mobilised and transferred to the Reserve Battalion of the West Riding Regiment. After a period of training, on the 6th September, he was moved to the Home unit prior to his posting to France on the 10th of January 1917. He joined his unit in time to take part in the British Offensive named the 2nd Battle of Arras, a city in the North of France. The action took place between the 9th of April and the 16th of May 1917. A region around the River Scarpe became the focus of the fighting with the First Battle of the Scarpe taking place between the 9th and 14th of April. A second battle, much shorter, followed from the 23rd to 24th of April. The Third Battle of the Scarpe was started on the 3rd of May. The battle was fought from Monchy along the Scarpe valley. No significant advance was made, and the following day the attack was halted due to heavy losses.

Robert was one of the 158,000 plus casualties the allies sustained during the Arras Offensive. Although treated by some as an allied victory the attempt to break through the German lines was not achieved. Very little had changed strategically or tactically.

He is remembered on Bay 6 of the Arras Memorial and Gargrave Wesleyan Chapel Bronze memorial plaque, now in St. Andrew's Church. His name is inscribed on the Gargrave War Memorial

3RD MAY

William Burton
"Craven's Part in the Great War" -
Clayton 1919

37746 Private William Burton

Durham Light Infantry
B Coy 18th (Service) Battalion
(1st County)
31st Division

William Burton was born at Lenton, Nottingham in 1887, to Edwin, a blacksmith, and Mary Anne, a dressmaker. He was the second son of the family. His brother Edwin, named after his father, was born two years earlier. 1889, saw the arrival of William's sister, Florence. Fanny, William's future wife, was the cousin of Ernest Aldersley also a Gargrave soldier. She gave birth to Mildred, on the 20th of July 1909. William married Fanny Aldersley of Gargrave in 1910. The couple took up residence in West Street Gargrave.

William was a gardener by occupation. While in Gargrave he was an under-gardener at Gargrave House. He went on to secure gardening positions at Scale House, near Rylstone, and Moorfield House in Silsden where he was appointed Head Gardener.

It was while he was working at Moorfield House that he took the decision to enlist with the Durham Light Infantry. He joined the 18th (Service) Battalion, a 'Pals' Battalion in Keighley on the 9th of August 1916. The Battalion was a unit of the 31st Division which was part of Kitchener's 4th New Army. After three months of training, he and the other recruits were sent to France. A further period of trench warfare training followed. On completion of the training, in preparation for the Arras Offensive, the 31st Division moved into assembly trenches near Oppy on the night of 2nd and 3rd of May. There was heavy shell fire during this operation. William, and two other men were killed when a shell exploded as he was moving up the line with the 18th Battalion, Durham Light Infantry. For a great while, no official news from the War Office reached Mrs Burton, now living at Reservoir House, Winterburn, but she was sent a letter from two comrades in arms from William's Battalion;

"Dear Mrs. Burton,

It is with deep and heartfelt sympathy I write to tell you that Will was killed in action on Thursday, May 3rd by a shell, on his way to the trenches, and the same shell also killed Fred Murphy and Tom Mitchell. We have all been pals together since coming out here, and we feel the loss of all of them as if they were brothers. This is the saddest task I have ever undertaken to write you, but I feel we would rather we told you. May God be with you in your hour of trial, comfort you, and strengthen you to face the future. Your grief is shared to a smaller extent by his sorrowing pals who have proved his worth out here in all circumstances.

Sincerely your friends

W. E. INGHAM and Wm. MEARES."

On the 3rd of February 1956, almost 40 years later, the 'Craven Herald & Pioneer', reported that:

"Recently a French farmer ploughed up a grave in which there were the bodies of five soldiers of the Durham Light Infantry, and with one of the bodies was a silver cigarette case with the initials and date W.B. 1895 in the centre. There was also a silver-plated dessert spoon bearing the initial B together with the regimental initials DLI.

The cigarette case and spoon have been sent by the Imperial War Graves Commission to Mrs Fanny Burton of Reservoir House, Winterburn, near Skipton, who has identified them as belonging to her first husband. Mrs Burton says she well remembers the silver cigarette case as her first husband came home for a 24-hour leave before departing for France and she asked him to leave the cigarette case at home as he might lose it. ..."

William was interred in the Canadian Cemetery No.2, Neuville-St. Vaast and is remembered on the Gargrave Roll of Honour, Gargrave War Memorial and Silsden War Memorial.

Canadian Cemetery No.2, Neuville-St. Vaast
Photograph by Ray Jones 2014

Photograph by Ray Jones 2014

3RD MAY

William Spedding
"Craven's Part in the Great War" -
Clayton 1919

265402 Corporal William Spedding

West Riding Regiment
2/6th Battalion
62nd (2/1st West Riding) Division

The son of Frederick Wilson and Maria Spedding, (née Taylor), William Henry Spedding was born at Gargrave in 1898. His father Frederick was born at Austwick and Maria at Niffany, near Skipton, Yorkshire. In 1901 the family were living at 32, River Place, Gargrave and in 1911 the family were residing at Low Green, Gargrave.

William enlisted with The 2/6th Battalion West Riding Regiment based in Skipton. He was with them through as they battled along the Western Front finally taking part in the Battle of Bullecourt, an action of the Battles of Arras.

The aim of this engagement was to break through the Hindenburg Line, a string of strongly held German defensive trench systems, to capture Hendecourt-lès-Cagnicourt, a strategic position and stronghold of the German army. Troops of the 62nd (2nd West Riding) Division were involved in the attack on Bullecourt. The village was taken, and despite the determination of the German forces to take back their lost position, the 62nd Division held the gained ground.

The Battles of Arras were unsuccessful as the German forces recovered enough to force a stalemate. Neither force gained an advantage both the British and German forces suffered appalling losses. Henry was reported missing after the engagement, his body was never recovered.

A single mention that he was missing was published toward the end of a lengthy article by the Craven Herald on the 5th of May 1917.

William Spedding's name is inscribed on bay 6 of the Arras Memorial, Gargrave War Memorial and on the Gargrave Wesleyan Chapel Memorial plaque in the St. Andrew's Church, Gargrave.

4TH MAY

Herbert Platt
"Craven's Part in the Great War" -
Clayton 1919

40031 Private Herbert Platt

York & Lancaster Regiment
12th (Service) Battalion.
(Sheffield)
31st Division

Herbert Platt, born in 1896, was the son of Samuel James and Maria Jane Platt, *nee* Rawling. Samuel James was born at Oundle, Northamptonshire and Maria at Bramley, Yorkshire. In 1901 four-year-old Herbert was living at 70, High Mill, Gargrave with his mother, brothers 22-year-old James, Henry 19, George aged 12, and 7-year-old sister Mary.

Herbert worked as a clerk in the clothing industry before joining the York and Lancaster Regiment on the 6th December 1915. He was nineteen when he enlisted. Herbert undertook training as a Signaller. The unit he entered, the 12th Service Battalion, was raised in Sheffield by the Lord Mayor and City on the 5th September 1914. This unit was soon to be joined by the 14th Service Battalion which was formed on the 30th November 1914 by the Lord Mayor and City in Barnsley.

The army was undergoing a massive restructuring in the early years of the Great War, and the following year both units moved to Penkridge, on Cannock Chase where they joined the 94th Brigade of the 31st Division. From here they moved to Ripon where they underwent further basic training, In August they were placed under the aegis of the War Office and were re-deployed to Salisbury Plain for additional training. Following a relatively short spell of intensive training, the troops were mobilised for war in December 1916. Their first move was to Egypt to help in defence of the Suez Canal. In February 1916 the units were informed that they were to move again, this time to the Western Front in France. On the 27th of February, the advance parties departed. The main body of the force moved out during early March. Disembarkation at their destination began on the 6th of March, and the move was completed on 16th March when the final units arrived.

The units took part in several actions during the 1916 Somme Offensive. The Battle of Albert, starting on the 1st July was a notable British defeat. The British Fourth and the French Sixth armies were involved in this action which was extremely costly to the British who suffered a devastating loss of 60,000 casualties on the first day.

Herbert managed to survive this first catastrophic action and went on to escape injury during the ensuing attack on Sere during July 1916, the Battle of the Ancre November 1916 and Operations on the Ancre during February and March 1917.

The final recorded battle that Herbert was involved in took place during the Third Battle of the Scarpe. This action was in Oppy Wood on the 3rd May 1916.

The 31st Division in XIII Corps had moved into trenches in the Gavrelle sector near Arras. From here on the 3rd of May, they advanced toward Oppy. The attack was led by the 92nd Infantry Brigade and the 93rd Infantry Brigade.

The 16th West Yorkshire Regiment, 15th West Yorkshire Regiment and the 18th West Yorkshire Regiment supported by the 18th Durham Light Infantry were also involved in the action.

The units had formed up on the evening of the 2nd May ready to move off shortly after midnight. They had chosen a brilliant moonlit night for the attack. The Germans had seen the movements and were fully prepared with their defences. They sent several artillery bombardments on the readying troops; The attackers were also laying down a creeping barrage in the hope that the Germans would be put out of action. Immediately they set off behind their creeping barrage they were met with devastating machine gun fire.

Those that managed to get into Oppy Wood were quickly driven back. Only one company, C Company of the 11th East Yorkshire Regiment reached the target, Oppy Village. Not one of C Company returned.

Herbert is remembered on Bay 8 of the Arras Memorial, Gargrave's Wesleyan Chapel Roll of Honour, which can now be seen in St. Andrew's Church, and Gargrave War Memorial.

12TH MAY

William Gill

235189 Private William Gill

Prince of Wales Own West Yorkshire Regiment
2/7th Battalion (Leeds Rifles)
62nd (2nd West Riding) Division

William Gill, born in Gargrave in 1898, to Percy and Jane Gill, née Dobby. Percy was born at Gargrave and Jane at Leeds, Yorkshire. The family resided at 15, East Street in Gargrave. Sadly, Percy passed away in 1904. Jane and her son William continued to live at the same address on East Street for some years eventually moving to Chesenley Stile, Wadsworth near Hebden Bridge.

William enlisted in Halifax, with The 2/7th Battalion of the Leeds Rifles, a Territorial unit. In January 1917 the unit was mobilised for war and sent to France. They landed at Le Havre and were to engage in various actions on the Western Front.

The last conflict William was to participate in was the Battle of Bullecourt, part of the Arras Offensive, this battle took place between the 3rd and 17th of May 1917. The final attack on Bullecourt commenced on the 12th of May with companies B and C of the 2/7th Battalion West Yorkshire Regiment, the 185th Trench Mortar Battery and a section from the 21st Machine-Gun Company. This force was called to attack and take the enemies strong point at a position known as the Crucifix, alongside the 2nd Australian Division.

The attack started at around 4.0 a.m. Some two hours later it appeared as if the objective had been achieved. At approximately 06:30 hours (6.30 a.m.) a spotter plane reported The 2/7th being seen in trenches holding the Crucifix position. Communication was lost between Field HQ and the Battalions and at 8.0 p.m. another spotter plane reported that the German forces were now back in control of the Crucifix. The 2/7th suffered five known fatalities, thirty-one missing and thirty-two wounded during this battle. William Gill was one of the fatalities.

He is remembered in Bay 4 of the Arras Memorial, Gargrave War Memorial, Gargrave's Roll of Honour and the Gargrave Wesleyan Chapel Bronze memorial plaque.

22ND JUNE

Danson William Yeoman

34825 Private Danson William Yeoman

East Lancashire Regiment
1st Battalion
11th Brigade
4th Division

Born at Gargrave in 1897, Danson was the son of William Calvert and Emily Yeoman. William, a gardener, was from Carlton in Coverdale and Emily, née Garnett was born in Gargrave. At the time of the 1911 Census, they had moved from Gargrave to Nelson where William Calvert had secured a head gardener position.

Danson 13 now had a younger brother Christopher born while the family were still in Gargrave in 1902.

Danson enlisted with the 1st Battalion of the East Lancashire Regiment, a regular army unit which served on the Western Front from 1914 until 1918. Danson was with the 11th Brigade of the 4th Division during the Battle of the Scarpe. In the Spring of 1917, the British Army launched a series of attacks at Arras in an attempt to dislodge the enemy from their position, capture some ground and possibly take prisoners. The offensive action started on the 9th of April, and at the end of May, there was little gained except an ever-increasing cost in lives and fighting men. Six of the Lancashire Battalions took part in the battles, the 11th East Lancashires entering the battle in May. The struggle to maintain the positions and prevent the German army pushing their opponents back carried on through May until well into June. On the 22nd of June, the day when Danson died, the units had started to move toward Oppy Wood and a new battle on the 28th of June.

Danson William Yeoman was buried at Crump Trench British Cemetery, Fampoux, Plot I, Row A, Grave 18. His name is inscribed on the Gargrave War Memorial and the family gravestone in St. Andrew's churchyard, Gargrave.

Crump Trench British Cemetery
Photograph by Ray Jones 2014

Courtesy of Martin Thompson

14th July

Riley Chew
"Craven's Part in the Great War" -
Clayton 1919

168040 Gunner Riley Chew

Royal Garrison Artillery
2nd Army Pool

Riley was born at Grindleton in 1889 to William and Millicent Chew. In 1891 they were living at Little Monetent, Stoops Lane, Bolton by Bowland, Clitheroe where William was a tenant farmer. By the time of the 1901 Census, the family had moved to Springheads, Bolton by Bowland. Riley, now 12, had been joined by four younger brothers; John 8, William 5, James 2, and newborn Thomas. The family had also been blessed by the addition of two daughters; Mary Ann 5, and Alice 4.

Grandfather Riley a retired farmer of 79 was also living with the Chew family. Riley left the family home to take up a post as a farm labourer with Thomas Whitaker at Bale House, Farm West Marton, Skipton, Yorkshire. He later moved to Hellifield as a farm labourerworking for Tom Moon at Old Hall, Halton West, Hellifield. In 1916, Riley married Maude Busfield, aged 24, the daughter of a dairy farmer at Moor Head, Swinden, Hellifield. Riley's mother and father moved to Scaleber Farm, Mosber Lane, off Marton Road Gargrave.

Riley enlisted with the Royal Garrison Artillery in February 1916. After training, he was sent to join his unit with the British 2nd Army in May 1916, during the operations on the Ypres Salient. It was during the lead-up time to the Third Battle of Ypres that enemy artillery fire on the positions held by units of the 2nd Army Pool fell directly onto the trench shelter where Riley was resting. He was killed outright in his sleep on the 14th July 1917.

The Craven Herald published the following on the 27 July 1917;

"A HELLIFIELD HERO - GUNNER R. CHEW, R.G.A.

We regret to say that news has been received of the death on the battlefield of Gunner R. Chew, R.G.A., husband of Mrs. Chew, Swindon Moor Head, Hellifield, and son of Mr. and Mrs. W. Chew, Scaleber Farm, Gargrave (late of Bolton-by-Bowland). The sad news came in the following letter, dated July 15th, from Second-Lieutenant A. K. Gowan:- "I regret to have to inform you that your husband, Gunner R. Chew, was killed yesterday morning by a shell in his sleep. He had only been with us a short time, but in his work he had showed his worth as a soldier. I offer to you and his relatives and friends my sincere sympathy in your sad bereavement. He was buried today behind the lines."

The Rev. E. G. Wells, Army Chaplain, has also written a letter of sympathy to the widow, in which he says:- "I was called to take the funeral and his body was laid to rest in the cemetery here near the ruined village church in the presence of his captain and several of his comrades. I understand that the cellar in which he was living was blown in by a shell, and from what I can hear I don't think he can have suffered."

Twenty-eight years of age, Gunner Chew enlisted in February last, and went to the front on May 29th. He was formerly a farm labourer for Mr. Moon, of Halton West, Hellifield. A memorial service is to be held at Halton West Church on Sunday at two o'clock."

Riley was laid to rest in Dickebusch New Military Cemetery Extension Plot ii, Row B, Grave 8. He is remembered on Bolton-by-Bowland War Memorial; Gargrave War Memorial and Roll of Honour; Halton West War Memorial and Halton West Mission Church Memorial Plaque.

Photographs by Ray Jones 2014

16th August

Ernest French
Private Collection – Dennis French

32221 Private Ernest French

Shropshire Light Infantry
6th (Service Battalion)
20th (Light Infantry) Division

Ernest was a member of the French family who can trace their family roots back to Suffolk in the 1820s. His father was Caleb, an Embsay born member of the Frenches. Caleb's father, Abraham was initially from Suffolk where his family had fallen on hard times. It is possible that the family had been workers in the textile industries in the Suffolk region. The Norwich crepes and worsted material were falling out of fashion, and the introduction of machine spinning and weaving in Yorkshire and Lancashire was making the hand spinners and weavers obsolete. With little alternative work available, Abraham took the offer of employment and a paid barge boat passage North to restart his life. After moving between jobs, he married Agnes, a young woman from Eastby and settled in Embsay to work in the local cotton factory. Caleb, Ernest's father, married Elizabeth Whitaker of Gargrave and set up home at 17 East Street. Ernest was born on 15th November 1885, the fourth child of Caleb and Elizabeth. Ernest's eldest brother, William was 6 years old, brother James, 4, and sister Agnes, 3 years old.

The children were joined by sister Margaret in 1891 when the family was living at Raybridge in Gargrave. By 1901, the family had moved to Barnoldswick and Ernest, now 16, was working as a cotton weaver. The 1911 census shows that Caleb, now 58, moved to Trawden with his family, Elizabeth his wife, daughter Margaret Ellen 21, Horace 10, Ida 8, and Gladys 6. Ernest has left the family home and is living with his elder sister, Agnes and her husband, Willie Priestley at Barrowford. Ernest is now working as a Coal Carter. Ernest married Susannah Ramsbottom of 17, Ashfield St., Keighley in 1912. Susannah was born 26th August 1883.

The 6th (Service) Battalion was formed at Shrewsbury Sept 1914 as part of the Second New Army (K2) and then moved to Aldershot to join the 60th Brigade of the 20th Division. In April 1915 the Battalion moved to Larkhill, Salisbury Plain for further training.

On the 22nd July 1915, the Division was mobilised for war. The Division landed at Boulogne and immediately undertook trench familiarisation and training in the Fleurbaix area. During 1916 20th Division were actively involved in the Battle of Mount Sorrel (from the 2nd to 13th June), the Battle of Delville Wood (15th July to the 3rd September), the Battle of Guillemont (3rd to 6th September), the Battle of Flers-Courcelette 15th to 22nd September, the Battle of Morval (2nd to 28th September), and the Battle of Le Transloy (1st until 18th October).

The German forces had suffered a costly failure at the Battle of Verdun fought between the 21st February and 18th December 1916. Defences were constructed during the winter of 1916-1917 to enable retirement from the Somme in the face of an increased force in the expected Anglo-French attacks. Withdrawal of German troops took place during February and March 1917 following British assaults on the Ancre Valley. The last battle that Ernest saw was during the Third Battles Of Ypres. This was a long drawn out operation, with several actions taking place. The fighting commenced on the 31st of July and continued until the 10th of November 1917. The Battle of Langemarck, fought between the 16th and 18th August 1917, was the second major Allied attack of the Third Battle of Ypres. The aim of the battle was to gain control of the high ground south and east of Ypres. Eight Divisions were deployed across the front from a point named Inverness Copse in the South, to a position North-West of Langemark. The 20th (Light Infantry) Division and the 29th Division as part of XIV Corps were on the Northern most end of the line.

The French Army units with supporting French artillery covered the Western Flank. The two Divisions in the north, the 30th and 29th, succeeded in advancing between 1,000 and 1,500 yards reaching all of their objectives and occupying the waterlogged ruins of Langemarck village. The success was not without cost. Units attacking the line at other positions came under fierce opposition resulting in catastrophic losses. Ernest was just one of an estimated 15,000 casualties. A high cost for the few hundred yards gained.

Ernest is commemorated on the Barrowford War memorial, Tyne Cot Memorial and the Keighley WW 1 Roll of Honour, a hand-bound Book of Remembrance with a calligraphic inscription in red and black ink. The book is held in a purpose-built glass case within Keighley Public Library.

20TH SEPTEMBER

Autbert C. C. Dutton
"Craven's Part in the Great War" -
Clayton 1919

Corporal Autbert Christopher Cedric Dutton

South African Infantry,
3rd Regiment (Transvaal & Rhodesia)
9th (Scottish) Division

Autbert, more popularly known as Cedric, was born on the 13th December 1897 at Lothersdale to join the family of the Reverend Charles Adolphus, the resident Vicar of Lothersdale, and Helen Dutton. Cedric was the youngest member of the family, joining Charles 20, Stephen 17, Winifred 16, Dorothy 6, Brenda 5, and Eric just three-years-old. Most of the family emigrated to South Africa between 1911 and 1916, except for Winnie who moved to Shepton Mallet. Cedric was sent to Hereford Cathedral School and on his sixteenth birthday left the school to join his family in South Africa.

Soon after the outbreak of World War One, Cedric joined the South African Armed forces serving with the Intelligence Corps. He was involved in the suppression of the German-inspired Maritz rebellion of the Boers in 1914. Later in his career in the South African Army, he became secretary to General Smuts. Cedric was to move on from this position to the 1st Infantry Brigade (South Africa). He underwent a period of training from December 1915 and on the 23rd January 1916 was sent into action taking part in the Senussi Campaign in Libya and Egypt. The Senussi were waging a German and Ottoman-backed guerrilla campaign against the British forces in North Africa. On the successful completion of the Senussi Campaign in February 1916, the Brigade was transferred to the Western Front in France where they joined the 9th (Scottish) Division in time to take part in the Somme offensive which raged for 141 days from 1st of July 1916 until the 18th of November 1916. Fourteen or more consecutive individually named battles took place during the Somme offensive.

The South African contingent took part in several of these battles and more. The final battle for Autbert Christopher Cedric Dutton was the Battle of the Menin Road Ridge which started on the 20th and lasted until the 25th of September 1917. The action was a part of the Ypres Salient, still in the Somme area with the aim of capturing Fortuin and Borry Farm.

The South African Brigade advanced toward Borry Farm after laying down a barrage of high explosive shells. A thick mist helped them to over-run the main strong points, except for four pill-boxes around Potsdam House. These were attacked and eventually captured after suffering heavy losses. When the advance on the final objective was launched, the South African Brigade came under German machine-gun fire from Hill 37. It was during these events that Cedric lost his life.

The Craven Herald published the news of Cedric's death on the 12th of October 1917

"GARGRAVE – CORPORAL A.C.C. DUTTON:

A Sixth Son Pays the Price

We regret to state that Corporal Autbert Christopher Cedric Dutton, sixth and youngest son of the late Rev. C. A. Dutton, Rector of Lothersdale, and of Mrs. Dutton, Gargrave, was killed in action on September 20th in the Ypres Menin battle. No particulars are at present forthcoming, except the following letter from his captain:–

"Dear Madam,

On behalf of my company, allow me to convey to you our deepest sympathy in the loss of your gallant son. He was killed, bravely doing his duty, in the advance on the 20th inst. I had a great opinion of him. It is a great blow to you to lose such a boy, but may I say it, there is consolation and pride in the knowledge that you were permitted to be the mother of such a man, who made the supreme sacrifice in the cause of liberty and right.

With deepest sympathy, believe me,

yours faithfully,

S. W. TOMLINSON, Capt."

Mr. Dutton went out to South Africa at the age of 16, where four others of his brothers are doing good work for their country. He was a boy of exceptional ability and trustworthiness. During the Rebellion in South Africa, engineered by Germans at the beginning of the war, he was one of the Secret Intelligence Staff under the Provost Marshal (Major H. W. Hamilton Fowle). He had several interesting German relics relating to this period, viz., photographs of captured German officers, amongst them that of the officer who commanded the poisoning of the wells in German South-East Africa; the flying officer in his aeroplane who harassed their lines of communication; together with passports, identification papers, &c. He then became secretary to General Smuts, at that time Minister of Defence and Finance, and was on excellent terms with his honoured chief. It is recorded that on a certain occasion the General said to him "What is this 'Tipperary' I hear so much of?" Someone entering the chief's office later was amused to find young Dutton giving the General vocal demonstration of the soldiers' popular marching song.

Deceased gave up a career full of promise at the age of 17 to enlist as a private with troops bound for England. After three months' training in South Africa and finishing the course in England, he was drafted to Egypt, and was there in action against the Senuše. He was seriously wounded on the Somme last year, and was three times offered a commission, but he preferred to remain with those he had been with from the first, and had come to regard as friends. He was educated at Hereford Cathedral School and was killed at the age of 19½ years."

Cedric is remembered on the Menin Gate Memorial, Gargrave War Memorial and Gargrave Roll of Honour, and the Lothersdale Christ Church Memorial Tablet. A private memorial tablet can also be seen in Lothersdale Christ Church.

Menin Gate Interior
Photograph by Ray Jones 2014

9TH OCTOBER

Ben Dobby
"Craven's Part in the Great War" -
Clayton 1919

Private Ben Dobby

Alexandra, Princess of Wales Own (Yorkshire Regiment)
6th (Service) Battalion
11th (Northern) Division

Ben Dobby, born 1892 to Thomas and Sarah Ann Dobby, née Moss. He joined the family of four girls, Sarah 11, Hannah 5, and three-year-old Elizabeth. Mary, another daughter to the family, arrived in 1894. In 1891 the family were living in East Street, Gargrave moving to North Street sometime prior to the 1901 Census. In February 1904, Ben's mother, Sarah Ann, died at the age of 42. She was buried in St. Andrew's Church yard on the 24th of February. 1904. Hannah, Ben's sister, married a David Wood, a platelayer from Rylstone at St. Andrew's Church Gargrave on the 6th of June in 1908.

She moved to Park House, Eldroth Clapham Station where her husband worked as a platelayer for the Midland Railway Company. 1911 Eldroth, Yorkshire Census shows Benjamin Dobby, aged 18 years, boarding with his sister, Hannah and her husband. Ben was employed as a platelayer with the same company as his brother-in-law. Ben moved from platelaying and took up a post closer to home as a farm servant at the Craven Heifer Inn on Grassington Road near Skipton.

It was during his period of service with the Craven Heifer that Ben decided to join the army. He enlisted on the 11th of February 1916 at Halifax. The unit he was appointed to, the 6th (Service) Battalion had been newly created as part of Kitchener's New Armies and had served in Gallipoli in 1915, and Egypt from January to July 1916 before being moved to the Western Front in July 1916. Ben was sent to join the regiment in France on the 9th of August 1916, in time to participate in the Battles of Ypres, also known as Passchendaele.

His unit was involved in the fighting around St. Julien on the 19th of August, the Battle of Polygon Wood, from the 26th of September and the Battle of Broodseinde on the 4th of October before Ben's final involvement on the 9th of October 1917 at the Battle of Poelcapelle. This last action was ordered by General Haig who planned to renew the attack on enemy positions occupying the high ground around Pilckem Ridge. The attack was to be preceded by a creeping barrage provided by the artillery units. The 'creeping barrage' is described in more detail later in this chapter.

The weather was not favourable for such an attack, the heavy continuous rainfall had made the ground difficult for the heavy artillery guns to be brought into place leaving the creeping barrage as relatively ineffectual. It did not weaken the resolve of the German defenders, nor cut through the defensive barbed wire entanglements as planned.

The advancing troops were attempting to cross a landscape which was almost entirely flooded, with no cover from enemy fire other than flooded shell craters. Many shells from the creeping barrage failed to explode because the ground was too soft to activate the detonators. A halt to the advance was called around midday, and the troops had to withdraw. The survivors of the attack reached their 'home' trenches by the end of the day. Seven-thousand men were lost from an attacking force of thirty-thousand with all but one of the objectives failed. Ben, struck in the head by a deadly piece of flying shrapnel, was one of the many soldiers who lost their lives on this day.

The Craven Herald issued the following report on the 19th of October 1917

> *"ANOTHER GARGRAVE SOLDIER PAYS THE PRICE*
>
> *On Tuesday morning Mr. Thomas Dobby, North Street, received official information that his son, Private Ben Dobby, Yorkshire Regiment, B.E.F., whose photo we give above, had been killed in action.*
>
> *His captain, L. Dawnay, writes:– "He was taking part in an attack when he was shot through the head by a piece of shrapnel and was killed immediately. I hope you will accept my deepest sympathy in your great loss. He did his duty up to the time of his death, when he made the greatest sacrifice of all."*
>
> *Private B. Dobby was a fine, well-built young fellow and enlisted at Halifax on February 11th 1916, going to France on August 9th last. Prior to enlisting he was a farm servant with Mr. Tyrer at the Craven Heifer Inn, near Skipton".*

He is remembered on Panel 52 to 54 and 162A. Tyne Cot Memorial, Gargrave War Memorial and the Gargrave Roll of Honour.

Photograph by Ray Jones 2014

12TH OCTOBER

William Draper Dickinson

Private William Draper Dickinson

Queens Own (Royal West Kent) Regiment
7th (Service) Battalion
18th (Eastern) Division

Born in 1893 at Langwathby, near Kirkby Stephen, Cumberland (now renamed Cumbria), William Draper Dickinson was the son of William and Elizabeth Ann Dickinson, née Draper. William's father was the station master at Langwathby in 1901. William at the age of seven was the eldest child in the Dickinson family. He had two sisters, Rose Ann 6 and Edith just three. The 1911 census return for Langwathby shows that William Draper Dickinson has left home and that the Dickinson family had an addition of another daughter, Ada born in 1903. William had found employment at Crackenthorpe, near Appleby as a labourer at the farm of Thomas Horn. He eventually moved to Gargrave where he was employed as a railway porter and found living quarters in High Street, Gargrave.

On the 20th of November 1915, William attended the recruiting office in Keighley and enlisted with the 4th (Hallamshire) Battalion of the York and Lancashire Regiment, a Territorial force initially based in Sheffield. His service records do exist but are severely damaged by fire, and some documents have been destroyed completely. Those that remain show that he embarked from Folkestone on route to Boulogne to join the 34th Infantry Base Depot at Etaples on the 6th July 1917, transferred to the 3/4th Battalion of Queens Own (Royal West Kent) Regiment on the 7th of July 1917, and subsequently posted to the 7th (Service) Battalion. William and the 7th Battalion were involved in the Battle of Pilckem Ridge in July, the Battle of Langemarck during August, and the First Battle of Passchendaele on the 12th of October 1917 at Poelcappelle in Belgium.

The First Battle of Passchendaele was the final action that William would take part in. The battle was an Allied attempt to take control of the area around Passchendaele. This was no easy task, the extremely wet weather and previous armed struggles by both the opposing forces had created an extremely muddy pock filled terrain. It was planned that the attack should take place following a creeping barrage created by the British artillery units.

The creeping barrage was to lay down a torrent of explosive shells around 100 yards (91.44 metres) ahead of the line the troops as they moved forward. Each barrage was to last eight minutes before shifting to the next position. The whole time of the barrage was planned to be six hours and forty-six minutes. Artillery movement was restricted by the conditions which stopped the movement of large guns into the area. The exhausted and low-spirited Allied troops could only make a small advance before being driven back by the intense German counter-attacks. The battle lost the Allied forces some 13,000 fighting men. William was one of these brave men.

William's name is inscribed on Panel 106 to 108. Tyne Cot Memorial. He is commemorated on the Gargrave War Memorial, the Gargrave Roll of Honour, Langwathby War Memorial and the Midland Railway War Memorial at Derby.

Inscription on Tyne Cott Panel
Photograph by Ray Jones 2014

28TH NOVEMBER

Harry Banks
"Craven's Part in the Great War" -
Clayton 1919

266245 Private Harry Banks

Duke of Wellington's (West Riding Regiment)
2/6th Battalion
62nd (2/West Riding) Division

In 1898 Henry and Mary Banks welcomed newborn Harry into the family living at 14 River Place in Gargrave. In 1901 Henry was a cotton mule spinner at a local mill, his eldest son, Richard, twenty-one, was working as a farm labourer and his eldest daughter, Hannah, nineteen, was a cotton rover. His two younger daughters, Jane, eleven, and Florrie, nine were attending school. Harry was now three. On the 8th of August Harry's mother, Mary, passed away at the age of fifty-two. She was buried in the grounds of Saint Andrews Church. In 1911 the census returns for Gargrave show that the Banks family had moved to South Street in Gargrave. Henry is still working as a cotton mule spinner; his eldest daughter Hannah has left home, and the remaining family were all employed as cotton spinners or winders. Harry stayed in the textile industry taking up a position as a weaver at Shuttleworth's of Earby.

Harry enlisted in the West Riding Regiment early in the war, when he was only seventeen years old. He was mobilised and sent to the Western Front on the 8th of February 1917. On the 7th of February, the 62nd West Riding Division was ordered to advance into the front-line trenches left vacant by the German army and hold them. The trenches had been entirely obliterated by constant artillery bombardment, leaving only craters full of slimy mud. The going was treacherous with more than one soldier losing his life by drowning after slipping into the deep cesspits the shells and constant rain had created.

After securing the objective at Beaumont Hamel, the Division took part in the Advance to the Hindenburg Line, the first attack on Bullecourt and then went on to carry further actions between the 29th of June and the 19th of November. The incident in which Harry Banks received the injury that would eventually take his life was the 4th and final phase of the Battle of Cambrai, the Capture of Bourlon Wood.

The line to be held by The 2/6th ran through Bourlon Wood, just below the Village of Bourlon. Sniping, sporadic machine-gun fire and period of an artillery shell bombardment carried on during the rest of the night until daybreak. Harry was admitted to a field hospital with gunshot wounds to the head where he sadly succumbed to his injuries. His passing was reported in the Craven Herald on the 14th December 1917

"ANOTHER GARGRAVE LAD KILLED

A few days ago a telegram reached Mrs. Adams, 18, River Place, with the sad news that her brother, Signaller Harry Banks, of the West Ridings, had succumbed in hospital to a gunshot wound in the head on the 28th November. He joined up three years ago, went across on February 8th last, and received his severe wound in action, dying at the age of 20 years. Prior to enlisting he worked as a weaver at Shuttleworth's Shed, Earby. We give his photograph above. At the Parish Church, the Rev. A. C. Blunt, vicar, very feelingly referred to the sad event at the close of last Sunday evening's service, and the congregation stood during the playing on the organ by Mr. E. Burlend, of the Dead March."

Harry was interred in Plot VIII, Row A, Grave 10, Grevillers British Cemetery, near Bapaume northern France. His name is inscribed on the Gargrave War Memorial, the Gargrave Roll of Honour and the Gargrave Wesleyan Chapel Bronze memorial plaque now on display in the St. Andrew's Church, Gargrave.

Above left - Harry's headstone at Grevillers British Cemetery Right - Cemetery Entrance
Photographs by Ray Jones 2014

3RD DECEMBER

Thomas Clark Bentham
"Craven's Part in the Great War" -
Clayton 1919

240442 Private Thomas Clark Bentham

5th East Lancashire Regiment
'A' Coy 2/5th Battalion
66th (2/East Lancashire) Division

Born in 1894 at Gargrave, Thomas Clark Bentham was the son of Joseph and Sarah Jane Bentham. The 1901 Census for Gargrave shows the family living at 13, South Street in Gargrave. Joseph is described as a Giggleswick or Settle born Master Butcher with his wife, Sarah whose maiden name was Clark. Their three children were all born in Gargrave with Thomas being the eldest. Minnie, the older of the two daughters, was born in 1896, and Thirza arrived in 1899. The family were fortunate to be able to employ a domestic servant, Edith Roberts, a young lady from Hampshire. By the time of the 1911 Census the family had moved to Colne in Lancashire and were living at 24 Derby Street. Father Joseph was still in the meat trade, and his family had increased in size. Sarah, the youngest child, had joined the family in 1902. Thomas was now seventeen and working as a telephone clerk.

Thomas enlisted with the East Lancashire Regiment late in 1913 and was allocated to the 1/5th Battalion. The 5th Battalion was a Territorial Force which was formed at Burnley in August 1914 as part of the East Lancashire Brigade in the East Lancashire Division. On the 10th of September 1914, the unit had mobilised and departed from Southampton bound for Egypt. Thomas, after enlistment and subsequent training, joined the unit in the Balkans on the 10th of May 1915. His unit took part in the landing at Cape Helles in Gallipoli and the action in the hills around the village of Krithia. In December 1915 they returned to Egypt. On the 2nd of February 1917, the Division arrived in Marseilles to make their way to the fighting on the Western Front. They were allocated to III Corps of the 4th Army. They continued to move northwards on to Flanders where they took part in the Battle of Passchendaele. It was an action during the Battle of Passchendaele that lost Thomas his life.

The Craven Herald made the following announcement on the 4th of January 1918

"GARGRAVE - DIED OF WOUNDS

> *News has been received of the death from wounds in France of Private Thomas*
> *Clark Bentham, 8, Earl Street, Colne, formerly of Gargrave, and a grandson*
> *of the late Mr Thos. Clark, of Settle. He was wounded December 2nd last,*
> *and died the following day, aged 24 years..."*

He is buried in Potijze Chateau Grounds Cemetery, Plot I, Row D, Grave 27. The cemetery can be found to the North East of Ieper (Ypres), Belgium. Thomas is commemorated on the Colne War Memorial, 54 Albert Road Colne Pendle Lancashire and his name is on the Gargrave war Memorial.

Potijze Chateau Grounds Cemetery
Photographs by Ray Jones 2014

1918

12TH JANUARY

Christopher Wane
"Craven's Part in the Great War" -
Clayton 1919

J/40880 Able Seaman Christopher Wane

Royal Navy
H.M.S. Opal

Christopher Wane, born at Gargrave on 27th March 1895 was the son of James and Agnes Wane, née Metcalfe. In 1901 the family were living in Barnoldswick, at Gill House, Coates. They moved to Skipton and in 1911 the census shows Christopher, now 18, working as a cotton weaver and living in Skipton, at 52, Otley Street with his sister, Isabella and brother-in-law, George Edward Aldridge.

Christopher enlisted with the Royal Navy on the 7th July 1915. He attended a short spell of training from the 9th of July until the 16th of July 1915 at the Portsmouth naval barracks, then known as H.M.S. Victory, named after Nelson's flagship. After training, he joined the crew of H.M.S. Excellent on the 17th July 1915 as an Able Seaman. He stayed on board the Excellent until the 31st of March 1916. He then was assigned to H.M.S. Opal. The Opal was with the 12th Destroyer Flotilla at Scapa Flow, an extremely large safe anchorage for ships hidden between in the islands of the Orkney archipelago in the North Sea.

On January 12th, 1918 the destroyers H.M.S. Opal, H.M.S. Narborough and the Cruiser H.M.S. Boadicea were on night patrol to apprehend German warships laying mines off the coast. The weather conditions were dreadful, with a blizzard threatening, and was deteriorating rapidly. By 5.30 p.m. fearing that the destroyers may be swamped and capsize, the Boadicea ordered them back to Scapa Flow. After four hours, a somewhat garbled message *"have run aground"* was received at 9.27 p.m. This was the final signal from the two ships.

It was two days until the wreck of H.M.S. Opal was found, battered and with no one left alive on board, on the Clett of Crura on the Eastern coast of South, a steep rock stack a little way off the massive sheer cliffs of Ronaldsay island's coast. H.M.S. Narborough met the same fate and was found a small distance away. Except for the sole survivor, Gunner Sissons of the Narborough, the whole of the two ships companies, 188 sailors, were lost to the sea.

The Craven Herald published the following accounts of Christopher's final voyage on the 1st of February 1918

GARGRAVE YOUTH DROWNED BY THE WRECK OF H.M.S. 'OPAL'

Able Seaman Christopher (Kit) Wane, son of Mrs. Wane, Marton Road, Gargrave, met with a watery grave when H.M.S. 'Opal' was wrecked during a fierce gale and snowstorm in a heavy sea off the Scottish coast on January 12th.

Joining the Navy on June 7th 1915, he was in the Jutland Battle on June 1st 1916 with the 12th Destroyer Flotilla. On June 3rd 1916, told to escort H.M.S. 'Hampshire', they had to turn back owing to rough weather, then returned to the scene of the disaster and picked up several bodies. On July 1st 1917, he was promoted to A.B. and was home on leave from December 13th to 24th last. Prior to joining the Navy he worked for the New Brighton Saw Mills Company Limited, and at Holden's Weaving Shed, Skipton, and was a member of the 'Pride of Gargrave' Lodge of Oddfellows. He was a steady and particularly bright lad and well known in both Gargrave and Skipton Football circles. He was aged 22 years.

On Sunday night the Vicar referred to the sad event from the pulpit, and the organist played a solemn Adagio from Beethoven. His older brother Richard is now serving on H.M.S. 'Royal Sovereign.'

Christopher Wane is remembered on panel 9 of the Portsmouth Naval Memorial. His name is inscribed on Gargrave's Roll of Honour and Gargrave War Memorial.

Portsmouth Naval Memorial
Photograph by Ray Jones 2014

5TH FEBRUARY

Hebden Walker
"Craven's Part in the Great War" -
Clayton 1919

235533 Private Hebden Walker

Alexandra, Princess of Wales Own (Yorkshire Regiment)
7th (Service) Battalion
17th (Northern) Division

Born in 1889 at 21 River Place, Gargrave Hebden was the son of Edwin and Elizabeth Walker. It appears that Hebden was named after his uncle, Hebden Walker, who lived on South Street, Gargrave. The family remained at River Place from the Census of 1891, until the 1911 Census showing no change in the family of mother Elizabeth, father Edwin, Hebden now 21 and the younger brother James twenty years of age. Hebden's work is described as a "Stripper and Grinder" in the card room of the local cotton factory. James was a "Mule Room Piecer" while their father, William was the "Card Room Overlooker". The family eventually moved to Earby where Hebden was employed as a weaver with J Birley Ltd.

In September 1917, Hebden enlisted with the Durham Light Infantry as 350905 Private Walker. He was soon to be transferred to the 7th (Service) Battalion of The Green Howards (Alexandra, Princess of Wales Own Yorkshire Regiment), as Private 235,533 Private Walker.

The 7th (Service) Battalion was formed as part of Kitchener's Second New Army (K2) in September 1914 at Richmond. After moving a number of times in the United Kingdom, the unit was mobilised for action in July 1915 and sent to the Western Front to take part in many battles during the time of landing at Boulogne and 1916 when Hebden joined the unit in France. In February 1918, Hebden suffered a toe injury which became infected leading to "septic poisoning" now generally termed sepsis or septicaemia. Sepsis can cause the immune system to react severely and affect the entire body. He was admitted to Number 16 General Hospital at Le Treport. No 16 General Hospital has been recorded as being in operation in Le Treport from January 1915 until February 1919, however other sources state the unit was taken over by the United States Army in June 1917.

The diagnosis of pneumonia as the cause of Hebden's death is entirely in keeping with the effects of sepsis as it can cause severe problems in breathing.

The Craven Herald published news of Hebden's death on the 15th February 1918

"EARBY SOLDIER'S DEATH FROM PNEUMONIA

Private Hebden Walker, P.O.W.'s Yorkshire Regiment, as being due to pneumonia following an attack of septic poisoning in the toe. Deceased, who was 29 years of age and single, was the eldest son of Mr. and Mrs. Edwin Walker, 37, Longroyd Road, Earby, and late of Gargrave. He was admitted to hospital about a fortnight prior to his death, and a few days later the parents received a telegram stating that he was dangerously ill with pneumonia. Private Walker joined up in September last. In civil life he was a weaver employed at Messrs A. J. Birley Ltd., a member of the Rechabites, and a well-known fancier and member of the National Homing Society. His brother, Sergt. James Walker (Military Medallist), only recently returned from furlough after three years in France, and is now serving as instructor in signalling with the Army in Italy."

He is buried in the Mont Huon Military Cemetery, Le Treport Plot VI, Row E, Grave 10A. He is remembered on the Earby and Gargrave War memorials, and his name is included on the Gargrave Wesleyan Chapel Bronze memorial plaque.

Mount Hue=on Military Cemetery
Photograph by Ray Jones 2014

11TH APRIL

William Gilbert Briggs
"Craven's Part in the Great War" -
Clayton 1919

265610 Private (Signaller) William Gilbert Briggs

Duke of Wellington's (West Riding Regiment)
1/6th Battalion
49th (West Riding) Division

William Gilbert was born in Gargrave in 1896 to William and Phyllis Briggs. The second child of the family, named Phyllis after her mother, was two years older than William Gilbert. The next addition to the family born in 1899 was Dora. Olive arrived in 1900 with Constance the last to join the family in 1902. The family lived in accommodation provided by William senior's employers at Eshton Hall where he was employed as an estate joiner,

Prior to enlisting with the West Riding Regiment, William was working at Eshton Hall maintaining the private electrical system which provided the power for the Hall and ancillary buildings.

After enlistment, William was sent with his regiment to the Western Front. His unit was eventually involved with the Battle of Messines. This Battle included the target of Bogaert Farm on the 10th of April 1918. The German 6th Army commenced their attack on the British positions on the 9th of April. On 11th April, during these fierce battles, William's life was cut short by a German missile, probably an artillery shell, described as a bomb in the Craven Herald article published on 26 April 1918.

"Signaller William Briggs, Skipton

Another Skipton Territorial to lay down his life for the great cause is Signaller William Briggs, only son of Mr. and Mrs. Wm. Briggs, of 8 High Street, Skipton. In a letter to the bereaved parents a pal says that Signaller Briggs was in a trench on April 18th with his Sergeant and Corporal when a bomb fell in the midst of them and killed deceased and the Sergeant. Formerly in charge of the electric installation at Eshton Hall, Gargrave, Signaller Briggs, who was 22 years of age, was mobilised with the local Territorials at the outbreak of war, and had been at the Front three years. He was on leave quite recently. Deceased's senior N.C.O. writes:- "He was one of our best men and the loss of so good a signaller will take a long time to replace."

He is commemorated on the Tyne Cot Memorial, Zonnebeke, West-Vlaanderen, Belgium, Skipton War Memorial, Holy Trinity Church Skipton memorial plaques, Gargrave War Memorial, Gargrave Roll of Honour and Gargrave Wesleyan Chapel Memorial Plaque.

William Briggs' name is marked above on this Tyne Cot Memorial tablet.
Photograph by Ray Jones 2014

27TH MAY

Joseph Hird
"Craven's Part in the Great War" -
Clayton 1919

13548 L/Corporal Joseph Hird M.M.

8th Border Regiment
8th (Service) Battalion
25th Division

Joseph Hird was born at Hollinghow, Eskdale, Cumbria in 1883 to a farming family headed by William Hird and his wife, Esther. The family at the time of the 1891 Census showed William and Esther with five children; Elizabeth aged eight, Joseph 6, Hannah 6, Henry 3 and Mary aged two. There were also three live-in Servants; George High, Henry Youdell and Elizabeth Cook. The 1901 Census shows the family had grown to include Sharpe aged 9, Eleanor 8, John 5 and William aged three years. No servants were listed as living in. Joseph married Jane Sharpe on the 17th of March 1908 and moved from the family home to Randlehow, Eskdale where they had two children, Margery and William Sharpe. Father in law Richardson Sharpe, a retired farmer, was living with the family at the time of the 1911 Census. Joseph eventually moved with his family to Gargrave as landlord of the Swan Inn.

Joseph enlisted with the 8th Border Regiment 8th (Service) Battalion which was raised in September 1914. His unit was sent to France on the 26th of September 1915. By the 30th September, the Division was fully assembled in the region of Nieppe. Over the next three years, Joseph was to see several Battles of Somme in 1916 including, Albert, Bezantin Ridge, Pozieres Ridge and several other minor skirmishes. During 1917 he would have taken part in the Battle of Messines and the Battle of Ypres and in the final year of the War, the battles of St. Quentin, Bapaume, Estaires, Messines, Bailleul, Battles of the Lys and his last involvement in the war, during the Battles of the Aisne.

It was on the first day of this Battle that Joseph was hit by machine-gun fire while attempting to bring casualties from the German artillery bombardment to safety. He was struck in the head and died instantly.

The Craven Herald published the following report on the 14th of June 1918

"Mr. Joseph Hird, Gargrave

Last weekend Mrs. Hird, of the Swan Hotel, Gargrave, received news that her husband, a stretcher-bearer, had been killed when assisting in removing a wounded comrade on May 27th. Mr. Hird, a native of Eskdale, in Cumberland, was thirty-five years of age and joined up about three years ago. His brother, John, was serving along with him at the time, and in a letter says:– "He had just got on the top to help to bring in one of our men who had been wounded when a German machine gun opened out, and a bullet hit him in the head and killed him instantly. He never spoke a word."

His body was buried close to where he fell in ground now occupied by the enemy. The Vicar very feelingly referred to his death in his Sunday evening sermon, and Mr. Burland played the Dead March in Saul on the organ, the congregation standing meanwhile."

Joseph is remembered on the Soissons Memorial and the War Memorial at Eskdale Cumbria and Gargrave, Yorkshire. His name is included in the Roll of Honour displayed in St. Andrew's Church, Gargrave.

Soissons Memorial, Aisne, France.
Photograph by Ray Jones 2014

29TH MAY

Ben Roper

205167 Private Ben Roper

Duke of Wellington's (West Riding Regiment)
1/7th Battalion
147th Brigade of the 49th Division

On the 22 December 1883, Ben Roper was born in Leeds to Joseph and Elizabeth Roper. In 1891, Elizabeth, now a widow, was living with her family in East Street in Gargrave. In July 1891, records show that Elizabeth sadly passed away and now rests in St. Andrew's Churchyard. The children moved to live with their grandmother, Beatrice Carr, at 28 River Place Gargrave. The 1901 census return for Gargrave shows the family still living at River Place. Ben was now 17 and working in the Cardroom at Low Mill in Gargrave. By 1911, Ben had moved to Wennington in Lancashire and was working for a local farmer, Edward Atkinson. In 1912 he married Lilly Pawson (née Hodkinson).

Ben enlisted in Halifax with the 1/7th Battalion of the West Riding Regiment, a Territorial Force unit, which was initially based at Milnsbridge, now a district of Huddersfield. After several moves, his unit was to engage with the enemy during the Third Battle of the Aisne, also known as Operation Blücher-Yorck. The Third Battle of the Aisne commenced on the 27th of May and stretched along a line from Soissons and Reims. In this region, the line were weak and had not been fortified leaving the troops more vulnerable to attack. The German 'Feuerwalze' or Fire Dance, a creeping barrage of artillery fire, travelled with ruthless efficiency through the exhausted defenders. Losses during the duration of the fight amounted to *one hundred and thirty-seven thousand* allied troops. Despite the inadequacy of the defences, the German armed forces casualty numbers were not far behind at 130,000. Ben was one of the many men that died here.

He is remembered on the Tyne Cot Memorial Panel and the Gargrave Methodist Chapel Roll of Honour now on display in St. Andrew's Church, Gargrave.

18TH JULY

George Harrison Mason
"Craven's Part in the Great War" -
Clayton 1919

476530 Sapper George Harrison Mason

Corps of Royal Engineers
461 Field Coy
62nd (2/West Riding) Division

George Harrison Mason, born in Gargrave on the 10th of April 1894, was the son of William Luthwaite, a plumber by trade and his wife, Elizabeth. William was born at Skipton, Yorkshire and Elizabeth at Barrow-in-Furness, Lancashire. The family were initially from Skipton moving to Gargrave in late 1893 or early 1894. They stayed in Gargrave for about ten years living on High Street. Around 1895 the family returned to Skipton to take up residence at 51, Castle Street. In 1910 George's father passed away at the age of 43 Elizabeth Mason eventually married Richard N. Myers in 1914. George himself married Florence Ada Hartle two years later in 1916.

George first joined the Territorial Force of the Royal Engineers as (T) 3417 Sapper George H. Mason he was temporarily transferred to the Royal Artillery with the service number of (T) 1480. Finally, he was returned to the main force of the Royal Engineers and allocated the service number 476530 and rank of Sapper. As a member of the Territorial Force George would have agreed to serve overseas and signed the "Imperial Service Obligation" form.

It is most likely that George was with one of the Royal Engineer tunnelling companies, nicknamed "the Moles". These companies specialised in the construction of tunnels under enemy lines to enable troops to move forward to an attack position in secrecy and to facilitate laying explosive charges beneath enemy positions. The Royal Engineers also designed, and built, frontline fortifications in addition to developing defences against chemical and subterranean warfare. It was during his duties that he suffered an injury which necessitated amputation of a leg. He never recovered and died in one of the ten military hospitals at Rouen.

George is commemorated on the Skipton War Memorial. His grave can be found at Block Q. Plot II. Row B. Grave 3. in the St Sever Cemetery Extension, Rouen.

27TH JULY

Bruce Bradley
"Craven's Part in the Great War" -
Clayton 1919

Trimmer Bruce Bradley,

H.M.H.S. Llandovery Castle

Born at South Street, Gargrave on 20th October 1881, to John and Margaret Ann Bradley, née McKell. John, a woodman by occupation, was born at Thornton in-Craven and Margaret at Gargrave. The family, living in South Street, Gargrave, was a large one. Bruce was the youngest of a family of eight children. Edward, 21 and the eldest was working as a Roller Coverer in the local cotton factory, probably Airebank Mill, Robert aged 19 was a cotton mule spinner, Isabella 16 was employed as a cotton reeler, George at 11 was a part-time cotton doffer and part-time scholar, Wallace aged 2, was at home with three-month-old Bruce to keep him company. Bruce's father died in 1885, leaving his wife, Margaret, a widow. The 1901 census finds Bruce boarding with his married brother, George, in Hellifield at 7 Thorndale Street. Bruce eventually moved to Burnley and for many years lived with his sister at 2 Layfield Street in Burnley Lancashire.

Bruce joined the Merchant Navy Fleet as a Trimmer. The trimmers were members of the 'down-below' team of workers known by other crewmen as "The Black Gang", working in the boiler room. They had the most physically demanding job, working in temperatures of 100 degrees plus Fahrenheit (about 40 degrees plus Celsius). The name trimmer seems to have come from the fact that they needed to keep the piles of coal, both in the bunkers and within reach of the firemen, evenly adjusted so that the ship remained on an even 'trim'. The boiler rooms were the most vulnerable in a torpedo attack and very seldom could the stokers and trimmers escape alive. Even if they did, they would be wearing minimal clothing and would freeze to death very quickly in the cold North Sea. Bruce's Merchant navy career lasted for 9 years, during which time he had seen the ships he was working on suffer from submarine torpedo attacks thrice.

He eventually was allocated to the Llandovery Castle, a former Union Castle liner, which was re-commissioned as a hospital ship on the 26th July 1916 and assigned to the Canadian Armed Forces. There was a medical staff of 102 in addition to the usual ship's crew. For two years H.M.H.S. Llandovery Castle carried out her work of carrying the wounded and sick to safety, until July 1918 when the unthinkable happened, a torpedo attack on a registered hospital ship.

Bruce Bradley was recorded as lost in the sinking of the Hospital Ship, S.S. Llandovery Castle on 27th July 1918. This ship was sunk by a German U boat (U 86), Captained by Lieutenant Helmut Patzig, 116 miles W of Fastnet (Ireland); 234 were drowned/shot, and only 24 survived in one of the most infamous maritime incidents of the war. It is more than likely Bruce died in the bowels of the vessel and was spared witnessing the events that followed.

U boat U 86
Public Domain

The ship was internationally registered as a hospital ship which meant that under Maritime Law it should have been immune from attack. It was carrying all the required items of a hospital ship when it sailed from Halifax, Nova Scotia for Europe with many doctors and nurses of the C.A.M.C. (Canadian Army Medical Corps) on board. The German U-boat commander, Patzig, knew that the Llandovery Castle was a hospital ship and had been shadowing it for some time. He attacked it with torpedoes, against orders from his own High Command. In records from the subsequent trial in Leipzig, survivors reported that the submarine came alongside the lifeboat of the ship's Captain. Captain Sylvester, who was accused by Patzig of carrying ammunition and US soldiers, clearly denied both these accusations. Before the U-boat moved away from the lifeboat, a German officer told Captain Sylvester to "Get away quickly" which he did. Captain Sylvester had been the last to leave the stricken ship and had managed to get all possible survivors into the lifeboats. He moved away, and survivors saw the U Boat swing around again and then start machine-gunning the lifeboats full of doctors, nurses and other survivors.

Only the captain's lifeboat survived with 24 souls on board; all the other people on the ship were murdered.

The German authorities obviously felt that the actions of the Captain and Officers on U 86 were unacceptable and manifestly contrary to international law as they had been duly notified that the Llandovery Castle was a hospital ship. Accordingly, they handed over the Captain, Patzig and the two officers who were on deck when the boats were attacked. Patzig disappeared before he could stand trial, the other two were tried and found guilty of murder and sentenced to 4 years. They both allegedly "escaped" before the end of their sentences.

It was established in the Leipzig trial that despite orders, Patzig decided to sink the Hospital Ship and that he and the officers decided to cover up the crime by killing all survivors, several German witnesses confirmed this.

Although branded a war criminal, when the Second World War broke out Patzig offered his service again. Patzig was on the staff of BdU "Befehlshaber der Unterseeboote" (Commander of Submarines) from February to June 1940 until he took command of the former Dutch boat UD 4 on 28 Jan 1941. He commanded that boat, but carried out no patrols, until 15 Oct 1941 when he again served in staff positions until retirement on 3 May 1945.

News of the attack reached Bruce's sister who was informed that her brother was missing in action in July 1918. On the 17 August 1918, the following article was published in the Burnley Express

> "*VICTIM OF HUN PIRATES*
>
> *Mrs. Ireland, of 2, Layfield-street, Burnley, has just been officially notified that her brother, Fireman Bruce Bradley is now presumed dead as the result of enemy action on the night of June 27th while serving on "Llandovery Castle." He had previously been reported missing in July last. The unfortunate sailor had served for over nine years on the sea, and on three previous occasions the different vessels had been torpedoed. Previous to joining the "Llandovery Castle" he served on the "Orita." Fireman Bradley was 37 years of age and a single man. He was a native of Gargrave, but settled many years ago with his sister, Mrs Ireland, in Burnley.*"

The names of the merchant ships lost during the 1914-1918 conflict are recorded in alphabetical order on the walls of the Tower Hill Memorial in London, together with the names of the 12,000 crewmen who perished. Bruce is also remembered on the Burnley Roll of Honour, and the Gargrave War Memorial.

1ST AUGUST

Frank Ayrton
"Craven's Part in the Great War" -
Clayton 1919

62480 Private Frank Ayrton

Kings Own (Yorkshire Light Infantry)
5th Battalion
62nd (2nd West Riding) Division

Frank Ayrton, born at Gargrave in 1899, was the son of John Thomas and Annie Elizabeth Ayrton, née French. John was born at Gargrave and Annie at Embsay, Yorkshire. Frank was born into a family of three. His sister Agnes aged 12, Ethel 8 and brother Hebden 7 made up the rest of the family group. Two years later Ann, his younger sister, was born. At the time the Ayrton family were living at Airebank Terrace in Gargrave.

This was a convenient address for his father's work at Low Mill as a Cotton Mule Spinner.

Prior to enlisting in the Army at Keighley, Frank was employed as a cloth-looker by Mr R. Brooks, Westfield Shed. Frank initially joined the 8th Training Reserve Battalion, a Young Soldier unit. His service number during his period of training was 93785. This was changed to 62480 on completion of training when he was allocated to the King's Own (Yorkshire Light Infantry) 5th Battalion, presumably just after his 18th birthday.

In June 1918, he went to France to join his unit, fighting in the Second Battle of the Marne, one of a number of actions which took place during 1918 to counter the German 'Spring Offensive. He was involved in the Battle of the Tardenois, an action within the Battle of the Marne. On the 20th of July during he was seriously injured, a wound from which he would not recover.

After being treated for his wounds by the Field First Aid unit, Frank was taken to Saint Germain. Here injured British soldiers were hospitalised in a convent that had been turned into a British Military Hospital. His brother, Hebden, who was serving in the Army Service Corps in Italy, managed to gain leave for a compassionate visit to the hospital. He was able to be with Frank for a brief period before the final day.

On the 22nd of August, the Craven Herald published the following article:

"FORMER GARGRAVE SOLDIER DIES OF WOUNDS

Private Frank Ayrton, K.O.Y.L.I. who died at Saint Germain, France, on August 12th, from wounds received on July 20th, was 18 years of age, and the son of Mr. and Mrs. J. T. Ayrton, 163, Gisburn Road, Barnoldswick (formerly of Gargrave). He had only been in France ten weeks. When a report of their son's precarious condition was received by the parents, the latter cabled to another son serving in the A.S.C. in Italy, who obtained facilities for visiting his brother at Saint Germain and was thus enabled to be with him for a couple of days before the end came. Private Ayrton was a particularly bright and promising lad and connected with the Wesleyan Sunday School. Up to the time of his joining the Army he was employed as a cloth-looker by Mr. R. Brooks, Westfield Shed."

Frank lays at rest at the St Germain-Au-Mont-D'or Communal Cemetery Extension. The cemetery is situated 14.5 kilometres north of Lyon to the east of the village of St Germain-Au-Mont-D'or on the Rue du Souvenir. He can be found in Row B Plot 13.

He is remembered on the Gargrave Roll of Honour, and his name is inscribed on the Gargrave and Barnoldswick War Memorials.

St Germain-Au-Mont-D'or Communal Cemetery Extension
Photograph by Ray Jones 2014

30TH AUGUST

William Edward Parrott
John Airton Photography
Private Collection - Barbara Preston

G/44798 Private William Edward Parrott

Duke Of Cambridge's Own (Middlesex Regiment)
1/7th Battalion
56th (1/1st London) Division

Born in Gargrave on 15th June 1884, William Edward Parrott was the son of Benjamin and Elizabeth Parrott. formerly Weatherill, née Hartas. Benjamin was born at Keighley and Elizabeth at Helmsley, Yorkshire. William's half-sister, Mary Elizabeth Weatherill was the mother of Tom Hartas Gill. The Parrott family lived at 30 River Place, Gargrave from around 1883 and are still recorded as living at the same address during the 1911 census.

In 1909, William married Sarah Elizabeth Langstroth and took up residence at 31 River Place, just next door to his father who was now living with his wife Elizabeth and his two youngest children, Sarah, 28 a rover in the cotton mill and Benjamin 23 who worked as a cotton bobbin carrier. Sarah was a cousin of Edward Fawcett, Robert Thompson and John William Ward all originating in Gargrave. Sadly the cousins also lost their lives during the war.

William's military records are incomplete. From the snippets available there is confusion as to the exact units he served with. It appears that he did serve first in the Durham Light Infantry as 351111, or 20886 Private W. E. Parrot followed by a period with the London Regiment as a Private with the service number 45184 and with the Middlesex Regiment as Private G/20886 Parrott.

The 1/7th Battalion Territorial Force of the Middlesex Regiment, Middlesex Brigade. Home Counties Division was initially based at Hornsea from 4th August 1914 until mobilisation between the 5th and 9th of August. In February 1915, they moved to the Western Front, arriving in Le Havre in March. The unit was involved in a great many actions during its period at the front and stayed until the cessation of hostilities on the 11th November 1918. The final action that the unit took part in was the Battle of the Scarpe which raged between the 26th and the 30th of August 1918.

William was killed on Friday, August 30th, 1918 and is interred at H.A.C. Cemetery, Écoust-St. Mein in Plot V, Row H, Grave 24. He is remembered on the Gargrave Wesleyan Chapel memorial plaque in St. Andrew's Church, and his name is inscribed on the Gargrave War memorial.

W.E. Parrott's grave marker at H.A.C. Cemetery
Photograph by Ray Jones 2014

Cemetery, Écoust-St. Mein
Photograph by Ray Jones 2014

2ND SEPTEMBER

Ernest Aldersley
"Craven's Part in the Great War"
Clayton 1919

154978 Private Ernest Aldersley

Machine Gun Corps
No 2 Battalion
2nd Division

Ernest Aldersley, born 1900 at Arncliffe, Yorkshire, was the son of Jeremiah and Rose Aldersley, née Jowett. Jeremiah was born at Gargrave and Rose at Arncliffe, Yorkshire. Ernest was the cousin of Fanny Aldersley, the wife of William Burton. In 1901 the family had moved to Higherland in Gargrave.

Ernest initially enlisted as 298098 Private Aldersley with the Royal Engineers. This changed early in 1918 when the Battalion machine gun sections were transferred to the Machine Gun Corps. Initially, the sections were grouped into Brigade Machine Gun Companies with three companies allocated to each Division together. A fourth Battalion was added to the Divisions at a later stage to form a Machine Gun Battalion. The Battalion then took the number of the Division they had been allocated to. Ernest became 154978 Private Aldersley, No. 2 Battalion (Machine Gun Battalion), 2nd Division.

During the Battle of Vaulx-Vraucourt, Ernest was killed by a shell while in action on the 2nd September 1918. The action in which Ernest lost his life reversed the defeats suffered during the German Spring Offensives in the early months of the last year of the war. Here the Germans had received reinforcements from the Eastern Front after Russia signed a cease-fire. The Germans had forced back the Allies across a wide area of the Western Front with the aim of taking Amiens.

The Germans named this offensive "Operation Michael", and it came within a few miles of Amiens, taking Bapaume and Albert - and almost took Arras. However, the allies struck back, and by late 1918 they had recovered all the German gains. This area was held by British troops, with French and US armies to the south.

On the 20th September 1918, the Craven Herald published this article:

"KILLED ON HIS 19TH BIRTHDAY

The sad news has reached Mr. and Mrs. J. Aldersley, West Street, that their only son, Ernest, was killed by a shell while in action on the 3rd inst. Authentic news through the War Office is not yet to hand, but his pal, Private Charles Goddard, sends the information to his parents in a very sympathetic communication. It appears they were fast friends, having been companions for some time. It was young Aldersley's first baptism of fire, and on his nineteenth birthday. A well-built strapping young fellow, he was, prior to enlisting, a Canal Office clerk and clerk at Delaney's Gargrave quarries. The deep sympathy of the whole parish goes out to his bereaved relatives. At the Parish Church the Dead March was played in his honour on Sunday night after very feeling references to the event by the Vicar at the close of his sermon."

Ernest was laid to rest in Plot II, Row H, Grave 25. Vaux Hill Cemetery. He is remembered in the Gargrave Roll of Honour, and his name is included on the Gargrave Wesleyan Chapel Memorial Plaque, both housed at St. Andrew's Church, Gargrave and his name is inscribed on the Gargrave War Memorial.

Ernest Aldersley's grave marker at Vaux Hill Cemetery
Photograph by Ray Jones 2014

12TH OCTOBER

John Leslie Berry
From "The British Roll of Honour"

Second Lt. John Leslie Berry

6th West Riding (Duke of Wellington's) Regiment
9th (Service) Battalion
17th (Northern) Division

John Leslie Berry was born on 24th October 1897, to Mr and Mrs John Berry of Gargrave Near Skipton.

Before enlisting with the West Riding Regiment, John worked at Messrs. Rose, Hewitt and Co., Broughton Rd. Shed, Skipton. On September 28th, 1914, a month before his seventeenth birthday he joined the 6th West Riding (Duke of Wellington's) Regiment. Following his training and subsequent mobilisation, on June 18th, 1915 he was sent to France. From that date until September 13th, 1917, he was continually in the line.

Although he was engaged in many severe engagements, often finding himself in positions of extreme danger, he escaped injury. During his active service of two-and-a-half years. He showed his capabilities of leadership and was promoted to lance-corporal. In September 1917, he returned to England to train for a commission. He very successfully completed his officer training and on May 27th, 1918, received his commission. The following August he returned to France, joining the 9th Battalion, West Riding Regiment. Sadly, less than two months later, on October 12th 1918, he fell at Neuvilly in the Cambrai sector, while leading his men to the attack in the victorious encounters which led to the capitulation of the German forces and the armistice.

The Craven Herald published the following on 25 October 1918:

> *"MORE SKIPTON SACRIFICES*
>
> *Second-Lieutenant J. Leslie Berry, West Ridings*
>
> *We regret to record the death in action on October 12th of Second Lieutenant J. Leslie Berry, West Riding Regiment, one of the three soldier sons of Mr. and Mr. Berry, 48 Broughton Road, Skipton. This fine young officer enlisted in September 1914, at the age of seventeen, and if he had lived until Thursday of last week he would have had five birthdays in the Army. He went to France in 1915, and after*

two and a half years' active service, at which time he had been promoted to Lance Corporal, he accepted a commission and came to England for the customary training. He returned to the Front about two months ago. For a short time before enlisting he was in the employ of Messrs Rose, Hewitt and Co., Broughton Road Shed. Two brothers are also serving: Gunner William Berry, who is suffering from shell shock, with the Machine Gun Corps, and Edmund in the Air Force.

Mrs. Berry has received the following letter from Lieutenant Colonel Arthur Driver, of Silsden:- "It is my very painful duty to have to inform you that your son was killed on the morning of October 12th, while leading his men to the attack. He is a great loss to the Battalions, for although he had been with us so short a time he was greatly respected by all ranks for his cheerful bearing and great gallantry in action. Please accept our deepest sympathy on behalf of the officers and men of the Battalion in this your very great loss."

John is interred at the Selridge British Cemetery Montay Row I. C. plot 17. His name is inscribed on the Skipton War Memorial.

Selridge British Cemetery Montay
Photograph by Ray Jones 2014

12TH OCTOBER

Richard Wharton
"Craven's Part in the Great War!"
Clayton 1919

12139 Sergeant Richard Wharton

Duke of Wellington's (West Riding Regiment)
9th (Service) Battalion
17th (Northern) Division

Richard was the brother of Percy Wharton who lost his life on the 3rd of September 1916.

His career in the British Armed Forces began when he enlisted with the Duke of Wellington's Regiment in 1914. On the 12th of July 1915, he was mobilised and moved to the Western Front with his Unit. By the 17th of July, the unit had assembled south of St Omer to join the 52nd Brigade in the 17th Northern Division.

The 9th (Service) Battalion was involved in a number of actions between 1915 and 1918, the first being the successful battle to regain Hooge. During 1916, the unit took part in an unsuccessful first attack on the Bluff, a large mound on the south bank of Ypres–Comines Canal near St Eloi south-east of Ypres. In 1917 the Division saw the several of the Battles of Arras including the First and Second Battles of the Scarpe, Action at Roeux, and at Ypres, the First and the Second Battles of Passchendaele. The following year, 1918, the Battles of St Quentin, Bapaume, Albert, Second Battle of Bapaume, Battle of Epehey, Cambrai and finally for Richard, The Pursuit to the Selle.

On the 1st of November 1918 the Craven Herald published the following announcement;

> *"EARBY – A Third Bereavement*
>
> *Sergeant Richard Wharton, Duke of Wellington's Regiment, killed in France on October 12th was the second son lost in the war by Mr. and Mrs. Michael Wharton, 8 George Street, Earby, who have also lost a son-in-law. Sergt. Wharton, who was 27 years of age and unmarried, enlisted immediately after the outbreak of hostilities, and had spent three years and four months on the Western Front. Three other sons and a son-in-law are still in the ranks, one of these (Sergeant Alan Wharton) being in France.*
>
> *Amongst the letters of sympathy received by the bereaved family is one from Second-Lieutenant Honeyman, who writes:– "Sergeant Wharton was our*

company Lewis gun sergeant, and was attached to my platoon. He was a brave soldier, who never shirked his duty - far from it. He was always keen about his work and encouraged many of our young recruits to take a deep interest in Lewis gunnery".

He was buried at Neville."

Sergeant Wharton was formerly employed by Messrs A. J. Birley Ltd., Albion Shed."

Richard's burial place can be found in Plot II, Row D, Grave 3 at the Selridge British Cemetery, Montay. After the armistice eighty-six British Soldiers were moved from Neuvilly British Cemetery and re-interred at Selridge. This may account for 2nd Lt Honeyman's statement above, *"He was buried at Neville"*.

He is remembered on the Gargrave War Memorial, Earby War Memorial and the Earby Conservative Club memorial plaque and Roll of Honour.

17th November

William Richardson
Private Collection - Barbara Preston

67044 Gunner William Richardson

Royal Garrison Artillery

Born in Liverpool in 1894, to George and Rose Ann Richardson. Both parents were born in County Cavan in Ireland. The 1901 Census shows the family living in Wenning View, Bentham. The family moved again between the 1901 and 1911 census, following the availability of work to Carleton, near Skipton where father George worked for the Rural District Council, and William found employment as a farm labourer.

William enlisted with the Royal Garrison Artillery on the 9th of November 1915 followed by his attestation at Dover Castle on the 10th of November 1915.

William married Minnie Preston of Carleton, near Skipton on the 26th of January 1916.

The marriage was reported in the Craven Herald on the 1st of February 1916

> *"CARLETON-IN-CRAVEN – MILITARY WEDDING*
>
> *A pretty wedding was solemnised at the Parish Church on Wednesday afternoon, (26th January 1916) the contracting parties being Miss Minnie Preston, fifth daughter of Mr. and Mrs. Preston, Aire View, and Pte. William Richardson, of the R.G.A. stationed at Dover. The bride who was given away by her father, was neatly attired in a gown of white silk voile and carried a bouquet of white chrysanthemums. She was attended by Miss Richardson as bridesmaid. Mr. Frederick White, of Elslack, acted as best man."*

The young couple set up home at Trees Cottages, Gargrave.

William returned to his unit, and on the 30th of April 1916, he was mobilised and sent from Soton (Southampton) with the 7th Anti-Aircraft Battery to Le Havre reaching the unit's destination on the 1st of May 1916. William stayed with the British Expeditionary Force moving between artillery units until April 1918 when he was repatriated suffering from multiple wounds to be admitted to Edmonton Military Hospital on the 7th of April. He stayed as a patient until the 10th of June 1918 and was discharged and given three weeks furlough.

He then went on to serve with The R.G.A. Crosby Battery also known as Fort Crosby. This unit was part of a coastal defence system intended to provide protection for the port of Liverpool. It appears that he had a brief period at the Seaforth Battery, at a site now occupied by Seaforth Dock, not too distant from Crosby Fort. William stayed with this unit until struck down by pneumonia. He was admitted to the nearby Seaforth Hospital on Beach Road before being transferred to the British Red Cross Auxiliary Hospital, Windy Knowe, at Blundellsands, Liverpool which dealt exclusively with acute medical cases from Seaforth Hospital. He succumbed to the illness on the 17th of November 1918.

The Craven Herald published the following reports about William's passing;

22 November 1918

> "RICHARDSON – Sunday, November 17th, of pneumonia, at Windy Knowe Military Hospital, Blundell Sands, Liverpool, late of Royal Garrison Artillery, attached to Anti-Aircraft Gun Section, Gunner W. Richardson, the beloved husband of M. Richardson, South Street, Gargrave, and second son of George and Rose Ann Richardson, Coniston Cold, aged 25 years. Interred at Gargrave Parish Church today (Friday) at 2 p.m."

29 November 1918

> "GARGRAVE – DEATH OF GUNNER WM. RICHARDSON, R.G.A.
>
> This soldier, whose death appeared in our last week's obituary notices, was attached for over two years to the Anti-Air Gun Section in France. A telegram that he was seriously ill at the Seaforth Military Hospital reached his parents, but it was found, however, that he had been transferred to Blundell Sands Military hospital, suffering from pneumonia to which he succumbed, aged 25 years on November 17th. He joined the Colours in October 1915, went to France in April 1916, and suffered from shell shock. On March 17th 1918, he was seriously wounded in six places, losing a lot of blood. When recovered he went on Home Defence to Crosby Battery, Liverpool. Farm work at Newton Hall, Gargrave, and Knutsford, Cheshire, followed. Contracting a cold, he was sent to hospital where he died. His mortal remains were sent to his home at Gargrave on last Wednesday week, the funeral taking place at the Parish Church last Friday. The coffin had a Union Jack for its pall, a firing party and bearers attended from the Skipton Military Camp. The Rev. A. C. Blunt, vicar, and the Rev. E. T. Birch-Reynardson, of Carleton, officiated, and he was buried with military honours. He was the second son of Mr. and Mrs. Richardson, Coniston Cold. At the Parish Church on Sunday night, the Vicar very appropriately referred to his death, and Mr. E. Burlend played the Dead March at the close of the service."

William's grave is in the grounds of St. Andrew's Church. His name is inscribed on the Gargrave War Memorial, and the Roll of Honour on display in St. Andrew's Church.

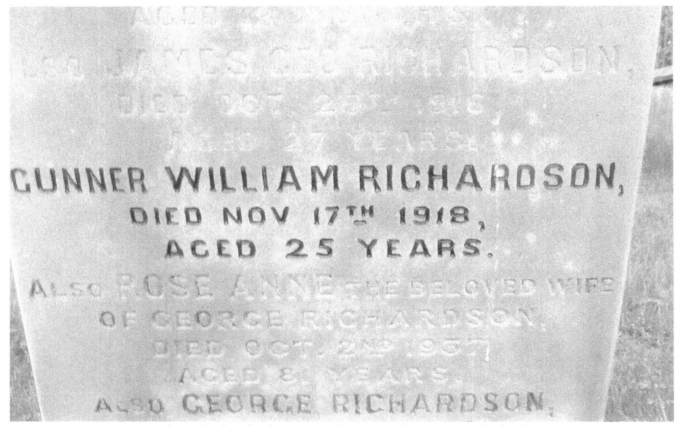

The Richardson family grave marker with Willam's name highlighted.
Photograph by Martin Thompson 2019

4TH DECEMBER

Thomas Asquith Gill
"Craven's Part in the Great War'"
Clayton 1919

108802 Driver Thomas Asquith Gill

Royal Garrison Artillery
121st Heavy Battery

Born on the 5th of August 1892, Thomas Asquith was the son of Luke and Annie Gill of Church Street Gargrave. Luke was a self-employed butcher and soon moved to larger premises at Bridge House Gargrave. The 1911 census shows the family living at this address. Thomas now 18, is working for his father as an assistant.

Thomas enlisted with the Royal Garrison Artillery being placed with the 121st Heavy Battery. As the term implies, Heavy Batteries dealt with heavy guns such as Howitzer and 60 pounders, firing 5-inch explosive shells over several miles. Because of their size, they needed stable ground and were usually positioned well away from the front line. More heavy weapons were introduced during the later years of the war with Railway Guns coming into use. These vast machines could send 9.2 inch, 12 inch and 14 inch rounds with exceptional accuracy up to 29 kilometres/18 miles away.

During his tour of duty in Belgium, Thomas contracted bronchial pneumonia and was admitted to a Casualty Clearing Station in Namur where he succumbed on the 4th of December 1918.

The Craven Herald published news of his death on the 20th December 1918

GARGRAVE – DRIVER TOM GILL, R.G.A.

Another Gargrave youth, whose photo we produce here, has to be added to the Craven Roll of Honour. Mrs. L. Gill, Bridge House, has received news from the Rev. T. Gordon Sharpe, Chaplain to the Forces at Namur, that her elder son, Tom, succumbed in hospital to a severe attack of pneumonia on Wednesday, November 6th, after two years' service as a driver in The R.G.A. The Chaplain says:– "Everything possible was done for him, and he received the very best of treatment. He was interred in the cemetery at Namur."

Mrs. Gill has a younger son, Leonard, serving in East Africa. Much sympathy is felt for this great blow to the family coming so soon after the death of his father. Deceased was a member of the Gargrave Rechabite Tent, and a memorial service was held and the 'Last Post' bugled on Sunday night at the Wesleyan Chapel, and the Vicar also referred to his death at the Parish Church. He was highly respected.

He is buried in Belgrade Cemetery on the Chaussee De Waterloo in the commune of St Servais to the west of Namur in Belgium. He lies in Plot IV, Row A, Grave 2. Thomas is remembered on the Gargrave War Memorial, the Gargrave Roll of Honour and the Gargrave Wesleyan Chapel memorial plaque on display in St. Andrew's Church, Gargrave.

1919

13TH FEBRUARY

Harry Gregson
"Craven's Part in the Great War"
Clayton 1919

293148 Air Mechanic 2nd Class Harry Gregson

Royal Air Force
1st Aircraft Depot

Harry Gregson, son of Bernard Crook and Mary Eliza Gregson, née Smith, was born in 1881 at Colne Lancashire. Harry's father, Bernard was living at Manningham near Bradford at the time. Mary and her three children, John William Smith-Gregson 5, Elizabeth Annie Gregson 2 and Harry just one month old, were living in a large double fronted at 75 Albert Road Colne with Mary's mother, Maria Smith.

Bernard Crook Gregson, Harry's father, was added to the 1891 Census as the son-in-law of Maria Smith. The family stayed at this address until the beginning of the 1900s with Bernard becoming head of the household. In the 1911 Census, the family is shown at a nine-roomed house 'Ash Mount' in Colne. There is no Ash Mount listed in Colne, but the house at 75 Albert Road is now the Ashville Guest House.

Harry, who worked as a Coach and Motor Body Builder in civilian life, enlisted as a Carpenter with the Royal Air Force on the 6th of September 1918. On the 27th September, he was posted to join the British Expeditionary Force and allocated to Number 4 Aircraft Depot at Guines. He was transferred to the 1st Aircraft Depot Saint-Omer on the 9th November 1918.

The RAF unit at Saint-Omer was a sizeable sprawling unit, at its peak, there were around four and a half thousand craftsmen engaged in maintaining, repairing and rebuilding aircraft and equipment. There were numerous large canvas aircraft hangars, workshops and Nissen huts for accommodation and administrative housing.

It was during his spell of duty at St. Omer that Harry became ill with acute bronchitis. The military medical facilities in and around St. Omer were not equipped to deal with Harry's illness, and so he was transferred to a Military General Hospital in Boulogne-sur-Mer. The illness overcame him on the 13th February 1919. He was interred in Terlincthun British Cemetery, Wimille Plot XIII, Row D. 3.

The Craven Herald published the following account on the 29th of February 1919

> *"GARGRAVE – AIRMAN'S DEATH IN FRANCE*
>
> *We reproduce the photograph of Mr. Harry Gregson (of the Royal Air Force), of Eshton, Gargrave, whose death from bronchitis in France, after a short illness, occurred on the 13th inst., at the age of 38 years. He was a native of Colne, by trade a motor-body builder, and prior to being called up was a member of the Gargrave Platoon of Volunteers. He leaves a widow and four young children residing at Eshton village".*

Harry is remembered on the Earby War Memorial, Gargrave War Memorial and the Roll of Honour on display in St. Andrew's Church, Gargrave.

Terlincthun British Cemetery, Wimille
Photograph by Ray Jones 2014

25TH JULY

Sam Rhodes

652918 Sergeant Sam Rhodes

Labour Corps
319th P.O.W. Coy

Sam Rhodes, born at Gargrave on the 23rd February 1885 was the son of Greenwood Rhodes, a Gargrave man, and Sarah Ann Rhodes, née Varley, originally from Embsay, Yorkshire. The family members who resided at 6, East Street in Gargrave at the time of the 1901 census included Mum, Dad, working as a cotton warper, and Sam aged 16 - a part-time student and postman, together with Sam's older brothers and sisters; Emily a cotton spinner 23, Annie a cotton winder 22, Timothy another cotton spinner 20 and Tom 18 a card room hand.

Sam married Betsy Isobel Lee in Gargrave at the St. Andrew's Church on the 16th of April 1904 and set up home in West Street where they had two additions to their new family; Eveline, born 1905 and Stanley who arrived in 1907. Sam was now a full-time postman.

On the 27th November 1914, while living at High Mill in Gargrave, Sam enlisted as a Territorial Soldier with the 6th Reserve Battalion Duke of Wellington's West Riding Regiment. Although the British Army Service Record for Sam Rhodes exists, it is incomplete with many records damaged or destroyed by fire. The account of his service has been gleaned from available, damaged documents.

Sam remained with the West Riding Regiment until late 1918 climbing through the ranks to be finally appointed as a sergeant. While serving in France on the 16 of April 1918, Sam suffered from a prolonged period of what was initially described as P.U.O. or Pyrexia of Unknown Origin. His illness was accompanied by diarrhoea, vomiting and loss of weight. The illness was eventually diagnosed as Trench Fever, a highly contagious rickettsial disease transmitted by lice, that infested soldiers in the trenches in the First World War. As symptoms of this infection last only a short period the illness is also known as 5-Day Relapsing Fever, the disease is completely incapacitating, and full recovery can take over a month with symptoms periodically recurring. He was treated and sent home to recuperate.

The Craven Herald published the following report on the 3rd of May 1918

"CRAVEN AND THE WAR

GARGRAVE SOLDIER INVALIDED

> *Corpl. Sam Rhodes, Park Place, Gargrave, of the West Riding Regiment, has been invalided to Blighty, suffering from trench fever, and is located at the Western General Hospital, Harpurhey, Manchester."*

Sam was not invalided out of the service, as reported above, but on 'convalescent' leave, and after recovery, went back to his unit in France. On the 13th of October 1918, he was transferred to the Labour Corps for the 'benefit of the Service' and allocated a new personal service number. He was then posted to 319 Prisoner of War Company in Pilsen. His appointment to Sergeant came on the 15th of March 1919 three months before his repatriation home for demobilisation on the 8th of July 1919. It was during his de-mob leave that Sam contracted pneumonia and died due to cardiac arrest on the 26th of July. In all probability, his heart was weakened by his rickettsial infection in April 1918.

The 1st August 1919 saw the following announcement in the Craven Herald;

Courtesy of Martin Thompson

"GARGRAVE – DEATH OF SERGEANT RHODES

In the prime of life, Sergt. Sam Rhodes, of the 2/6th Duke of Wellington's Regiment, died from pneumonia after about a week's illness at his home in Park Place, Gargrave, last Friday. Deceased enlisted in November 1914, and for about three years acted as cook to the troops in France, and lately was a guard at a German prisoner's camp. He had been at home only a short time anticipating demobilisation, when taken ill. Dr Cameron's assiduous attention being unavailing. He was 34 years of age and leaves a widow and two children to mourn his loss. Sergeant Rhodes, prior to joining up, was in the service of the Post Office, and was greatly respected. His remains were interred in the Parish Churchyard on Tuesday afternoon amid many signs of sorrow and regret. Many floral tributes were sent by relatives, friends and neighbours."

Sam is interred at St. Andrew's churchyard, Gargrave and is remembered on the Gargrave War Memorial and the Gargrave Wesleyan Chapel Memorial Plaque.

1921

17TH APRIL

Tom H Gill
Private Collection - Barbara Preston

Gunner Tom Hartas Gill

Royal Field Artillery
4th West Riding Battery

Tom was born on the 31st January 1898 to John William and Mary Elizabeth Gill at Paradise, Gargrave. His father worked at the Paradise Sawmill when Tom was born. He later became a railway plate-layer, and the family moved to River Place and then on to South Street. Tom, 13, the eldest of five children, was in full-time work as a cotton ring spinner doffer. Following available work, the family eventually relocated to Brierfield near Burnley, Lancashire.

The portrait of Tom, shows him wearing the regimental hat badge of the Royal Field Artillery. Unfortunately, at present, there is no military record pertaining to Tom Hartas Gill available to view. However, a Gunner 2041 T Gill from the 4th West Riding Battery of the Royal Field Artillery was listed as "Wounded" on the War Office Casualty List from the 30th of December 1915. It is possible that this record refers to Thomas Hartas Gill, but this has not been confirmed.

Tom was injured in his left leg. The tibia or shin bone was damaged, and the wound became infected due to constant abrasion while carrying out his duties on horseback.

Courtesy of Barbara Preston

He was eventually admitted to Victoria Hospital in Burnley during February 1921 where carcinoma of the bone was discovered at the site of the injury. After a long illness, Tom died at home in Brierfield on the Seventeenth of April 1921 aged 23.

He is remembered on the Gargrave Wesleyan Chapel Combined Roll of Honour and Memorial Plaque which is now on display at St. Andrew's Church. His is buried in St, Andrew's Churchyard.

Gargrave War Memorial
Courtesy of Martin Thompson 2019

THE SURVIVORS

BRAVERY AWARDS

Several Gargrave people who survived the conflict were honoured for their bravery in the war. Three men gained the DSO (Distinguished Service Order), awarded for distinguished service in war, and one received the French Croix de Guerre for heroic actions when facing the enemy.

Four men from Gargrave were awarded the MM (Military Medal). This medal was introduced in 1916 as an award for

'acts of gallantry and devotion to duty under fire'

by non-commissioned members of the armed forces of Great Britain and the Commonwealth countries. Although established in 1916, retrospective application was allowed from 1914.

The Military Meda

The Distinguished Service Order

The Croix de Guerre.

In an earlier chapter, mention was made of some of the soldiers who returned to the village after the war. Men who had previously served in the forces were Archie Armistead, John Gill and Arthur Nicholson. John and Arthur were both awarded the Military Medal and more about them can be found in the following pages.

JOHN GILL

John Gill was awarded the Military Medal on two occasions, giving him the right to wear a Military Medal and Bar. John Thomas Gill was born at 4 East Street, Gargrave in November 1882. His eighteen-year-old mother died in childbirth, so he was brought up by his grandparents, thinking them to be his mother and father. At the age of 16, he discovered the truth about his parents and ran away to join the army. Although his family tried to find him and bring him home, they were too late and he was on a ship to South Africa to fight in the Boer War.

He was demobilised with the rank of Acting Sergeant and fully intended to return as a regular soldier, but an encounter with a young lady changed all that.

John Gill, standing, holding a swagger-stick with a seated colleague.

John Gill, with Kate.
Courtesy of the Dennis French Collection

He met and married Kate Austin, who had come to Gargrave to work as a nanny for the curate's children. At the time of their marriage, John was working as a butcher with his uncle Luke Gill.

At the outbreak of the First World War, Sergeant Gill enlisted in the Duke of Wellington's Regiment and then transferred to the Northumberland Fusiliers for the duration of the war.

John was wounded more than once during his wartime service and suffered as a result of war gas attacks. He was admitted to hospital to recover from his injuries.

In the photo left, we see John in military hospital patients uniform, with Kate and daughter Kathleen. The photograph was possibly taken at the Skipton Military Infirmary on Gargrave Road, formerly the Workhouse and later known as Raikeswood Hospital. It was usual for repatriated wounded soldiers to be hospitalised at establishments near their home.

In August 1918, the 100 Day Offensive was launched, which was the final push that ended the conflict. The Northumberland Fusiliers were involved in the second Battle of Bapaume, attacking German positions along the Albert-Arras railway. It was during these actions that John was recognised for his bravery.

John with Kate and daughter Kathleen at a military hospital. Kathleen is holding onto Daddy's cane.

The commendation on his first Military Medal was for:

"Invaluable service as Company Sergeant-Major in keeping platoons in touch throughout a dense fog in an advance on the railway at Achiet-le-Grand, and in collecting men for an attack on an enemy machine gun, he accompanied men in the attack and by his personal example greatly encouraged the men who were suffering heavy casualties, and by refusing to leave the company although wounded by machine gun fire."

After a break for rest and recovery, the Fusiliers were back in action and for his action on 27 September, John Gill was awarded a second Military Medal. The citation described his actions:

"During the operations east of Havrincourt the company to which he belonged lost all of its officers before arriving at its first objective and Sergeant-Major Gill took command and succeeded in capturing the enemy's position. Here he reorganised the company which had suffered heavily, and continuing the advance, he overcame the enemy position in the sunken road, and trenches had to be cleared before reaching he second objective. In conjunction with a company on his right, the final objective was captured and consolidated. The Warrant Officer's personal example and leadership were a magnificent incentive to those under him and contributed very materially to the success which his company enjoyed."

After the war, John ran the butcher's business from Bridge House and later on from a shop in South Street, after the Co-op had moved to the High Street. He served in the Home Guard in the Second World War and he and Kate retired to Wakefield to live near their daughter. He died there in 1960, aged 77.

JOSEPH BURROW

Joseph Burrow of Garris Farm, Church Street, was awarded the Military Medal for his deeds just ten days before the Armistice. Under fire, in the Battle of Valenciennes, he gallantly rescued a fallen comrade. Gunner Burrow joined the West Lancashire Regiment of the Royal Field Artillery on his 18th birthday in October 1914. Earlier in the war, he was severely wounded at Messines in June 1917. Joseph returned to Gargrave to run the family farm and, in 1945, was sadly killed by a train whilst crossing the railway line between his fields. He was very deaf and didn't hear the train whistle.

ARTHUR NICHOLSON

Another Military Medal holder was Arthur Nicholson, who had worked as the chauffeur for the vicar. Arthur had previously served as a Territorial soldier, enlisting in 1908, although no information can be found about his first stint in the army. He was born in Appleby in 1886 and his family moved to Skipton in about 1890 where his father worked as a tailor. At the outbreak of war, he joined the Green Howards – the commonly used name for Alexandra Princess of Wales' Own Yorkshire Regiment. He and the 5th Battalion left Newcastle for Boulogne in April 1915 and moved to the Ypres Salient.

The Green Howard's gazette of September 1916 lists Sergeant Nicholson as wounded and in the following month's edition he is on the Military Medal awards list. No details can be found of Arthur's deeds, but his regiment was known to be fighting at that time in the region of St Julien, just north east of Ypres. The Craven Herald mentions that he received the MM and that he had been treated for his wounds at hospitals in Huddersfield, Brighouse and Redcar. In November 1916 he was guarding German prisoners of war in South Kensington and by mid-1917 had been transferred to the School of Musketry at Bisley, possibly as an instructor. He stayed there until demobilisation in 1919, after which nothing more is known about him.

FRED FOSTER

Fred Foster, born in Gargrave in 1896 worked for New Brighton Saw Mills before the war, making tree nails. He joined the Royal Field Artillery in 1917 and was awarded the Military Medal, but no further information has yet been found about his deeds.

NORMAN AYRTON ENGLAND

Norman Ayrton England went into the 2/6th Duke of Wellington's Regiment as a Captain, having previously served in the 3rd Duke of Wellington's Volunteer Regiment. His family manufactured worsted cloth at Britannia Mill in Bingley, and after his marriage in 1909, he came to live at Townhead, Gargrave. Together with Godfrey Ermen he helped to train the 6th Duke of Wellington's recruits in Skipton. The regiment sailed to France early in 1917. At some point, Norman transferred to the 8th West Riding Regiment (the Leeds Rifles) and in July 1918 while fighting in the Battle of Tardenois, they led a successful assault on the Montagne de Bligny. Acting Lt Colonel England was awarded the DSO for his part in the action and the entire battalion was awarded the Croix de Guerre by the French government. The translation of the citation in French says:

> "This Battalion d'elite, under the forceful command of Colonel Norman Ayrton England, from July 20th to July 30th, took a brilliant part in the heavy fighting that won us the Vallee de l'Ardre. On July 23rd, having cleared a path through the dense thickets of the Bois de Petit Champ, it captured a vital position despite continuous fire from enemy machine guns. On July 28th, 1918, with magnificent spirit it captured the Montagne de Bligny, strongly defended by enemy forces superior in number, and maintained the position in spite of heavy losses and the desperate efforts of the enemy to regain the ground."

As a civilian, Norman resumed his life running the family business and raising a family with his wife Dorothy at Townhead. In the 1930s he travelled to Buenos Aires on many occasions, probably to buy wool for cloth manufacturing. Norman died in January 1939 as a result of an accident when the car he was driving skidded off an icy road, crashed through a parapet and ended up in a culvert. He was cremated at Bradford, but a memorial service was held for him at St Andrew's.

Mathew Wilson and Robert Wilson

The Wilson family from Eshton Hall also had members that served in the forces. The 4th Baronet, Sir Mathew Richard Henry Wilson and his younger brother Robert Amcotts Wilson both saw action in World War One and were each awarded the Distinguished Service Order (DSO).

OTHER SURVIVORS

Where photos of the survivors are available, these have been included in this chapter, together with short biographies. When war broke out, there was a rush to enlist and many Gargrave lads joined or re-enlisted at this time, including Archie Armistead, William 'Jock' Bannon, John Hogg, William Inman, George William Taylor and John Herbert Weatherill. The original claim by the British Government was that the war would be over by Christmas. This turned out to be false optimism and recruiting carried on. The 1915 batch of recruits included the following lads: James Bradley, Ben Parrott, Mark Sheriff, Fred Slater, Stanley Weatherill, Roland Wilkinson and James Preston.

Courtesy of the Dennis French Collection

This group photo, taken in 1916 or 1917 shows, left to right: George William Taylor, Arthur Langstroth, James Parkinson and James Roland Bradley. They had joined up at various times in the war. George Taylor had enlisted in September 1914, James Bradley in January 1915, James Parkinson in September 1916 and Arthur Langstroth in November 1916.

ARCHIE ARMISTEAD

Courtesy of Dorothy Pighills

Archie Rufus Armistead was born in Gargrave in 1888 to John and Louisa. Archie was the eldest of 16 children, three of whom died in infancy. In the 1911 census, John, Louisa and 12 children were living in a six-room house in Church Lane. By this time, Archie had already enlisted in the Duke of Wellington's 2nd Battalion and was stationed at Tidworth Military Camp in Wiltshire.

He transferred to the Machine Gun Corps in 1915 and spent some or all of the war in India. He was demobilised in 1919 with the rank of Sergeant.

After the war, Archie returned to Gargrave and in 1923, married Clara Langstroth. His occupation at the time of his marriage was given as a horse driver. Later, he worked as a road foreman and was a volunteer air raid warden in the Second World War. Archie died in 1971 and was buried at St Andrew's Church, Gargrave.

WILLIAM (JOCK) BANNON

Jock Bannon was born in Renfrewshire, Scotland in 1894. Both his parents were from Ireland. It is possible that he came to Gargrave just before the outbreak of war, as some Scottish labourers were working on demolishing the old Gargrave House.

He enlisted with the Argyll and Sutherland Highlanders and was deployed in France from May 1915.

Jock was wounded and spent some time in the War Hospital in Skipton. The Workhouse Infirmary was requisitioned in

Courtesy of the Dennis French Collection

1917 for soldiers that were recovering from their wounds. Up to 100 soldiers could be accommodated at any one time.

Jock married a local girl, Mary Elizabeth Bradley just after the war. They lived in South Street. In the 1939 register, Jock's occupation was given as a bricklayer and Mary was described as a dealer in sweets and confectionery. Jock died in 1974 and was buried at St Andrew's Church, Gargrave.

JOHN HOGG

Courtesy of the Dennis French Collection

John was born in Edinburgh in 1891. His father John Thomas Hogg was in the 6th Dragoon Guards and had moved around the country between various barracks. In Canterbury he met and married Charlotte, they then spent time in Leeds and Edinburgh before coming to Gargrave in about 1895. Here they lived at High Mill Cottages and John Snr was a labourer at the Saw Mill.

At the time of the 1911 census, they were living below the Conservative Club, where Charlotte was the caretaker. John Jnr was working as a cotton spinner.

He is recorded on the Gargrave Roll of Honour as serving in the Royal Engineers, but this photo shows him in the dress uniform of the Dragoons.

It is likely that he changed regiments during the war. After demobilisation, he married and moved to Keighley and then ended his days in Leeds.

However, his brother Eric and his sister Norah both made their homes in Gargrave. Eric married Grace Fawcett and Norah married Jerry Aldersley.

WILLIAM INMAN

Courtesy of Barbara Preston

Billy Inman was born and baptised in Gargrave in 1889. His parents were Robert and Sarah (née Hartas). His mother's sister Elizabeth was the grandmother to Tom Hartas Gill (by her first marriage) and mother to Ben and William Parrott by her second marriage. Billy's father died when he was only two years old and Sarah worked as a housekeeper to an older, single lady in order to provide a living for her and Billy. In 1901, Billy was living with his Aunt Elizabeth and the rest of the Parrott family in River Place, listed as an adopted son.

Billy got married at the end of 1910 to Harriet Elizabeth Atkinson, a Gargrave lass. They went to live with Harriet's mother in Keighley where Billy worked as a labourer in a textile mill.

He joined the 3rd King's Own Hussars. This regiment were part of the 4th Cavalry Brigade that spent most of the war fighting in Northern France and Flanders. After the war, Billy and Harriet continued to live in Keighley.

Courtesy of the Dennis French Collection

GEORGE WILLIAM TAYLOR

George's father, Alfred William Taylor was from Bank Newton, but moved around the area to find work as an agricultural labourer. As a result, George was born in Hawes in 1897, but spent his early years at Buttersett, then Langcliffe, before the family relocated to Gargrave just before the war.

He joined the Duke of Wellington's Regiment at the outbreak of war. This photo was probably taken in 1917 and shows that George has three wound stripes on his sleeve. After July 1916, soldiers could wear these for any wounds or gassing received after 4th August 1914.

George spent the rest of his life in Gargrave, working as a labourer / bricklayer.

JOHN HERBERT (JACK) WEATHERILL

Jack was the eldest of four sons born in 1895 to John and Clara Weatherill. Jack and his three younger brothers, Stanley, Henry and Edward would all be involved in the First and Second World Wars. In 1911, the family lived at 11 River Place, Gargrave.

Jack enlisted in the Duke of Wellington's Regiment in 1914 at the age of 19. After initial training, he went on active service to France, but he was wounded and returned to England to recover.

He had earlier been recommended for officer training, so upon recovery was transferred to the Officer Training Corps at Lichfield. On completion of his course, he was commissioned as a 2nd Lieutenant in the 3rd Cheshire Regiment.

In August 1917, Jack joined the Royal Flying Corps and undertook his pilot's training at Thetford, Hounslow and Stamford. He graduated in May 1918 as a qualified pilot, signaller and bomber. The Royal Flying Corps became part of the Royal Air Force in April 1918 and Jack became part of the No 4 Squadron.

Snapshots of Jack Weatherill's Armed Services Career.

Jack the recruit   *Lt. Jack of the Cheshires*   *Pilot Jack of the RAF*

Courtesy of Audrey Weatherill

After further training for reconnaissance work, he was posted to northern France and flew over the battlefields with an observer as a passenger who was spotting artillery and taking aerial photographs. The plane used for this work was the Royal Aircraft Factory RE 8.

After the Armistice, Jack was posted to No 5 Squadron as part of the occupation forces in Germany from March to September 1919, based at Hangelar Aerodrome near Bonn. RAF Rhine was tasked with maintenance and repatriation of aircraft. There was still aerial photography to be carried out and Jack was flying Bristol BF planes around Bonn, Cologne and Düsseldorf.

Jack married his sweetheart Constance Wiles in 1924 and they lived happily together in Gargrave.

Courtesy of Audrey Weatherill

In 1940, he rejoined the services as Group Officer in the Royal Observer Corps for the West Yorkshire and East Lancashire areas.

WILLIAM STANLEY WEATHERILL

Usually known as Stanley, he was the second son of John and Clara and younger brother of Jack. Stanley was born in 1897 and prior to the war worked as a groom. He joined up in November 1915 into the 14th Northumberland Fusiliers.

He married Dorothy Mary Pearce in 1928 and they moved to Grassington, where Stanley died in 1950.

Courtesy of Audrey Weatherill

HARRY WEATHERILL

Courtesy of Audrey Weatherill

Harry was born in Gargrave in 1900, the third son of John and Clara and younger brother of Jack and Stanley. He joined the conflict in May 1918 and worked as a ship's radio officer. One of his jobs was in a Spanish port where he reported on German ships being supplied and refuelled in neutral Spain. He returned to the Merchant Navy Service after the war until 1922.

He married Alice Churchman in 1928 and they lived in North Street. In the 1939 register, Harry's occupation was given as a lime burner's clerk. He was part of the Royal Observer Corps in The Second world War. Harry died in 1983 in Devon.

JAMES ROWLAND BRADLEY

Courtesy of the Dennis French Collection

James was born in South Street, Gargrave in 1897. He was the seventh of ten children. His father Robert worked as a plate-layer on the railway. James was usually called by his middle name, Rowland. Both he and his brother Edward worked at Airebank Mills before joining the Royal Field Artillery.

This photo was taken about two years after he enlisted and appears to show a wound stripe on his left sleeve. He also appears to be wearing riding jodhpurs, so possibly rode the horses that pulled the gun carriages.

His sister, Mary Elizabeth Bradley married Jock Bannon.

BEN PARROTT

Ben was born in Gargrave in 1888 and lived at 30 River Place with his parents Benjamin and Elizabeth. Elizabeth (née Hartas) had previously been married to John Weatherill, so their household in 1891 included five Weatherill children and three young Parrotts. Ben's older brother William was to be one of the war casualties.

According to the 1911 census, Ben, his father and his siblings all worked at Airebank Mills. Later in 1911, Ben married Elizabeth Barker up in Penrith. Their first daughter Ethel was born there and their second daughter Lilian was born in 1913 after they'd moved to Burnley, where he worked as a farm labourer.

Ben Parrott.
Courtesy of Barbara Preston

Ben enlisted into the Royal Field Artillery in February 1915 and served as a driver for the duration of the war.

Elizabeth died in 1919 and Ben remarried – to another Elizabeth. They had three children together and lived at West Marton, then East Marton. After the Second World War, the family relocated to Keighley until Ben's death in 1959.

MARK SHERIFF

Mark was born in 1884 near Huddersfield and came to work in Skipton as a young man, where he met and married Elizabeth Alice Chapman in 1903. They moved around the Craven area and came to Gargrave in about 1913, where their four youngest children were born at Trees Terrace.

Mark joined up at the beginning of 1915 and served in the Northumberland Fusiliers until demobilisation in February 1919. The family lived in one of the 'Homes for Heroes' built at Eshton Flatts for returning servicemen.

Later, he moved to Stanbury, then Halifax and Mark died in Burnley Hospital in 1951.

Courtesy of the Dennis French Collection

FRED SLATER

Fred was born in Gargrave in 1889 and lived in Water Street with his parents Alfred and Elizabeth and siblings Edward and Arabella. Prior to the war, he worked as a cotton spinner at Airebank Mills and then enlisted into the Prince of Wales' Own West Riding Regiment in February 1916. After initial training and home service, he served in France for two years. In July 1918, he was promoted to the rank of Corporal and transferred to the Yorkshire and Lancashire Regiment until he was

Courtesy of the Dennis French Collection

demobilised in September 1919 and placed on the Army reserve list. In 1922, he married Margaret Pearson and settled down in Gargrave.

ROLAND WILKINSON

Courtesy of D Mc Robert

Roland Robert Wilkinson was the grandson of Robert Wilkinson, who founded the New Brighton Saw Mills. His early years were spent at New Brighton, but in 1911, the census records him as living in Windermere and working as an apprentice nurseryman.

Although he initially enlisted in December 1915, it seems that he was not required – possibly due to his slight build and poor eyesight. However, he was recalled in May 1918 and joined the Royal Garrison Artillery and at this point in time, his occupation was a draughtsman. His service record shows that he needed different glasses to correct his eyesight, and he was almost immediately transferred to the East Lancashire Regiment, but posted to Scarborough. Unfortunately, much of his war record in illegible, but it could be that he was seconded to the Royal Navy Wireless Telegraphy Station that monitored the positions of the German warships. After the war, Rowland spent most of his adult life back in Gargrave, living in one of the cottages at New Brighton.

JAMES PRESTON

James was a farmer's son, born in Long Preston in 1899. He went into service at the age of 12 as a groom and farm labourer. Although he was underage, he joined the Lancashire Fusiliers in 1915 and saw action in France and Belgium. He was a skilled marksman and wore the crossed rifles badge on his uniform. His back and legs suffered from shrapnel wounds, from which he recovered, but he had some pieces of shrapnel in his back for the rest of his life.

He married Patty Bradley in 1916 and after the war, they settled in Gargrave and raised a family of three sons and three daughters. During the Second World War, James worked at the Steeton Munition Dump and was also a member of the Gargrave Home Guard.

James lived in Gargrave until his death in 1969

1916 CONSCRIPTION

As insufficient volunteers were coming forward, compulsory enlistment came into force in 1916.

PERCY JOHNSON

Percy Johnson (in uniform), his father (John Thomas Johnson), his sisters and his brother. Ca 1914.
Courtesy of the Dennis French Collection

Percy Johnson was the second of eight children, all born in Gargrave. The family were Wesleyans and lived at Old Hall Fold, at the top of West Street.

Percy's father John Thomas Johnson was originally from Lancashire, but came to Gargrave when his widowed mother (Sarah) married Thomas Burrow Wiseman. The family settled in River Place, where four more children were added to the family. The youngest of John's half-brothers was Richard Wiseman, who was killed in the war.

John married Sarah Garnett (daughter of Jesse Garnett of Gargrave) in 1890 and went on to have eight children. These were Alice, Percy, Sarah Jane, Lily, Eveline, Cicily, Clara and Cyril. Their mother Sarah died in 1910 and some time after the 1911 census (when they were still at Old Hall Fold), the family moved to Wadsworth, near Hebden Bridge.

Percy enlisted in June 1916 into the 4th Battalion (Territorial Force) of the Duke of Wellington's Regiment. The Battalion was at its annual summer training camp at Marske when the war broke out and was recalled to its home base of Halifax. The family group photo was probably taken in 1914, when Percy first joined the army. Percy's war record is in existence, but much of it is illegible. During his service, he met and married Beatrice Durrant, who lived near York. After the war, they settled in Nun Monkton.

JAMES PARKINSON

Courtesy of the Dennis French Collection

James was a Gargrave lad, born in 1898, the fourth of the five children of Richard and Ann. The family lived in Trees Terrace, and James' father Richard worked as a railway plate-layer.

James enlisted in September 1916, three months after his 18th birthday, into the Navy. His ship was HMS Euryalus which was deployed out in the Indian Ocean and Far East.

After demobilisation, James returned to Gargrave and married Minnie Muncaster in 1921. At the time of his marriage, and when their children were born during the 1920s, his occupation was given as a tennis racket stringer. When the New Brighton tennis racket business closed, James and his family moved to Bradford where he found similar work.

Courtesy of the Dennis French Collection

ARTHUR LANGSTROTH

Arthur was born at 7 East Street in 1894. He was the youngest of the six children of Christopher and Elizabeth. His father Kit and older brother Joe were in the church bell-ringing team. He joined the 10th Battalion of the Duke of Wellington's Regiment in November 1916.

Arthur married Grace Harling and they lived in River Place for many years.

In 1917 and 1918, about 35 more men enlisted. The exact number is not known, as the Roll of Honour does not include all Wesleyan and Catholic recruits. These last three are ones where photos have been obtained.

CHARLES ALFRED GILL

Charles came from Ilkley, where he was born in 1888. He came to Flasby before the war to work as a horseman on Richard Swales' farm. When he married Elizabeth Ellen Dobby in 1912, he was working as a railway plate-layer and living in East Street.

Charles enlisted into the Duke of Wellington's Regiment in August 1917. After the war, he returned to Gargrave and spent the rest of his life here, until his death in 1956.

Courtesy of the Dennis French Collection

ROLAND LOFTHOUSE

Roland was born in 1895 into a Wesleyan family. They lived in the cottage next door to the Liberal Club. The family members were:- grandmother Sarah, parents William and Annie, Roland and his sisters Mildred and Norah. In the 1911 census, their occupations showed that William was the chauffeur to Dr Cameron, Roland was a grocer's errand boy, working for the Co-op and his mother and grandmother were both dressmakers.

Courtesy of the Dennis French Collection

At the rear of their cottage is a separate building with a large south-facing window. This may have been used as a workshop, firstly by Roland's great grandfather (one of the village tailors) and then by Sarah and Annie for their dressmaking.

Roland enlisted in September 1917 into the Prince of Wales' Own West Yorkshire Regiment. From his war record, it appears that he spent the war on home service duties. In 1923, he married Charlotte Clarke and they moved away to the Blackpool area where he died in 1943.

DOCTORS AND NURSES

Both the village doctors took short term commissions in the Royal Army Medical Corps. Dr Herbert Wales went in September 1915 to serve in Egypt. On one of his visits home on leave, the Gargrave male voice choir assembled outside Mevell Hall and serenaded his return with a rendition of "When Evening's Twilight Gathers Round". Dr Wales was known for his fine singing voice and participated in many of the village musical events, so this was a most appropriate home-coming.

Dr Alexander Cameron, having looked after the village medical needs in the absence of Dr Wales, then went off to 'do his bit' in 1917 and was posted to East Africa.

Ethel Burlend
Courtesy of the The Burlend family.

ETHEL BURLEND

The Roll of Honour in St Andrew's Church has only one woman on it. This is Ethel Burlend, the daughter of Edward Burlend, the church organist and previously headmaster of the Church School. She was born at Tosside in 1887 and in 1891 the family were living in Long Preston where her father was the school headmaster. They moved to Gargrave in 1900 when Edward took on the job of the head of the National (Church) School. She had two older brothers and a younger sister. Initially they lived in Airebank Terrace and then moved to one of the new houses in Church Street. Ethel trained as a nurse at Leeds and then went to work at Leicester Infirmary. At the outbreak of war, she was working as a theatre sister, she joined the Territorial Force Nursing Service (TFNS) and immediately transferred to the 2nd Northern War Hospital at Leeds.

At the beginning of 1916, Ethel and a group of other nurses were posted to France. She was to serve here until the end of the war, at the military hospitals in the Boulogne and Calais areas and later at casualty clearing stations just behind the battle lines. For her services in the war, she was awarded the British War Medal, the Victory Medal and also an oak leaf emblem for being mentioned in dispatches.

The TFNS uniform was a blue-grey cape with scarlet facings with silver 'T' at each corner. The dress was of blue-grey material the same colour as the cape, with a band of the same material edged with scarlet, worn on the right sleeve six inches above the wrist, to wear on duty in the hospital. White linen collar and cuffs and white muslin cap.

Ethel never married and died in Sussex at the age of 80.

Her brother, Edward Ernest Burlend served as a padre in the war and later became the Rector of Rufford in Gloucestershire.

LIFE AFTER THE WAR

PEACE CELEBRATIONS

Although the Armistice was in November 1918, the official peace celebrations didn't take place until July 1919. An extra bank holiday was declared, there were huge parades in London and communities all over Britain held their own events.

The streets and houses of Gargrave were festooned with flags and bunting, but the most lavish decorations were to be found inside Airebank Mills. John Brindle and his workforce had hung streamers from the machinery and in the card room was a display of pictures of Lord Kitchener, David Lloyd George, Sir David Beatty and Marshal Foch (the Supreme Allied Commander). Underneath was the slogan:

"Don't Worry, Work."

The mill opened its doors to the public so they could have an opportunity to inspect the latest machinery and equipment.

At 11 am, the returned servicemen and the Volunteer Platoon paraded in uniform, headed by Benjamin Walls and the Drum and Bugle band. An open air service was held on Low Green and both the vicar and the Wesleyan minister addressed the throng. In the afternoon, there were sports and athletic competitions, organised by Dusty Rhodes, followed by a 'free meat tea' for children, ex-servicemen and residents over the age of 70. The day was rounded off with a parade, drawing appreciative comments about

> "the gay colouring and crafty devices that had been brought into requisition".

After the euphoria of the peace celebrations, it took time for life to return to some sort of normality. Of course, for those families who had lost their menfolk and for those with life-changing injuries, things would never be the same again.

There was still a lot of war work to be done. Equipment that could be salvaged was brought back from the front, prisoners had to be guarded and an army of occupation was deployed in Germany.

Another huge and difficult undertaking was to exhume the bodies of servicemen from isolated graves and small cemeteries and rebury them in larger official war cemeteries.

This meant that it was well into 1919 before many troops were repatriated. The German prisoners of war in Britain also had to wait to go home.

The War Memorial

In London, a temporary war memorial that had been erected for the peace celebrations was replaced in 1920 by the Cenotaph, designed by Edwin Lutyens, and positioned in Whitehall as a national monument to the fallen. All over the country, cities, towns and villages planned their own memorials.

The Gargrave war memorial in Coronation Square was unveiled by Norman England at a special service on 9 January 1921. At the dedication service, the address was given by the Rev Blunt, vicar of St Andrew's, the lesson was read by Jonathan Dodgson from the Wesleyan Chapel and the last post was played by three boys from the Scouts Band. The money to pay for it had been raised by public subscription, the costs coming to £220. Initially, there were 25 names on the plinth of the memorial, but a further 13 were added soon after. The complete list of names on the war memorial is given in appendix E.

As the volume of traffic increased, the War Memorial was eventually moved from the middle of the road to its present location after Trees Terrace was demolished.

The War Memorial in its original position in The Square
Courtesy of the Dennis French Collection

THE GREAT GARGRAVE SELL-OFF

1919 turned out to be a momentous year in the history of the village. Sir Mathew Richard Henry Wilson, the 4th Baronet, who had succeeded to the title in 1914, was gradually selling off his estates. He had already sold books, furniture, works of art and household goods, and now he started on his property.

All the Eshton Hall Estate properties and farms in and around Gargrave were put up for auction in May 1919. Also included in the sale were the Stainton Cotes estate and the Wilson's Arms at Threshfield.

Images on this page have been scanned from a copy of the original Estate Sale Catalogue.

IN 102 LOTS.   MOSTLY WITH EARLY POSSESSION.

In the Beautiful Craven District
GARGRAVE

Bradford 22 miles.   Leeds 28 miles.   Keighley 12 miles.   Nelson 14 miles.   Skipton 4 miles.

Outlying Portions of the

Eshton Hall Estates
extending to

1,200 ACRES
FREEHOLD and comprising

Paget Hall (253 Acres), Ivy House (30 Acres) and
Well House (43 Acres) Farms.

110 ACRES OF ACCOMMODATION LAND
of First-Class Quality, in Small Lots.

High Lying, Ripe Building Land
Close to Gargrave Station. The Major Portion of the

VILLAGE OF GARGRAVE
with its Principal Houses and their Stabling and Grounds, MEVILLE HALL,
KNOWLES HOUSE, BRIDGE HOLME, GREENHEAD and others.

Twelve Shops & Canal Warehouse, Two Fully-Licensed Hotels
and One Inn, also 170 Smaller Houses and Cottages.

THE STAINTON COTES ESTATE, 734 ACRES
which includes STAINTON COTES HOUSE, a Gentleman's
Tudor Manor House and 435 Acres,
Kelber Farm (167 Acres) and Haughfield Farm (132 Acres),
all Good Grazing Farms; and the

WILSON ARMS HOTEL, Grassington,
a First-Class Modern Fully-Licensed Hotel. The whole producing at Low Rentals

£3,840 per annum

For Sale by Auction by Messrs.

JOHN D. WOOD & Co.
AT THE TOWN HALL, SKIPTON,
On Thursday and Friday, 29th & 30th May, 1919,
At Two p.m. Each Day.

Solicitors: J. H. VANT, Esq., Settle.

Lot 11 (Coloured Red on Plan No. 2).

A Gentleman's Comfortable Residence

known as

"Meville Hall"

HIGH STREET, GARGRAVE,

stone built and slated, and containing: *On the Ground Floor*, Entrance Hall, Dining Room, Morning Room, both with bay windows, Surgery, Consulting Room, Lavatory, Kitchen, Scullery, Larder, etc. *On the First Floor*, Drawing Room (25-ft. by 17-ft.), Five Bed Rooms, Bath Room, etc. *On the Second Floor*, Three Bed Rooms.

The Outbuildings

are also stone built and slated, comprising Barn, Motor House, Stabling, Lofts, etc. There is a Tennis Lawn, a large high walled Kitchen Garden and Croft, the whole extending to

2a. 0r. 24p.

Let to Dr. H. Wales on a yearly tenancy at £61 15s. per annum.

Outgoings:
Tithe apportionment 10s. 5d. Land Tax 1s. 1¼d.

Lot 54 (Coloured Green on Plan No. 2).

Gargrave Sanitary Laundry

A Fine Range of Modern Red Brick and Slated Buildings at present used as a Laundry, but readily

Adaptable to other Commercial Uses.

The Modern Model Laundry contains Covered Loading Entrance, Office, Sorting Room, Large Ironing Room, Wash-house, Private Wash-house, Engine and Boiler House, Living Room, Scullery, Bed Room and Out-offices.

The Stable

has Stalls for two horses, a Loose Box, Van House and Lofts over. The steam engine, boiler and shafting are included in the sale. There is also a capital

Drying Ground.

All is in working order, and let on a yearly tenancy to Miss Sargisson, at a rent, including insurance, of £34 17s., tenant paying rates. Also in a separate building of similar construction

THE BATHS

containing

Hairdresser's Shop.

Three fine clay-enamelled slipper baths and lavatory, at present in hand. The whole extends to about

1r. 15p.

N.B. J. W. Coulthurst, Esq., is equal half owner of Lot 54.

Images on this page have been scanned from a copy of the original Estate Sale Catalogue.

The larger houses were sold individually, and the rows of terraced cottages were sold in blocks.

A Block of
Thirteen Cottages

and back premises and

A Corner Shop

situated in

RIVER PLACE, GARGRAVE.

all stone-built and slated and producing

Per £94 19s. 4d. Annum.

No. 1 contains Parlour, Kitchen, Scullery and Four Bed Rooms.

Nos. 2, 3 and 5 contain Parlour, Kitchen and Three Bed Rooms.

No. 4 is a Corner Shop with Cellar and Room over.

Nos. 6, 7, 8, 9 and 10 contain Living Room, Scullery and Three Bed Rooms.

Nos. 11, 12, 13 and 14 contain Living Room, Scullery and Two Bed Rooms.

SCHEDULE.

No. on Plan.	Occupier.		Rental.		
			£	s.	d.
1	J. Weatherill ...	...	9	2	0
2	Mrs. G. Sewell ...	...	7	7	4
3, 4, 5	S. Reeder ...	...	20	0	0
6	Miss Slater ...	...	6	14	4
7	N. Gray ...	...	7	16	0
8	J. Gray ...	...	7	3	0
9	A. Gray ...	...	6	14	4
10	A. E. Lawson ...	...	6	14	4
11	H. Rhodes ...	...	5	8	4
12	R. Kirkbright ...	...	6	10	0
13	J. Bradley ...	...	6	1	4
14	H. Saunders ...	...	5	8	4
			£94	19	4

Tenants pay rates. All are weekly tenancies, except Nos. 3, 4 and 5, which are half-yearly.

Some properties were bought before the sale day, as Sir Mathew wanted to give tenants a chance to buy their home or proprietors to buy their business premises.

The following took advantage of this offer:

Dr Wales: Mevell Hall for £1,200
Luke Gill: Butcher's shop and residence Church Street £575
Fred Green & Son: Canal warehouse and land £1,475
Mr C. W. Thomas: Bridgeholme £975
Mr J. Aldersley: Three cottages and gardens at Higherland £270

Over the two days of the auction sale, many other properties changed hands – including:

Mr John Brindle: Grouse Hotel £1,700
Frank Hardisty: Two shops on the corner of West St. and High St. £650
Walter Gill & Sons: Bicycle repairing & mechanics shop £140
John Such: Post office, house & garden £500

Paget Hall Farm was bought by the West Riding County Council with the intention that it would be split into smallholdings for the benefit of discharged soldiers and sailors. In fact, this never happened as the rents needed to make the project viable would have been too high. Some parcels of land on Eshton Road were sold to Skipton Rural District Council. These were used to provide eight houses for returning servicemen.

A few properties remained unsold and were retained by the Eshton Hall Estate to be sold at a later date.

For those that couldn't afford to buy their home, this meant a change in landlord, which sometimes caused problems. Mrs Annie Preston, who lived at Park House on High Street, was in danger of eviction. She was a widow in her eighties, living in a big house and the new owners offered her alternative smaller accommodation in Water Street, but she refused to move. She said that the other house was inferior and anyway, Sir Mathew had promised she could stay where she was. The owners took her to court, but because a recent change in legislation had made it harder to evict tenants, Mrs Preston stayed put. She did move out in the end, but maybe due to ill health, as she died a few years later at her son's house on East Street.

HOMES FOR HEROES

Four pairs of semi-detached cottages were built on land in Eshton Road. Each had a big garden, so that the owners could grow plenty of produce on these small holdings. They were allocated to returning servicemen, and the rents were set at 12s a week. Known at Eshton Flatts, the houses were completed in 1921/22.

The much higher rents (£31 a year) were being charged for several reasons. Rents had been frozen during war time to prevent landlords from profiteering when housing was much in demand. The rents on the Eshton properties that were quoted at the time of the 1919 sale would have been set before the war and would have been relatively low. The rent control legislation allowed for quite substantial increases in rents for new houses and the ones at Eshton Flatts had the benefits of huge gardens. They may well have been unaffordable to many of the men for whom they were intended.

The early residents were:

1   John & Ada Aspinall, then John & Elizabeth Birks
2   Fred & Stella Crawford, who stayed until the 1940s
3   John & Ann Lancaster, then Willie & Mary Sharples
4   Robert Chippindale, then James & Hannah Nuttall
5   Mark and Elizabeth Sheriff, until about 1940
6   Isaac and Maud Isherwood, then John Bownass
7   Tristram and Mary Cuthbert, until the 1960s
8   John and Sarah Oselton, until about 1947, then Tristram Cuthbert Jnr

Not all of these families were from Gargrave, which perhaps supports the theory that they were rather expensive. In the 1940s, the houses acquired names, instead of 1 – 8 Eshton Flatts. Number 6 was Heather View, 7 was Burnett Field and 8 was The Elms. Once more homes were built and house numbering was used, the row of cottages became 40 – 54 Eshton Road.

OTHER HOUSE BUILDING

In the early 1920s, more houses were being built. Development started along Skipton Road around the end of Eshton Road. A pair of houses was erected in the High Street, next to Victoria Hall, called Waverley and Kenilworth. In 1925, the first new house in Marton Road was built, as the village started to expand. A new police station was built in Eshton Road in 1926, the former police sergeant's house in the High Street having been part of the Eshton Estate sale.

WORK

NEW BRIGHTON SAW MILLS

This business had kept going during the war. As well as their railway goods, they were making sports equipment, having taken over J H Cleave. By 1918, they had closed the High Mill works and moved all production to the New Brighton site. They were making billiard tables and accessories and tennis and badminton rackets. An article appeared in The Sports Trade Journal of November 1921, describing how the company made their famous Koh-i-Noor brand of tennis rackets. Robert Wilkinson, son of the founder gave the journalist a guided tour of the factory, showing him how the ash tree trunks were sawn into the required components and how the racket heads were bent into shape before being left to dry and season. Assembling the rackets and stringing them with gut was a skilled process. It was claimed that 30,000 tennis rackets a year were being made. The visitor was most impressed by the modern workshops, good electric lighting and the friendly relations between all levels of the workforce. He did fail to mention the company's on-site tennis court and pavilion. No doubt this facility was for quality control and as well as providing some lunch-time recreation.

Tennis racket manufacturing at New Brighton Works ca. 1919.
Courtesy of the Dennis French Collection

These are a couple of pages scanned from the a copy of the firm's catalogue.

The telegram address is still Treenails, Gargrave – keeping the link to the company origins. Unfortunately, the post-war boom didn't last and the Saw Mill closed in 1933.

AIREBANK MILLS

The activities and fortunes of John Brindle's mill didn't get reported in the papers during the war or immediately afterwards, so nothing is known about this phase in the company's history. John retired in 1920, passing the company on to Thomas Openshaw, who had been working as his manager. The business was relaunched as Gargrave Mills (1920) Ltd and to raise capital, shares were sold. In the hope that their jobs would be secure, many of the workers bought shares, but this ultimately proved to be a waste of money, as they lost it all when the mill closed in November 1932. Once again, the village was plunged into despondency, just as it had been after the 1912 fire. However, salvation came from Slough, when Johnson & Johnson arrived in 1934 enabling Gargrave to move on and prosper.

GOFA TYRES

The Gofa Tyre Company moved into Middle Mill in 1920. This mill had originally been known as Low Mill, but in the 20th century, it became known as Middle Mill – probably due to its location on Middle Green. The company had been operating in Skipton since at least 1913 under the ownership of William Carter Platts and his business partners. The tyres had a metal mesh woven into the tread which made them more difficult to puncture. Their advertising slogan was "Go Farthest, Fare Best". They took over the whole of Middle Mill, but the venture was short-lived and went into liquidation in 1924. On the face of it, William Carter Platts was an unlikely tyre manufacturer. He was better known as an author and journalist writing about fishing.

OTHER WORK

Domestic workers were still in demand to help the wealthier families in the area. The railway, quarry, farms and the estates employed a variety of outdoor workers. Skipton Rural District Council had a depot in Gargrave providing labourers to mend roads.

Harry Turner's lorry in Skipton
Courtesy of the Dennis French Collection

The Sanitary Laundry closed its doors soon after the war and the building was taken over as a joinery works by Harry Turner.

Harry Turner's Reliant Works, now the Village Hall.
Courtesy of the Dennis French Collection

He also had a workshop in Skipton and trained and employed many of the village lads. After Clemence Franzee moved out of Story's House, the Turner family went to live there, being conveniently close to the works.

Businesses suffered considerable disruption and stoppages due to the coal strike in 1921. Coal was in short supply and as a result, gas production had to be suspended and the schools were closed due to lack of heating. In the same year, the cotton trade wages dispute also led to closures, making this a difficult year for the village.

TRANSPORT

One big change in the post-war era, was the increase in motoring. The business men, professionals and wealthy of Gargrave had motor cars. Some fell foul of the motoring laws and their misdemeanours and fines appeared in the local press. Burton Chapplow was fined 15s for failing to illuminate the rear number plate on his lorry and Miss Mary Dewhurst of Knowles House was fined £1 for not stopping in a parking place and causing the highway to be obstructed. Even the Rev Blunt was fined 10s for parking his car and obstructing The Grove at Ilkley.

Garages and motor engineering workshops were springing up everywhere to cater for the needs of car sales and maintenance. Walter Gill already ran a bicycle business in Gargrave. They were able to buy their premises in the 1919 estate sale. From then on, they expanded to sell and service motor bikes and cars. A Vulcan 20 HP eight cylinder 4/5 seater private car could be bought from them for £625.

Advertising card fro Walter Gill's business
Courtesy of Stuart Smith

This advertising postcard probably dates from the later 1920s, as the telephone number has now changed to Gargrave 2.

ALBERT BRINDLE,

Holme House, GARGRAVE,

Near SKIPTON.

Motor Engineering and Repairs.

CARS AND MOTOR CYCLES OVERHAULED.

REPAIRS EFFICIENTLY ATTENDED TO.

MOTOR LANDAULETTE FOR WEDDINGS AND PUBLIC HIRE.

TELEPHONE—11 SKIPTON.

Advert from early 1919.

A new contender for a share in Gargrave's motoring trade was Albert Brindle. He was the son of John Brindle, who had taken over the running of Airebank Mills in 1911. Albert joined the Royal Naval Air Service and was deployed at one of the airship stations on the east coast. Before the war, he worked as a stripper and grinder in a cotton mill and would have been maintaining the machinery. In the RNAS he worked as a mechanic and may have become familiar with motor engines at this time.

On his return to Gargrave, he started a motor engineering business at Holme House. The family were living at Endsleigh, but he may have been using one of the barns at Holme House. There was a reason for this location, as his sister Jane was married to Robert, son of Isaac Hitchon who farmed the land around Holme Bridge.

In 1919, Albert's father John bought the Grouse Hotel in the Eshton Estate sale and in the following year relinquished control of Airebank Mills to Thomas Openshaw. They didn't appear to run the Grouse as an inn. All the family moved in – John and his wife Alice, Albert and his wife Emma, and Jane and Robert Hitchon.

J. BRINDLE & SON,

Grouse Hotel Garage, GARGRAVE.

MOTOR ENGINEERING and REPAIRS.

CARS AND MOTOR CYCLES OVERHAULED.

REPAIRS EFFICIENTLY ATTENDED TO.

MOTOR LANDAULETTE FOR WEDDINGS AND PUBLIC HIRE.

28 SEATER CHAR-A-BANC, 1 to 7 days tours.

Bookings at –

CRAVEN MOTOR CO., High Street, SKIPTON.

JOHN SMITH, 11, Water Street, EARBY.

TOM GARNETT, 31, Skipton Road, BARNOLDSWICK.

HARRY McKELL, GARGRAVE.

TELEPHONE; 146, SKIPTON.

Advert from 1920.

The outbuildings were converted to a garage and in 1920 they were advertising repairs and vehicle hire. Incidentally, Albert was renowned as a singer. He appeared in many concerts and was the secretary of the Musical Society.

John Brindle died in 1922. The landaulette was advertised for sale at £460 and the 3-year-old char-a-banc for £650. In 1924 Albert, Emma and their children emigrated to New Zealand, and the business was for sale. It was described as having a showroom for ten cars, oil store, garage, workshop, electric lighting plant and enough land to park 50 cars.

A Norman J. Clark bought the Grouse Garage and ran it for a few years until the Pennine Buses moved in.

BUS SERVICES

As people began to travel further afield for work and leisure, regular bus services started to run. The first in Gargrave was run by Arthur Hull. Arthur Edward "Ted" Hull originally came from Loughborough and before the war was working as a mining student in Mansfield. He joined the Royal Naval Air Service and worked at various bases around the country before coming to Gargrave just after the war with his wife Florence and their first child. They initially lived in a cottage at Holme Bridge, where Albert Brindle had his first motor business. Although this is just speculation, it may be that Arthur and Albert met while in the RNAS, both gaining engineering skills and that Albert suggested that Arthur join him in Gargrave. Perhaps he drove the char-a-banc and the landaulette for the Brindle's firm?

A resident of Gargrave recalled that Arthur had (supposedly) found the chassis of an old Ford Model T in a field, added a flat back to it and started a light haulage company. At first he delivered coal and then ran a regular parcel service to Skipton. In 1921 he added a makeshift cover, installed padded boxes for seats and a ladder and the first passenger service between Gargrave and Skipton was inaugurated. As the route was gaining in popularity, a bus with proper bench seats was bought and because it looked like an orange box, the name stuck. The next vehicle was added to the fleet in 1923.

This was a 14 seater Model T Ford known to the locals as "It'll be reet". Even when the bus was full, he'd say "Get on, it'll be reet". Overloading the bus wasn't always "reet" as in March 1927, he was fined £1 for carrying 56 passengers on a bus licensed for 32.

The family were now living at The Crofts (now Kirk Syke), previously the residence of Dr Cameron, who'd moved to Northampton in 1921. Arthur's parents, Arthur and Annie joined them and two more children were added to the family. They installed an ex-RAF hanger in the yard to use as a bus garage and bought more vehicles. Two later acquisitions were a 26-seater Guildford and an E-Type Dennis 32-seater. Florence also drove the buses and is thought to be the first woman in Yorkshire to hold a Public Service Vehicle Licence.

Arthur Hull and the Dennis bus in Leeds
Courtesy of Sheila Pantin

The timetable from 1926 shows how good the bus service was between Gargrave and Skipton. Late night buses meant that people could go to the cinema in Skipton or to the theatre in Keighley. Early buses were laid on for workers.

The advertising on the reverse of the timetable is interesting, as it shows that with the departure of the Brindle family, the Grouse is again operating as a pub.

Towards the end of 1927, Arthur Hull sold his company to Pennine Motors of Skipton. The proprietors, Arthur Simpson and Jim Windle had been operating on the route between Skipton and Settle for the previous two years. They bought the Grouse Garage and moved some of their fleet to Gargrave in 1928.

A tale attached to Pennine's first bus of the day from Gargrave towards Settle was that it was timed to suit Miss Bertha McKell, to get her to Coniston Cold where she worked as a teacher. Bertha (sister of Harry McKell), was a single lady aged 36 who was living with her parents next door but one to the Post Office. Bertha was to have a long career in teaching.

Although Arthur had stopped running buses, he still lived at The Crofts, but had gone back to running a haulage company. In these years, he suffered several blows. His wife Florence died in 1928, aged only 31. At her funeral, floral tributes were sent from the pupils of the grammar schools, whom she used to drive from Gargrave to Skipton and back.

Hull's Bus Timetable for 1926

A fire in 1929 burnt out the garage at the back of The Crofts, destroying three cars and causing £1000 of damage. Sheila, their younger daughter recalled the terrifying night and how her grandparents took the children across the road to take shelter with neighbours. Another one of her memories was of the hand-operated petrol pump that stood in the yard. The petrol was supplied by Russian Oil Products Ltd at considerably lower prices than from the government controlled companies. This was quite legal, as an Anglo-Russian trade agreement had opened the oil market up to foreign competition.

"Ted" Hull remarried in 1930, moved away from Gargrave and settled in the Immingham area.

Pennine Buses continued to run the bus route from Skipton to Settle for many more years, eventually going out of business in 2014. The Grouse Garage had been closed some years previously, and the site converted to housing.

CHANGES ON THE HIGH STREET

There were few changes to the shops on the High Street in the post-war period. As the tailors and shoe makers retired, there were fewer people carrying on these trades and with better transport, it was easier to get to Skipton to buy clothes.

Gargrave had been without a saddler for about 15 years until the arrival of Harry Howard. Harry was from a family of saddlers in Swaffham, Norfolk. During the war, he'd been a saddler for the Norfolk Yeomanry and had then joined the newly formed RAF. He came to Gargrave to work as a gamekeeper at Flasby Hall and as Captain Preston could only pay him 10s a week, he was allowed to do some saddling in his spare time. Eventually this took all of his time and he opened a shop on the High Street, right on the corner, opposite The Swan. He and his wife Esther lived in the cottage next door and Harry spent many long years as the only saddler in the district, making saddles and harnesses and other leather goods.

At some time in the 1920s, the McKell family expanded their business interests. Harry and May McKell had previously taken over the running of the newsagents on the corner of the High Street and West Street from May's parents, John and Sarah Hyde. Now, they also had a café and newsagents just opposite Victoria Hall at 37 High Street. When Harry died in 1928, his widow May and their son 18-year-old Donald were running both businesses. Kathleen Reeder (Arthur Reeder's daughter) came to work for them and ended up marrying Donald. Eventually they gave up the corner shop and Donald and Kath concentrated on the shop at 37 High Street.

There were now two fish and chip shops – Arthur Jones' at Trees Terrace on Coronation Square and Stephen Reeder's at 4 River Place. Mr and Mrs Lucas had a café and Temperance Tea Bar next door at No 3.

COMMUNICATIONS AND INNOVATIONS

The war effort had halted the growth of new technology, but with the advent of peace, modernisation marched onwards.

TELEPHONES

More phones were being installed in private houses, shops and businesses. As the take-up of phone lines increased in the Craven Area, the Skipton exchange was over-loaded, local telephone exchanges were set up, and the numbering system was revised. Gargrave, Settle, Grassington and other places all had their own phone numbers.

The changeover from Skipton numbers took place in 1925 and the first ones on the Gargrave exchange were:

1	Lionel Dewhurst	Knowles House
2	Walter Gill & Son	Motor engineers
3	J H Preston	Flasby Hall
4	Arthur Hull	Garage, The Crofts, High Street
5	Grouse Hotel	
6	Robert Wilkinson & Sons Ltd	Sports goods & timber, New Brighton
7	Police Station	
8	Post Office and Call Office	Elsie Such, postmistress
9	Sir Mathew Wilson	Eshton Hall
10	Isaac Hitchon	Farmer & cattle dealer, Holme House

The local phone directory was published each year as part of the Craven Household Almanac.

In the Almanac, there is also a mention of a telephone exchange at Park Place and a public phone box at the Post Office.

Gargrave Post Office housed a public phone in the small porch-like structure at the entrance
Courtesy of the Dennis French Collection

POST

The postal system was very much the same as before, but changes to collections and opening hours prompted 'inconvenienced' of Gargrave to write to the Craven Herald.

"The latest time we can post a letter is 5.15 pm – compared to 7.40 before the war. The post office is shut between 12 and 1 and closes all day Tuesday. This closing is a wretched arrangement and leads one to wonder if the convenience of the public is considered at all."

In the following week's edition, postmaster Mr Such explained that the earlier collection time was as a result of the train timetables being changed.

MUSIC

LIST of
NEW MODELS
Season 1919-1920.

ZONOPHONE
Hornless Model
No. 2 (L.W.O.)

IS as fine an instrument of the internal horn type as one could wish for, and is equally suitable for use in drawing-room or garden. In appearance it is handsome and of generous, yet compact proportions.

SPECIFICATION.
English quartered oak, waxed finish, wood internal horn. Nickel-plated fittings. Size 8¾ in. × 17 in. × 17 in. Double-spring motor, 12 in. turntable, plays 10 in. and 12 in. records. Speed regulator. Goose-neck taper-arm, Zonophone sound box.

PRICE £10 10 0

Advert for the Zonophone Player

Gramophones had been around since the turn of the century, but were only bought by the wealthy. After the war, more people were aspiring to keep up with the latest technology.

J. Wood & Sons was a music shop in Skipton High Street that sold instruments, sheet music, records and gramophones. The Zonophone Hornless player was being advertised as the must have equipment for Christmas. For a cost of £10, this could *"Make your home resound with music this festive season"*. The 78 rpm records were priced at 4 shillings for a 10 inch record and 6s 6d for the 12 inch version.

Popular singers of the era were Harry Lauder ("Stop Your Tickling, Jock"), George Formby ("Grandfather's Clock") and Marie Lloyd ("My Old Man Said Follow the Van").

One of the most-recorded British bands of the time was The Black Diamonds. They had a prolific output from 1900 onwards of classical music, military marches, popular songs and dance music.

RADIO

This was a new innovation and after the BBC was founded in 1922, daily radio broadcasts started. A radio licence, that cost 10s, was required and most receiver sets were powered by batteries. The Council School had an aerial fitted in early 1924 and borrowed a receiving set to listen to a music concert from Manchester. In years to come, people would gather round the radio to keep up to date with matters of national importance or just to listen for pleasure.

ELECTRICITY

This modern convenience was slow to arrive in Gargrave and the village still wasn't connected up in 1925. Some buildings generated their own electricity, for example, New Brighton Saw Mill, Middle Mill and Eshton Hall.

Over the years, numerous discussions had taken place, starting before the war with a proposal for a hydroelectric scheme. These resumed in 1920 when Colonel England was asked to get expert advice, but a few months later, the scheme was abandoned due to lack of support. The following year, a committee was formed to consider an electricity supply, but again, nothing happened.

After much prevarication, the village eventually got mains electricity from the early 1930s. The Council School was wired up in 1931, but the Church School had to wait until 1939.

RECREATION

The residents of Gargrave continued to make their own entertainment, with the churches and clubs hosting concerts, plays and lectures. The Victoria Hall was used as a theatre for visiting actors and singers. Messrs Bracking & Turnbull's "Merry, Mirthful Mummers" performed their variety show for three nights just after Christmas 1921. This must have gone down well, as Mr Vaughan Bracking returned a couple of years later with his "Unique Concert Party" of humorous songs and sketches. Local musicians joined in, with Tom Rhodes on the violin, Arthur Reeder providing more comedy and Miss Davis and Miss Gray playing the piano.

The Victoria Hall was the venue for Robert Wilkinson's treat for the New Brighton Saw Mills employees. A report of one of these events said that workers and friends were entertained with songs and sketches, there was dancing to Tom Rhodes' orchestra and that Mrs McKell and Mrs Hardisty won the musical chairs competition.

Sporting activities resumed, with the cricket and football sides playing again. Herbert Gladstone Rhodes was busy organising athletic meetings. He was a renowned runner who had arrived in Gargrave in 1914, as an employee of J H Cleave at High Mill. Herbert, nick-named 'Dusty' started to train the village youth and to organise events. Dusty served in the army, however, he was wounded early on and returned to Gargrave to become a founding member of the Volunteer Platoon and competitor in the inter-platoon sports.

In 1925, Dusty commissioned medals for an athletics competition. These were made by Fattorini's of Bradford and were silver, with an enamelled centre piece with the Gargrave coat of arms.

A cinder track was laid on Low Green for athletic training and events. Traces of it could still be seen many years after it fell out of use. This photograph shown below shows Dusty in full running gear on the cinder track. The houses on the left of the picture are on East Street and the barn on the right has been converted to dwellings.

Dusty Rhodes on Low Green cinder track.

Going to the cinema was now much more convenient, thanks to the bus services running to Skipton. In the early 1920s all the films were silent and the incidental music would be provided by the cinema organist. There were two cinemas in Skipton – The Gem Picture Palace in Sackville Street (now The Plaza) and the Premier Picture Palace in Keighley Road. The Premier eventually closed as a cinema, and the building was taken over in the 1970s by the Co-Op who used it as a supermarket before demolition of the structure and the development of the site to build Sunwin House, a bigger and better Co-Op store. Now the Co-Op has gone and a number of different retail outlets and other ventures occupy the 'new' building.

Education and Welfare

The Schools

Both the village schools improved their performances in the years after the war and more pupils gained scholarships to the Skipton grammar schools. The curriculum was more varied. An increasing importance was put on physical education and time was set aside for drill, games and organised sports. The children were taken out on educational visits to Skipton Castle, Liverpool and Leeds. One group went on a tour around Gofa Tyres, where Mr Carter Platts explained the manufacturing process. The Church School organised trips to London to visit Westminster Abbey, the Tower and Hampton Court. The Council School organised exchange visits with a school near Rotherham. Their children came to Gargrave to be shown around the area and in return, our children spent a weekend with them, visiting a colliery and a steel works.

Although the schools still had to close down for outbreaks of infectious diseases, more care and attention was being given to the health and welfare of the pupils. School doctors, nurses and dentists made regular visits to check on the children. Dr Wales and medical officers from West Riding County Council gave talks to parents and children to improve health education.

Health Care

For adults, medical care could be obtained by subscribing to the Friendly Societies or by just paying for it. The workhouse infirmary (in Skipton) was the last resort for the desperate. People rallied round to help their own in times of need. When James Hargreaves broke his leg playing football, the football club and colleagues at New Brighton Saw Mills raised money to pay for his hospital care. The Oddfellows helped one of their brothers in distress. They bought a three-wheeler bath chair for Brother Herbert Wild, made of wicker, with a waterproof cover and costing £20.

The District Nursing scheme was just about functioning, as it struggled for funding and was sometimes without a permanent nurse. There were also temporary nurses who provided care. One of these was Annie Wane, wife of Thomas Bentley Wane, who operated a carrier service. Annie would travel around the district during and after the war, dressing the wounds sustained by injured soldiers. Her young daughter Nancy would sometimes go with her to help by holding the sterile equipment and dressings. As a young girl, the sight of such terrible injuries stayed with her for life.

There was no permanent dentist in Gargrave, but in 1919, Mr Sloane was advertising that he visited Gargrave every Tuesday afternoon.

CAMPAIGN FOR MORAL PURITY

In 1921, the Bradford Diocese launched the White Crusade for purity. At an all-male gathering at the Parochial Hall, a speaker from Keighley condemned the 'wild oats' attitudes that were prevalent in some quarters. Men were implored to curb their animal passions and think of the effect that venereal diseases had on children – blindness and insanity. He deplored the existence of these diseases which caused so much suffering for parents and children and a degeneration of body and soul.

During the following week, there was a White Crusade meeting for the ladies. Proceedings were opened by Rev Blunt, who then withdrew to leave the ladies to their discussions. What transpired at that meeting wasn't reported.

In general, the health of the village seemed quite good, judging from the ages of those buried at St Andrew's. Many residents were lasting well into their 70s (and some beyond) in an age when life expectancy was about 55 years. If infants made it to the age of 5, they generally survived all the childhood diseases that regularly caused the schools to close. Interestingly, the Spanish flu epidemic of 1918 didn't affect deaths in Gargrave, as the numbers of burials in the years 1918 and 1919 were the same as during the war.

EPILOGUE

Although life had settled back to normality in the years after the war, there would be more troubles ahead. The depression and the Second World War could not have been foreseen by the inhabitants of Gargrave. This, however, is another story.

Appendices

A EMPLOYMENT STATISTICS

A large proportion of the village workforce was employed in the Airebank cotton spinning mill. This was consistently the largest source of employment in Gargrave. As a percentage, the figures were: 40% in 1891, 35% in 1901 and 39% in 1911.

This information has been found from the census returns, but as a ten-yearly snapshot, it just indicates a trend.

Although no accurate figures exist, the numbers must have fluctuated even between 1901 and 1911. The mill shut down in 1904 and families moved away, but then it restarted, and jobs were restored.

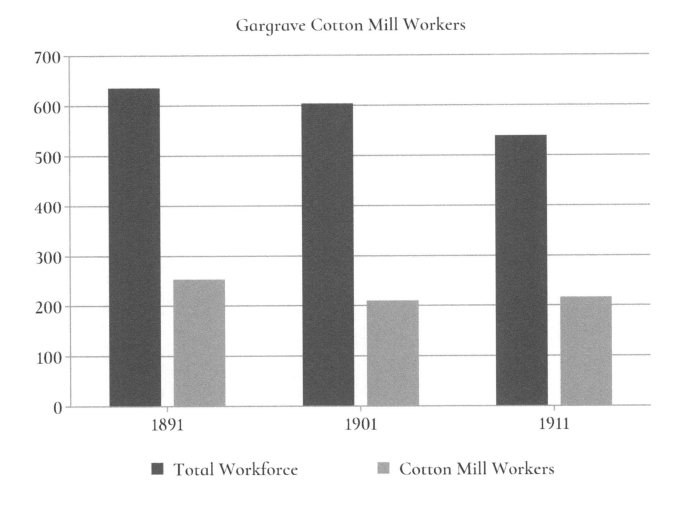

A substantial number of people worked in agriculture and in other types of outdoor work on estates, as can be seen in the next graphs.

The following two graphs show the distribution of employment by different sectors, comparing 1901 with 1911.

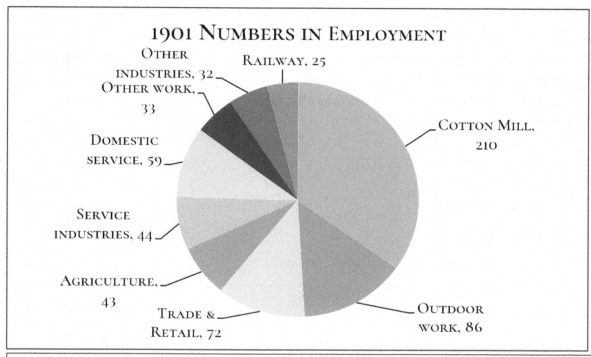

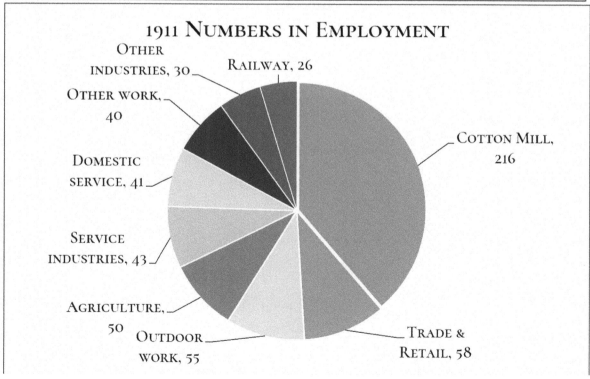

B   COTTON MILL PROCESSES

The raw cotton arrived at the mill in bales. It was cleaned in the blowing room, rolled into a mat called a 'lap' and then went into the carding room. The carding process combed and straightened out the cotton fibres and stretched them into long slivers. These slivers were drawn into loosely twisted strands known as 'roving'. The roving was then spun into the finished cotton yarn. Two types of spinning processes were used at Airebank Mills – ring spinning and mule spinning. Many of the processes required nimble fingers and were carried out by women and children. Keeping the spinning process running smoothly involved changing the full bobbins for empty ones and preventing breakages.

SOME OF THE COTTON MILL JOBS

CLEANING AND CARDING

SCUTCHER	*Separates the raw cotton from seeds and other debris*
CARD TENTER	*Tends the carding machine*
ROVER	*Tends the roving machine*

SPINNING

DOFFER, BEAMER, CREELER	*Load and unload bobbins*
PIECER	*Mends broken threads*
RING AND MULE SPINNERS	*Worked the spinning machinery*

GENERAL JOBS

OVERLOOKER	*Foreman*
PIECER	*Mends broken threads*
STRIPPER AND GRINDER	*The men who maintained the machinery*
STATIONARY ENGINE DRIVER	*Ran the steam engine that powered all the machinery*

C Cost of Living in 1910

Money

Pre-decimal, the UK money system was split into pounds (£), shillings (s) and pence (d).

There were   20 shillings to the pound
And   12 pence to a shilling

Typical wages

Factory workers: Men   £70 pa
                   Women   £30 pa

Overlooker   £100 pa

Housing

In Gargrave, a two bed roomed cottage cost £6 a year to rent. For three bedrooms, £11-£12 a year and a larger five bed roomed house would be rented out for about £30 a year. Small cottages could be bought for £100 and a larger house for £600.

Other costs

Model T Ford £220
Bicycle £15
Loaf 1d
12 eggs 4d
Pint milk 1d
Letter post 1d
I lb apples 2d
Wrights Coal tar Soap bar 4d

In 1910, the goods a single pound could buy would be worth around £117 pounds in 2019. The table below shows the value of goods that money of 1910 could purchase in 2019.

1910	1s (5p)	5s (25p)	10s (50p)	15s (75p)	£1 (20s)
2019	£5.84	£29.20	£54.41	£87.61	£116.81

D Shops and Businesses

No	Location	Type of business	Before 1900	1900	1901	1902	1903	1904	1905	1906	1907	1908
1	Church Street	Shoemaker	James Hunt	James Hunt			James Hunt moved to a differe					
2	Church Street	Joiner		Fred Roberts								
3	Bridge End	Butcher		Luke Gill								
4	Trees Terrace	Fish & Chip Shop										
5	Trees Terrace	Clogger										
6	High Street	Painter and decorator		Samuel Hartley								
7	High Street	Painter and decorator										
8	High Street	Confectioner						Misses Hartley				
9	High Street	Newsagent	John Hyde	John Hyde								
10	West Street	Butcher	Richard Driver	Richard Driver								
11	West Street	Joiner										
12	North Street	Cabinet maker	Rudolph Franzee	Clemence Franzee								
13	Park Place	Iron monger	Robert Parkinson	Robert Parkinson								
14	High Street	Shoe maker		W & J Maudesley								
15	High Street	Blacksmith	Jonathan Dodgson	Jonathan Dodgson								
16	High Street	Dress maker	Sarah Lofthouse	Sarah Lofthouse								
17	High Street	Chemist										
18	High Street	Grocers & Drapers	John H Howarth	John H Howarth					Arthur Edward Wright			
19	High Street	Grouse Garage										
20	The Square	Pie Shop		Weatherill								
21	High Street	Saddler	James Wade	James Wade								
22	High Street	The Nurseries	John Horsman	John Horsman								
23	High Street	Shoemaker	Thomas Finister	Thomas Finister		Then Dorcas Finister ran it as a boar						
24	High Street	Tailor	Robert & John McKell	John McKell								
25	High Street	Post Office	Dorothy Varley	Dorothy Varley								
26	High Street	Saddler										
27	High Street	Garage / Cycle repairs										
28	East Street	Grocers	Hannah Wiseman	Tom Pighills								
29	4 River Place	Grocers	Isabella Procter	Isabella Procter		Stephen Reeder						
30	South Street	Grocers										
31	South Street	Shoemaker	Middlebrook	Sarah & Herbert Middlebrook								Herb
32	South Street	Co-op Grocers & Drapers	Founded in 1872	Various managers								
33	South Street	Newsagent	Absalom Hilton	Miss Ann Hilton								

	…9	1910	1911	1912	1913	1914	1915	1916	1917	1918	1919	1920	1921	1922	1923	1924	1925	1926	1927	1928	1929
ation in same area						James Hunt															
						Fred Roberts															
						Luke Gill															
											A Jones										
											Stephen Metcalfe										
						Samuel Hartley															
						Misses Hartley												Emily Simpson			
						John Hyde	Harry & May McKell														
k Hardisty						Frank Hardisty															
																		Harry Turner			
						Clemence Franzee															
							John Hyde														
						Jonathan Dodgson										Percy Dodgson					
						Sarah Lofthouse															
								James W Hardman												Willie Sugde	
							Stockdale and Helm											Check S & H date			
											John Brindle				Albert Brindle			Pennine Buses			
demolished																					
Anthony Clarke						Anthony Clarke															
ouse																					
						John McKell															
						Dorothy Varley				Such										Such	
																Harry Howard					
							Gill & Gott			W Gill & Son											
						Stephen Reeder										Mrs Lucas' Temperance Tea Bar					
							George Reeder														
ddlebrook						Herbert Middlebrook															

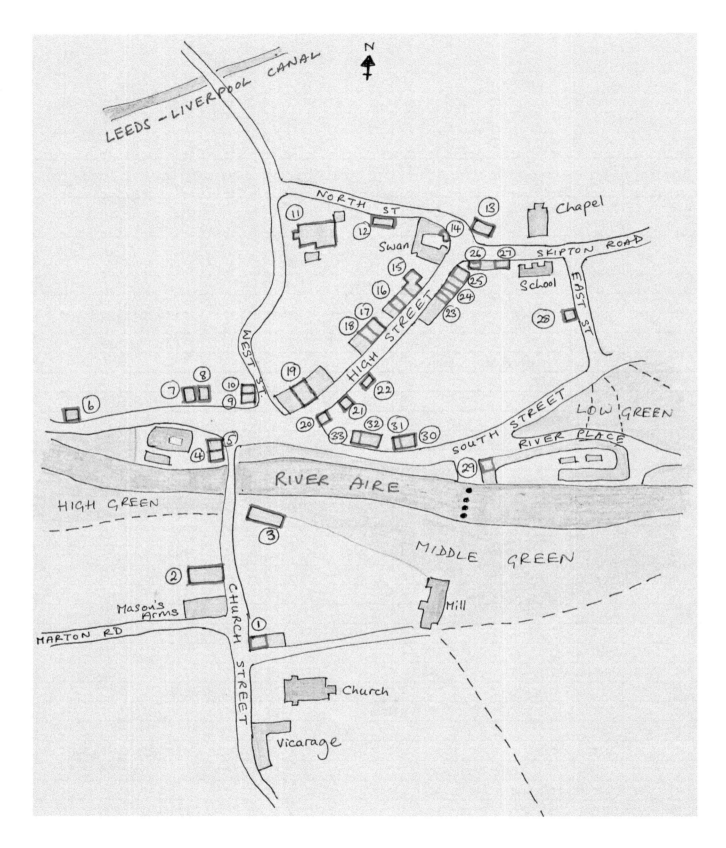

Sketch map showing positions of businesses - Not to Scale
From an original drawing by Sue Lyall.

E GARGRAVE ROLL OF HONOUR

ROLL OF HONOUR
EUROPEAN WAR 1914–1918.

Herbert Gladstone Rhodes — Yorkshire Regiment
George Lister — Royal Field Artillery
Percy Roe — Royal Engineers
Archie Armistead — Mechanical Transport Corps
Richard Wiseman — Royal Field Artillery
Cecil Armistead — W Yorkshire Regiment
Joseph Kirkbright — W Yorkshire Regiment
William Bannon — A & S Highlanders
C.H. Bromley — King's Royal Rifles
Arthur William Nicholson M.M. — Yorkshire Regt
Guy Bramwell — Northumberland Fus
Richard Chester — W Yorkshire Regiment
Joseph Hind — Border Regiment
Eric Dutton
John Herbert Weatherill — Royal Field Artillery
Walter Pope — E Yorkshire Regiment
Charles William Luff — W Yorkshire Regiment
George William Taylor — W Yorkshire Regiment
William Gilbert Briggs — W Yorkshire Regiment
George Antony Wane — Army Service Corps
Thomas Henry Wane — Yorkshire Regiment
Philip Preston — Northants Regiment
John Hogg — Royal Engineers
Ralph Porter Walker — W Yorkshire Regiment
Matthew Henry Wilson D.S.O.
Norman England D.S.O.
Godfrey Ermen — W Riding Regiment
William Surgener — Royal Engineers
Samuel Rhodes — W Yorkshire Regiment
Thomas Waterhouse
Joseph Burrow M.M. — Royal Field Artillery
Harold Chester — Royal Field Artillery
William Slater — Royal Engineers
James Roland Bradley — Royal Field Artillery
Mark Sheriff — Northumberland Fus
John Wane — Royal Engineers
Robert Lister — Lancashire Fusiliers
Tom Lister — Lancashire Fusiliers
John Henry Preston
James Edward Walker
William Walker
William Frank Pighills — W Yorkshire Regiment
John Gill M.M. & Bar — Northumberland Fus
Edward Bradley — Royal Field Artillery
James Lawson — Army Service Corps
Jack Garnett — Army Service Corps
Christopher Wane
David Walker — H.M.S. ...
Albert Brundle
Wilfred Chester
Cedric Dutton
Cyril Norman Dutton
Joseph Hitchin

Herbert Wales
Tom Rhodes
Richard Wane — H.M.S. Royal Sovereign
William Richardson
Fred Slater
William Gill
Jack Parkinson
Sidney Hebden
Edmund Howard
Jack Howard
Stanley Weatherill
Anthony Boothman — Royal Field Artillery
Ernest Emmott — West Riding Regiment
Edward Slater
James White
Hugh Henry Wiseman
Charles Thomas Hutton
Arthur Frank Pope — H.M.S. ...
Henry Cope
Arthur Cope
Ben Dobby
Joseph Summersgill
James Preston
Jeremiah Aldersley
Harold Maudsley
Edward Williams
Fred Summersgill
William Whittaker
Arthur Brindley
Stephen Capstick
Stephen Gill Wallbank
Arthur James Barker
John William Hitchon
Arthur Ormrod
George Wilfred Clarke
William Sargeant
Thomas Asquith Gill
William Burton
James Bazeley
James Hodgson
James Nuttall
Leonard Gill
Christopher Bateson
James Parkinson — H.M.S. ...
Cecil James Gill
George Reeder
Arthur Langstroth
William Kirby Foster
Horace Aldersley
Riley Chew
Edward Taylor
Charles Sydney Chester
William Turner

Frank Foster — H.M.S. ...
William Dickinson
Henry Hartley
Arthur Gamble
Rupert Parker
Tristran Cuthbert
Fred Foster M.M.
Robert Walker
Edward Oliver Chester
George Staff
Fred Mason
Charles Alfred Gill
Roland Lofthouse
Alexander Cameron
Frank Wainwright
Ernest Abberley
Robert Milner
Frank Ayrton
Henry Lawson
Bruce Bradley
Maurice Hyde
Tom Knight
Harry Weatherill
John Herbert Middlebrook
Henry Marshall Gill
James Chew
Richard Taylor
John Bonnass
Robert Riddle Bell
John Isherwood
Wilfred Mason
Albert Barrow
Edward Ernest Burland
Sam Chatburn
Horace Gordon Lord
Ernest Hebden
Harry Denison
Ethel Burland — T.F.N.S.
Joseph Ayrton

Richard Banks
Richard Black
Robert Burden
George Cullimore

Eric Rowland Gregory
John Henry Horner
William Lever
George William Metcalfe
Richard Moore
Edgar Nicholson
William Rimmer

Surname	Forename	Regiment, Service or Ship
Rhodes	Herbert Gladstone	Yorkshire Regiment
Lister	George	Royal Field Artillery
Roe	Percy	Royal Engineers
Armistead	Archie	Machine Gun Corps
Wiseman	Richard	Royal Field Artillery
Armistead	Cecil	West Yorkshire Regiment
KirkBright	Joseph	West Yorkshire Regiment
Bannon	William	Argyll and Sutherland Highlanders
Bromley	C. H.	Kings Royal Rifles
Nicholson	Arthur William	Yorkshire Regiment
Bramwell	Guy	Northumberland Fusiliers
Chester	Richard	West Yorkshire Regiment
Hird	Joseph	Border Regiment
Dutton	Eric	
Weatherill	John Herbert	Royal Field Artillery
Pope	Walter	East Yorkshire Regiment
Luff	Charles William	West Riding Regiment
Taylor	George William	West Yorkshire Regiment
Briggs	William Gilbert	West Yorkshire Regiment
Wane	George Anthony	Army Service Corps
Wane	Thomas Henry	Yorkshire Regiment
Preston	Philip	Norfolk Regiment
Hogg	John	Royal Engineers
Walker	Ralph Porter	West Yorkshire Regiment
Wilson	Matthew Henry	Middlesex Hussars
England	Norman	West Riding Regiment
Ermen	Godfrey	West Riding Regiment
Surgener	William	Royal Engineers
Rhodes	Samuel	West Yorkshire Regiment
Waterhouse	Thomas	West Riding Regiment
Burrow	Joseph	Royal Field Artillery
Chester	Harold	Royal Field Artillery
Slater	William	Royal Engineers
Bradley	James Roland	Royal Field Artillery
Sheriff	Mark	Northumberland Fusiliers
Wane	John	Royal Engineers
Lister	Robert	Lancashire Fusiliers
Lister	Robert	Lancashire Fusiliers
Preston	John Henry	Dorset Regiment
Walker	James Henry	Royal Engineers
Walker	William	Kings Own Royal Lancashire Regiment
Pighills	William Frank	West Yorkshire Regiment
Gill	John	Northumberland Fusiliers
Bradley	Edward	Royal Field Artillery

Lawson......................James...........................Army Service Corps
Garnett......................Jack...........................Army Service Corps
Wane......................Christopher..............HMS Opal
Walker......................David......................HMS Bartum
Brindle......................Albert......................Royal Air Force
Chester......................Wilfred......................West Riding Regiment
Dutton......................Cedric......................South African Infantry
Dutton......................Cyril Norman...........Royal Engineers (S.A.)
Hitchen......................Joseph......................56th Remount Regiment
Wales......................Herbert......................Royal Army Medical Corps
Rhodes......................Tom......................West Yorkshire Regiment
Wane......................Richard......................HMS Royal Sovereign
Richardson...............William......................Royal Garrison Artillery
Slater......................Fred......................York and Lancaster Regiment
Gill......................William......................West Yorkshire Regiment
Parkinson...............John......................West Yorkshire Regiment
Hebden......................Sidney......................Northumberland Fusiliers
Howard......................Edmund......................King's Liverpool Regiment
Howard......................Jack......................King's Liverpool Regiment
Weatherill...............Stanley......................Northumberland Fusiliers
Boothman...............Anthony......................Royal Field Artillery
Emmott......................Earnest......................West Riding Regiment
Slater......................Edward......................Royal Field Artillery
White......................James......................Royal Army Medical Corps
Wisemen......................Hugh Henry..............West Yorkshire Regiment
Hutton......................Charles Thomas........West Yorkshire Regiment
Pope......................Arthur Frank............HMS Fairy
Cope......................Henry......................Durham Light Infantry
Cope......................Arthur......................West Yorkshire Regiment
Dobby......................Ben......................Yorkshire Regiment
Summersgill...............Joseph......................King's Liverpool Regiment
Whittaker...............William......................York and Lancaster Regiment
Bradley......................Arthur......................Northumberland Fusiliers
Capstick......................Stephen......................Army Service Corps
Wallbank......................Stephen Gill..............Royal West Kent Regiment
Barker......................Arthur James............Tyneside Scottish
Hitchon......................John William............C.M.T.
Ormerod......................Arthur......................Northumberland Fusiliers
Clarke......................George Wilfred........King's Own Yorkshire Light Infantry
Sargeant......................William......................Army Service Corps
Gill......................Thomas Asquith.......Royal Garrison Artillery
Burton......................William......................Durham Light Infantry
Bazely......................James......................West Yorkshire Regiment
Hodgson......................James......................Royal Warwick Regiment
Nuttall......................James......................East Yorkshire Regiment

Gill	Leonard	Army Service Corps
Bateson	Christopher	Royal Garrison Artillery
Parkinson	James	HMS........
Gill	Cecil James	Royal Air Force
Reeder	George	North Staffordshire Regiment
Langstroth	Arthur	West Yorkshire Regiment
Foster	William Kirby	Royal Engineers
Aldersley	Horace	East Yorkshire Regiment
Chew	Riley	Royal Garrison Artillery
Taylor	Edmund	Royal Fusiliers
Chester	Charles Sydney	Army Service Corps
Turner	William	East Yorkshire Regiment
Foster	Frank	HMS........
Dickinson	William	Royal West Kent Regiment
Hartley	Henry	Royal Air Force
Gamble	Arthur	York and Lancaster Regiment
Parker	Rupert	Royal Field Artillery
Cuthbert	Tristram	Royal Air Force
Foster	Fred	Royal Field Artillery
Walker	Robert	HMM........
Chester	Edward Oliver	HMD........
Staff	George	HMS Victory
Mason	Fred	West Yorkshire Regiment
Gill	Charles Alfred	West Yorkshire Regiment
Lofthouse	Roland	Yorkshire Regiment
Cameron	Alexander	Royal Army Medical Corps
Wainwright	Frank	Coldstream Guards
Aldersley	Ernest	Machine Gun Corps
Milner	Robert	Machine Gun Corps
Ayrton	Frank	King's Own Yorkshire Light Infantry
Lawson	Henry	Royal Field Artillery
Bradley	Bruce	Hospital Ship SS Llandovery Castle
Hyde	Maurice	Machine Gun Corps
Knight	Maurice	West Yorkshire Regiment
Weatherill	Harry	Mercantile Marines
Middlebrook	John Herbert	West Yorkshire Regiment
Gill	Harry Marshall	Royal Air Force
Chew	James	Durham Light Infantry
Taylor	Richard	West Yorkshire Regiment
Bownass	John	West Yorkshire Regiment
Bell	Robert Riddle	Royal Marines
Isherwood	John	Army Service Corps
Mason	Wilfred	Royal West Kent Regiment
Barrow	Albert	West Yorkshire Regiment
Burlend	Edward Ernest	Canadian Forces

Chatburn.....................Sam.............................Machine Gun Corps
Lord...........................Horace Gordon.........Durham Light Infantry
Hebden.......................Earnest........................West Yorkshire Regiment
Gregson......................Henry...........................Royal Air Force
Burlend......................Ethel............................Territorial Force Nursing Service
Ayrton.......................Joseph
Banks.........................Harry
Banks.........................Richard
Black..........................Richard........................1st Surrey Rifles
Burden.......................Robert
Cullimore...................George
Davis..........................Thomas William.......Prince of Wales Own
Gregory......................Eric Rowland
Horner.......................John Henry
Lever.........................William
Metcalfe.....................George William
Moore........................Richard
Nicholson...................Edgar
Richardson.................William
Rimmer.....................William

F   Gargrave Wesleyan Chapel Memorial Plaque

Surname	Forename	Regiment, Service or Ship
Aldersley	Earnest	
Parrott	Edward	
Luff	Charles	
Rhodes	Sam	
Ayrton	Frank	
Yeoman	Danson	
Swales	James	
Walker	Hebden	
Gill	Thomas Asquith	
Wiseman	Richard	
Thompson	Robert	Kings Own Royal Lancashire Regiment
Banks	Harry	
Briggs	William	
Davis	Thomas William	
Spedding	William	West Riding Regiment
Bradley	Arthur	
Dobby	Ben	
Gill	Thomas Hartus	
Platt	George	Leicestershire regiment
Platt	Herbert	York and Lancaster Regiment
Ward	John	

Sewell...........................(Charles) Oswald.....Rifle Brigade
Roper............................Ben................................

G WW1 OPERATIONAL THEATRES OF WAR 1914-1920

In warfare, a theatre is an area or place, encompassing land sea and air, where military operations occur. There were seven distinct theatres of war during WW1. Each of these Theatres of War had several distinct operational areas which were identified by a code of a number and letter. WW1 Theatres of War included:

- Western Europe, allocated code number 1 and covering operational areas with code letters

1. France and Flanders also known as the Western Front

2. Italy

3. Balkans with Code: 2 and areas

4. Greek Macedonia, Serbia, Bulgaria and European Turkey

5. Gallipoli (Dardanelles)

Russia - Code: 3

Egypt – Initially Code: 3 which was changed in 1st January to Code: 4

4th/5th November 1914 - 18th/19th March 1916

18th/19th March 1916 - 31st October/1st November 1918

Africa – Until 31st December 1915 - Code: 4 then in 1st January

this was changed to Code: 5

a East Africa, Nyasaland and Northern Rhodesia

b South West Africa

c Cameroon

d Nigeria

e Togoland

Asia until **31st December 1915,**
Code: 5 and from **1st January and then allocated** Code: 6

a Hedjaz

b Mesopotamia

c Persia

d Trans Caspia

e South West Arabia

f Aden

g Frontier Regions of India

h Tsing-Tau

Australasia until 31st December 1915 **Code: 6 and from 1st January 1916** Code: 7

a New Britain

b New Ireland

c Kaiser Wilhelmland

d Admiralty Islands

e Nauru

f German Samoa

These codes were used by the British military for the compilation of records of service and medals.

The alphanumeric codes were slightly amended after 1st January 1916.

H   ARMY RANKS

The commissioned ranks are awarded a 'Commission' from the Sovereign. Warrant Officers, First and Second Class, hold a Royal Warrant from the Monarch, Non-Commissioned Officers, Lance Corporal to Staff Sergeant, may have an appointment.

Ranks with the prefix 'T/' are temporary and can be removed without detriment to the individual's service record. A temporary rank is given on active service and usually held only for the duration of the action. A temporary rank may be made permanent if there is a 'vacancy' for that 'A/' indicates the rank is 'acting'; the holder is to prove that he is worthy of the rank before it is made 'Substantive'.

The Household Cavalry, along with other cavalry units initially did not have Sergeants. As most cavalry units were once made up of 'gentlemen' it was deemed unseemly to have sergeant as a rank, the title having come from the same root as 'servant'. Instead, they have an equivalent rank of Corporal of the Horse with three stripes showing on the sleeve. A Lance Corporal of the Horse has two chevrons, and a Staff Corporal shows three chevrons surmounted by a crown on the sleeve. Most units have abandoned this rank.

A Bombardier in the Artillery Regiments is the equivalent of a Lance Corporal.

The rank of Private is equivalent to Gunner (artillery), Trooper (cavalry) and Sapper (engineers)

INFORMATION SOURCES

Web Site Addresses

1.   Archive.org
2.   https://www.ancestry.co.uk/
3.   1914-1918.invisionzone.com/forums/
4.   tankmemorial.vpweb.co.uk/
5.   www.carriere-wellington.com/
6.   www.cpgw.org.uk
7.   www.cwgc.org
8.   www.cwgc.org/default.asp
9.   www.fylde.demon.co.uk/welcome.htm
10.   www.historial.org/index.php/en/home.html
11.   www.iwm.org.uk
12.   www.kaiserscross.com
13.   www.lastpost.be/mainpage.htm
14.   www.mgbtours.com/
15.   www.nztunnellers.com/
16.   www.ramc-ww1.com/
17.   www.richardvanemden.com/
18.   www.skphotoscom.co.uk/index.html
19.   www.tank-cambrai.com/english/home.php
20.   www.wargravesheritage.org.uk/index.html
21.   www.westernfrontassociation.com/
22.   www.twgpp.org
23.   livesofthefirstworldwar.org
24.   wartimememoriesproject.com
25.   www.bbc.co.uk/news/uk-scotland-north-east-orkney-shetland-42647570
26.   www.gwpda.org/naval/opalnarb.htm
27.   en.wikipedia.org/wiki/HMS_Opal
28.   en.wikipedia.org/wiki/HMS_Opal_(1915)
29.   www.gwpda.org/
30.   www.revolvy.com/
31.   www.academia.edu
32.   www.loc.gov
33.   https://www.thegazette.co.uk/
34.   www.longlongtrail.co.uk
35.   www.1914-1918-online.net

36. www.bbc.co.uk/guides/z9bf9j6
37. wlb-stuttgart.de
38. www.nationalarchives.gov.uk/first-world-war/centenary-unit-war-diaries.htm
39. commons.wikimedia.org/wiki/Atlas_of_World_War_I
40. www.westpoint.edu/history/SitePages/WWI.aspx
41. ww1centenary.oucs.ox.ac.uk/
42. www.centenarynews.com/
43. www.imagesde14-18.eu/
44. www.researchgate.net
45. www.scarletfinders.co.uk   (WW1 nursing)
46.

BOOKS, MAGAZINES, ETC

1. "The Silver Jubilee Book: The Story of 25 Eventful Years in Pictures: 1910-1935" - Odhams Press Ltd, Lang Acre, London W.C.2 Published 1935.

2. "Fighting the Bosche Underground" - Harry Davis Trounce - New York Charles Scribner's Sons Published October 1918

3. "Craven's Part in the Great War" Compiled and Edited by John T. Clayton, Published by the Craven Herald 1919

4. "The War Illustrated Album De Luxe" Edited by J. A. Hammerton With Chapters by H. G. Wells, Sir Gilbert Parker And Sir Arthur Conan Doyle Published By The Amalgamated Press, Limited London, 1915

5. "The Illustrated War News." parts 1 to 98 - Published June 14th, 1916 to April 10th, 1918 by the Illustrated London News and Sketch, Ltd., 172, Strand, London, W.C.

6. "The History of the Great War" Volumes 1 - 8 Editor; Newman Fowler, Waverley Book Company LTD 96. Farrington Street London E.C.

7. "Letters from Mesopotamia" Robert Palmer, Printed for Private Circulation Only, London Women's Printing Society, Ltd. Crick Street, Piccadilly 1916

8. "The Story of the Great War", Volumes 1 to 8, by Churchill, Miller, and Reynolds, Published New York, P.F. Collier and son, 1916 - 1920

9. "True Stories of The Great War" Volumes 1 to 6, Editor-in-Chief Francis Trevelyan Miller (Litt. D., L.L.D.) Review of Reviews Company, New York 1917

10. "The Story of the 62nd (West Riding) Division 1914 - 1919" Volumes 1 and 2, Everard Wyrrall- Published by John Lane, Bodley Head Limited, Vigo Street, London1

11. "The New Army in Training" by Rudyard Kipling Published by Macmillan and Co., Limited St. Martin's Street, London 1915

12. "The Times History of the War" Volumes 1 to 21, Printed and Published by "The Times", Printing House Square, London. 1918
"Liverpool's Military Hospitals" Part XLV (45) Liverpool Courier 25 Nov 1919

13. "List of auxiliary hospitals in the UK during the First World War" redcross.org.uk/WW1

14. "Forgotten Fort Crosby" by Alison Burns BA (Hons) Archaeology, MA - ISBN 978-0-9929677-1-0 Published by Sefton Coast Landscape Partnership - 29 Oct 2015

15. "British Battalion s on the Somme" by Ray Westlake – ISBN 0 85052 374 5 - Publisher Pen and Sword Books 1995

16. "The Siege" by Russell Braddon- ISBN 224 61793 I - Publisher Jonathon Cape Ltd, 30 Bedford Square, London WC1

17. "Armenian Golgotha: A Memoir of the Armenian Genocide, 1915–1918" By Grigoris Balakian Originally published in Armenian as "Armenian Golgotha: Episodes from the Armenian Martyrology from Berlin to Der Zar, 1914 – 1920" published in Vienna by the Mekhitarist Press. Translated by Peter Balakian, published by Vintage Books 2010

18. "Passchendaele" by Peter Barton – ISBN 978 1 829 422 9 – Publisher Constable and Robinson 2007

19. "The History of Lumsden's Horse" Edited by Henry H. S. Pearse (War Correspondent) Longmans, Green, and Co. 39 Paternoster Row, London 1903

20. "The British Campaign in France and Flanders, Vol. I" by Arthur Conan Doyle published by Hodder & Stoughton, London, 1916

21. "The Memoirs of the 18th (Queen Mary's Own) Royal Hussars, 1906 -1922" Brig.-General Charles Burnett C.B., C.M.G. Published by Warren and Son, Limited 1926

22. "The History and Antiquities of the Deanery of Craven" by Thomas Dunham Whitaker, L.L.D. F. S. A. - First Edition 1805; Second Edition 1812 and Third Edition, (Edited by A. W. Morant), 1878.

23. The Little British Kingdom of Craven by N. Wood 1966 Northern History. 32. 1-20. 10.1179/007817296790175155.

24. The Ecclesiastical Parish of Gargrave. Volume 1 Flasby and volume 2 Gargrave – Harry M Gill

25. Craven Herald Archives held in Skipton Library

26. Yorkshire Post; Leeds Mercury, - British Newspapers online

27.   Craven Household Almanac
28.   "History of the Church and Parish of Saint Andrew, Gargrave" by Janet Dinsdale 1966
29.   St Andrew's Church Parish Magazines 1896 – 1904
30.   Little North Western Railway – Donald Binns
31.   Pennine Motor Services 1925 to 2000 – Donald Binns
32.   The Leeds and Liverpool Canal: A History and Guide - Mike Clarke
33.   The Aero Manual of Mechanical Flight 1909. Compiled by the staff of "The Motor"
34.   Dizzy Heights – The Story of Lancashire's First Flying Men. 1988 Chris Aspin
35.   Eshton Hall: The History of a Yorkshire Mansion - Peter Robinson

WAR DIARIES CONSULTED

1.   2nd Battalion Royal Sussex Regiment 1914 – 1916
2.   2/6th Battalion Duke of Wellington's West Riding Division (T. F.) 1914 - 1917

THANKS TO

George Ingle for all his input,
Graham Beck for unrestricted access to the Dennis French collection
Derrick McRobert,
Robin Platt,
Edith Parker,
The Burlend family,
David Hull,
Sheila Pantin
Enid French
Jean Dickinson and family

Thanks too for Remiscences from

Joe Langstroth,
John Wallace,
Enid White,
Dennis Ford,

IMAGE SOURCES

Soldiers Portraits -

Except where otherwise stated, all portrait images of the soldiers have been scanned from "Craven's Part in the Great War" - Edited by John T Clayton - Published by the Craven Herald 1919 and are now considered Public Domain .

 Other images where possible have been captioned and the source acknowledged.

INDEX

A

C

G

I

J

M

N

Q

S

Y

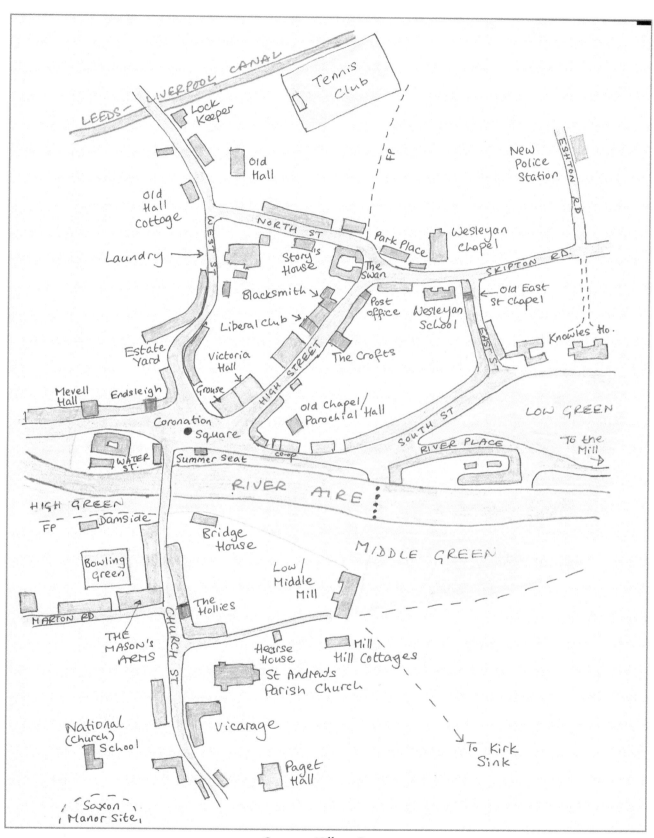

Gargrave Village Centre
From a sketch map by Sue Lyall

Lightning Source UK Ltd.
Milton Keynes UK
UKHW031929271019
352410UK00003B/11/P